Teaching Shelley's
Frankenstein

Approaches to Teaching
World Literature

Joseph Gibaldi, series editor

For a complete listing of titles,
see the last pages of this book.

Approaches to Teaching Shelley's *Frankenstein*

Edited by

Stephen C. Behrendt

Consultant Editor
Anne K. Mellor

The Modern Language Association of America
New York   1990

© 1990 by The Modern Language Association of America
All rights reserved. Printed in the United States of America

For information about obtaining permission to reprint material from
MLA book publications, send your request by mail (see address below),
e-mail (permissions@mla.org), or fax (212 533-0680).

Library of Congress Cataloging-in-Publication Data

Approaches to teaching Shelley's Frankenstein / edited by Stephen C.
    Behrendt, consultant editor, Anne K. Mellor.
        p. cm.
    Includes bibliographical references and index.
    ISBN 0-87352-539-6   ISBN 0-87352-540-X (pbk.)
    1. Shelley, Mary Wollstonecraft, 1797-1851. Frankenstein.
    2. Shelley, Mary Wollstonecraft, 1797-1851—Study and teaching.
    I. Behrendt, Stephen C., 1947- . II. Mellor, Anne Kostelanetz.
    PR5397.F73A6   1990
    823'.7—dc20   90-43124
    ISSN 1059-1133

Cover illustration of the paperback edition: Film still from Frankenstein,
Edison, 1910. Courtesy of Museum of Modern Art Film Stills Archive.

Third printing 1997
Printed on recycled paper

Published by The Modern Language Association of America
10 Astor Place, New York, New York 10003-6981

CONTENTS

PREFACE TO THE SERIES

In *The Art of Teaching* Gilbert Highet wrote, "Bad teaching wastes a great deal of effort, and spoils many lives which might have been full of energy and happiness." All too many teachers have failed in their work, Highet argued, simply "because they have not thought about it." We hope that the Approaches to Teaching World Literature series, sponsored by the Modern Language Association's Publications Committee, will not only improve the craft—as well as the art—of teaching but also encourage serious and continuing discussion of the aims and methods of teaching literature.

The principal objective of the series is to collect within each volume different points of view on teaching a specific literary work, a literary tradition, or a writer widely taught at the undergraduate level. The preparation of each volume begins with a wide-ranging survey of instructors, thus enabling us to include in the volume the philosophies and approaches, thoughts and methods of scores of experienced teachers. The result is a sourcebook of material, information, and ideas on teaching the subject of the volume to undergraduates.

The series is intended to serve nonspecialists as well as specialists, inexperienced as well as experienced teachers, graduate students who wish to learn effective ways of teaching as well as senior professors who wish to compare their own approaches with the approaches of colleagues in other schools. Of course, no volume in the series can ever substitute for erudition, intelligence, creativity, and sensitivity in teaching. We hope merely that each book will point readers in useful directions; at most each will offer only a first step in the long journey to successful teaching.

Joseph Gibaldi
Series Editor

PREFACE TO THE VOLUME

Frankenstein is undeniably one of the great and influential works of the English Romantic period. Particularly helpful for the student who may be intimidated by the poetry of Mary Shelley's contemporaries, the novel introduces such pervasive issues of the era as individual and class alienation, social conditioning, gender stereotyping, the conflict between rational intellect and intuitive emotion, and the revisionist Romantic view of the relation between God and humanity. *Frankenstein* provides not only a rich and complex text in its own right—written by a remarkable woman who was then about the same age as many undergraduates are now—but also an excellent vehicle for introducing students to the complexities of Romantic art and thought generally.

That *Frankenstein* is widely taught in courses whose primary focus is not Romanticism, however, suggests one of the needs that this volume seeks to address. The novel appears in a considerable range of courses in science fiction, gothic fiction, and the history of ideas, broadly and variously defined. Moreover, *Frankenstein* is increasingly visible in courses in women's literature and feminist inquiry, as well as in a dazzling array of literature surveys, both traditional and nontraditional. This collection of essays proceeds from a shared desire among the contributors to open up *Frankenstein*'s richness to instructors who may not have had sufficient time or opportunity to consider the daunting range of intellectual concerns and influences that Mary Shelley brought to bear in her enduring novel.

Because most students come to *Frankenstein* with interest and anticipation, the novel furnishes its own incentive to reading. But students' predictable preconceptions about *Frankenstein*, based on its many manifestations in film and popular culture, constitute a potential obstacle to interpretation and appreciation. Teaching strategies are, therefore, of particular importance in approaching *Frankenstein* in the classroom. It is not enough for the well-meaning instructor merely to suggest that the novel will not be what students expect it to be, for they will inevitably compare the text with their presuppositions about it. Such comparisons are often startlingly revealing and can result in fruitful learning experiences. All of us who teach or study *Frankenstein*, however, eventually become aware of the presence of a cinematically mythologized, popular-culture image of Frankenstein and his Creature that tries surprisingly hard to intrude itself between the novel's text and our perceptions of and responses to it. Hence the essays collected here reflect the diverse and creative ways in which instructors in courses and classroom situations of all sorts anticipate, deal with, and often actively exploit students' expectations.

The first section of this book, "Materials," offers some preliminary observations about the novel and its major issues, together with suggestions about primary and secondary materials that experienced instructors have found of interest and assistance in preparing to teach *Frankenstein*. As a preview to the essays in this volume, this section synthesizes much of the good advice provided by instructors in the survey that preceded the preparation of the volume and responds to some of their comments about what they regarded as desirable information.

In the "Approaches" section individual instructors discuss classroom strategies for teaching *Frankenstein*. These essays reflect a diversity of critical perspectives and methodologies, but each contributor has endeavored to maintain the pedagogical focus that characterizes the Approaches series. The single exception to this emphasis on the teaching process—and it is an exception only to an extent—is Wheeler Dixon's essay, a brief film history that will enable instructors to deal with the cinematic versions of *Frankenstein* in an informed fashion.

I want to begin my acknowledgments by thanking Joseph Gibaldi, general editor of this series, for his interest and encouragement at the outset of this project, his sage advice as it progressed, and his patience as it drew toward its conclusion. I am grateful as well to Anne K. Mellor for accepting my invitation to serve as consultant editor for the volume, for her careful and tactful readings of draft materials, and for her sound suggestions on ways to make the volume better. To our teaching colleagues I offer a profound expression of thanks. The responses to the preliminary survey of instructors were detailed and informative, the advice helpful indeed, and the enthusiasm infectious. In a profession in which one frequently hears laments about overwork, I am continually impressed by the generosity of spirit and of mind epitomized here in the lengthy, thoughtful, and stimulating responses of these colleagues; their comments reveal a deep and abiding love not so much for Mary Shelley's novel as for the whole enterprise of teaching. Of course, I also thank the scholars and teachers who contributed essays and who responded as promptly and graciously to my requests for revisions as they did to my editorial quibbling.

I am grateful to John Yost, vice chancellor for research and dean of graduate studies at the University of Nebraska; to Frederick M. Link, chair of the Department of English, for facilitating a reduction of my teaching load at the most crucial and time-consuming point in the preparation of this volume; and to Tim Duggan and Maggie Kerchal for their contributions to the preparation of the manuscript. Finally, I thank Patricia Flanagan Behrendt for her insightful readings and rereadings, her consistently good advice, and her unfailing support and enthusiasm, on which so much depends.

SCB

AN OVERVIEW OF THE SURVEY

Perhaps the most immediately striking aspects of the survey of instructors on which this volume is based are the tremendous diversity of courses in which *Frankenstein* is taught and the range of student levels and curricular interests of those courses. The novel appears most often, naturally, in the context of the British Romantic period and with surprising frequency in courses bearing titles like Romantic Poetry, where it can help to alleviate the real and pressing difficulty instructors face when none of the principal authors under consideration is a woman. Many instructors find that Mary Shelley's generally accessible novel both underscores and questions the primary themes and issues that recur in the works of the period's major poets. At the same time, many teachers present the novel as a work that stands on its own merits as a major literary achievement and articulates a vision that often differs significantly from those of other Romantic works. Modern criticism has come to perceive in much of Romantic poetry a systematic critique of the works of both predecessors (especially Milton) and contemporaries. Likewise Mary Shelley's *Frankenstein* contains a critique of the works and opinions of her parents, William Godwin and Mary Wollstonecraft, of her predecessors, and of contemporaries like Byron and Percy Shelley. In this sense the novel often functions effectively in Romantic literature courses both as sounding board and as measuring rod, quite over and above its value and function as a compelling literary performance.

The many other contexts in which *Frankenstein* is taught range from traditional historical surveys (of British, Western, or world literature) to genre courses like the novel (English or otherwise), gothic fiction, science fiction, popular literature (and its interdisciplinary cousin, popular culture), and horror literature. The novel also appears in special-topics courses like The Villain in Literature, Models of Male and Female Development, The Female Gothic, The Self and Its Doubles, and Christian Themes in Literature; in broad-based history-of-ideas courses like Science and Literature or Western Values; and in courses in women's studies and feminist literary criticism. Indeed, many instructors (some outside literature departments) report that *Frankenstein* is their principal pre-1900 vehicle for introducing feminist issues and feminist theory into their courses. Finally, nearly a quarter of the survey respondents report using the novel successfully in freshman English courses, a fact undoubtedly related to the powerful responses the novel elicits from readers who are about the same age as the nineteen-year-old Mary Shelley who composed it. Such readers typically react strongly and sympathetically to the ways in which the novel addresses issues of child rearing, education, rejection, ostracism, insecurity, alienation, and ethical responsibility for one's actions, issues that are very close to the intellectual—and, more important, the emotional—experiences of beginning college students.

Some 55% of the survey respondents spend a full week on *Frankenstein*. An additional 23% give more than four or five sessions to the novel, while 15% devote two full weeks or more to it. Not surprisingly, the novel's formal aspects pose the greatest initial difficulties for students, who regularly complain about the language and "style" of *Frankenstein* (my essay suggests two approaches to this problem). While 53% of the respondents report this negative response, several instructors share the contrasting view of one who writes, "I would expect students to find the often ponderous nineteenth-century discourse boring, but in fact they do not. Others teaching the book have mentioned the same thing to me." Additional stumbling blocks for some students are the novel's occasional inconsistencies, improbabilities, and seemingly forced coincidences, difficulties that are alleviated once the students become more familiar with the conventions of gothic fiction. More taxing for beginning readers of *Frankenstein* are the extended descriptions of nature, the intellectual apparatus (especially that relating to the Creature's education), and the De Lacey episode, subjects that are addressed in the essays that follow in this volume (e.g., those by Bowerbank; Mellor; Cantor and Moses). Many—perhaps most—of the students' criticisms stem from the novel's failure to fulfill their preconceptions about *Frankenstein*. Approaching the novel with notions generated by films and by a variety of Halloween-like caricatures of the Creature, students often find the story remarkably unsensational, the creation scene curiously truncated, and both the narrative and philosophical frames tedious and inexplicable. So profound are some of the expectations, one teacher comments, that students "feel cheated because the novel is not as exciting and does not move along as quickly as the movie."

Paradoxically, many respondents to the survey report particular (often initially unexpected) success in addressing and countering these very objections in their classes, which suggests why instructors do well to anticipate them and plan their teaching strategies accordingly. The narrative frames that shape and control the novel's structure, for instance, are regarded by more than half the respondents as so important that they demand detailed treatment in class. Many teachers report considerable increases in classroom enthusiasm as students begin to see what Mikhail

Bakhtin would term the *heteroglossia* that emerges from the use of different narrators with significantly different points of view (see the essays by Conger; Thornburg). By undermining the reader's expectation of an authoritative authorial voice, as Mary Shelley does in employing a narrative structure with clear ties to the rhetorical model of the skeptical debate, the author forces the reader to assume the role not of observer but rather of participant in a complex process of evaluation and judgment. Once students begin to understand that the destabilization of text—and therefore of authorial authority—is deliberate, they respond to the intellectual and emotional immediacy that results from their having to deal, personally and directly, with Frankenstein and the Creature and with their own crises of sympathy and discrimination. One of the novel's enduring strengths is that it permits readers neither retreat nor escape from the need to formulate and defend intellectual and ethical discriminations in the face of taxing, frequently contradictory, emotional demands.

Victor and the Creature, of course, receive the greatest share of attention in discussions of *Frankenstein*. Some two-thirds of the respondents emphasize various aspects of character in connection with the two figures, particularly in terms of the "double" (into which consideration Walton and Clerval also figure), while others encourage students to compare the Creature's predicament as the creation of a flawed creator with the reader's situation as the creation of a presumably perfect creator, the God of Christianity. This evocation of a divine creator also raises the issue of *Frankenstein*'s intertextuality, its overt and covert relations to other texts, as in this instance its connection with Genesis. Such intertextuality in fact figures largely in a variety of courses other than those in English literary history, as the essays included here demonstrate. Shelley's novel offers both a lens on, and a critique of, a diversity of texts typically regarded as Western cultural landmarks, texts whose themes are selectively reified even as their fundamental tenets are frequently modified, subverted, or flatly rejected by the author (see the essays by Mellor; Walling; Veeder; Bennett).

The Creature—whom I call by this name in keeping with the nonjudgmental language he applies to himself (*Frankenstein*, ed. Bloom 95)—is viewed by survey respondents in various ways: as a victim of irrational prejudice, as an example of the effects of physical and emotional deprivation (see Michie's essay relating the Creature to Marx's view of alienated labor), as a critique of Rousseauistic ideas about education articulated in *Emile*, and as a distillation of conflicting Enlightenment opinions about the "natural man" in the tradition of John Locke, Jean-Jacques Rousseau, and Etienne Condillac (see the essays by Cantor and Moses; Bennett). The Creature demonstrates dramatically that reason and its achievements (reasonableness, civility, language acquisition, etc.) are insufficient to human subsistence. Finding his needs for both physical and spiritual bonding denied, he resorts to wreaking havoc as his only means of retaliation. At the most fundamental level Mary Shelley forces her reader to wrestle with the Creature's own ambivalent nature. The reader must distinguish between an instinctive sympathy for a miserable and rejected being and the need to judge, fairly and objectively, not only the actions and responses of the Creature but also those of Victor Frankenstein (who eventually earns a measure of reader sympathy when he, too, becomes a "victim") and of other characters in the novel.

Despite being described in detail, the Creature remains only partially "visible"; his shadowy nature links him for many readers with the mind, the imagination, and the creative act, a bond reinforced in the "Author's Introduction" that Shelley added to the 1831 edition. As an entity possessed of the potential for both greatness and destructiveness, for moral good and moral evil, the Creature is an apt embodiment for the work of art (see the essay by Johnson and Georgianna), even as he is for the spirit of revolution. In this latter context the novel is often discussed as a mythic examination of the disastrous results of the French Revolution (see, for instance, Sterrenburg). Mary Shelley had, after all, spent the first eighteen years of her life in an England at war with France, a nation only a few miles from England's shores. In France, of course, an initial fervent and optimistic republican embrace of liberty, equality, and fraternity had deteriorated into years of bloody violence, dashing the hopes of meliorist political reformers like Shelley's father, the liberal political philosopher William Godwin, and her husband, Percy Shelley. Mary Shelley's own turn toward political conservatism, which becomes increasingly apparent in her subsequent writings, testifies to a considered recantation of idealism coupled with political pragmatism. In this political context, as in many other contexts, *Frankenstein* is much occupied with mythic patterns of experience, particularly in the myths of Adam and Prometheus and their negative and positive attitudes toward consciousness and in creation myths involving both Prometheus and the Creator of Genesis (see the Walling essay).

Instructors report that *Frankenstein* generates many lively discussions of ethical issues: the consequences of attempting to reach beyond conventionally accepted limits; the predicament of the scientist whose quest for knowledge yields uncontrollable destructive results; the catastrophic effects of the desire for revenge against an oppressor; the societal tendency to respond with horror and revulsion to what is different; and the responsibility toward, and the guilt resulting from, the individual's relations with others. All these issues propel students—and their teachers—into hazardous but stimulating investigations of ambivalences and ambiguities, as for instance when beauty, progress, and "the general good" are considered in their capacity to become both noble ideals and irresponsible or inadvertent sources of evil. Survey respondents are virtually unanimous in citing as one of the novel's greatest assets in the classroom its challenge to social, political, ethical, moral, spiritual, aesthetic, and intellectual complacency.

One locus of this broadly cultural complacency is particularly addressed within the context of feminist criticism and theory, both in traditional courses and in women's-studies courses (see the essays by Bennett; Wolfson; Feldman; Aldrich and Isomaki). *Frankenstein* is a central document in discussions of gender implications in writing, whether one explores what Toril Moi calls the Anglo-American feminist model, which locates social and ideological conceptions of gender systems in biological differences between men and women, or the French feminist model, which regards such social and ideological distinctions as manifestations of an essentially fallacious binary mode of thinking in Western culture (Mellor, "On Romanticism" 3–5). Two related topics to explore are the "masculinist" ideologies in *Frankenstein* and the assumptions about gender and artistic and intellectual creation that have long formed the bedrock of the Western literary-historical tradition.

Many teachers report productive discussions of such central topics as the archetypally male obsession with knowledge that often occurs in conjunction with the repression of all feelings except anger; the preference for rigid judgment over compassion; the overarching fear of domesticity; the gender implications of Romantic conventions and their relation to "female gothicism"; the motifs of "softness" and "ugliness" in the novel and their relation to gender stereotyping; and, from a Jungian perspective, Victor Frankenstein's egotism and his inability to integrate the feminine. Issues of this sort often coalesce in an approach that considers the novel, as one respondent puts it, "as a critique of the masculinist scientific tradition that separates knowledge/culture/objectivity/the masculine from feelings/nature/subjectivity/the feminine." Inherent here, too, is the larger issue of cultural conditioning, which can also be approached by considering how all the characters in *Frankenstein*, male and female, offer opportunities for exploring nineteenth-century gender politics, a subject that mediates between English literary history generally and the feminist emphases of the tradition of women's literature.

Finally, perhaps because of Mary Shelley's age when she composed *Frankenstein*, students tend to be more than usually interested in, and receptive to, biographical approaches (see Bennett's essay). Especially productive are discussions of Mary Shelley's complex and trying relationship with her husband, the consequences of their difficult life-style, and her anxiety about pregnancy, which owes much to her ambivalence about her mother, Mary Wollstonecraft, who died of complications resulting from

Mary Shelley's birth. The psychological burden of this event, together with the death of Shelley's first, premature child, sheds helpful light for students on the Creature's "birth" and subsequent history. Likewise, the whole history of parent-child relations (as both physical and literary or philosophical "creators" and "createds") among Mary Shelley's social and familial circle often provokes discussion and insights. So, too, does the consideration of *Frankenstein* as an intellectually sophisticated critique of the ideas and works of Mary Shelley's contemporaries.

I leave the last word of this overview to some of the survey respondents who were instrumental in its genesis. One instructor observed that

> students almost universally enjoy and are excited by *Frankenstein*. Non-majors as well as majors like it, freshmen who are taking a required course like it, men in a feminist course of almost all women like it, and even those fringe members of a class who are least likely to be excited by the material respond to *Frankenstein*.

This broad appeal underlies the not atypical comment of a teacher who wrote that "students *want* to write papers on *Frankenstein*. Freshmen, upperclassmen, graduate students all delight in it." Clearly, the acts of imagining, discovering, and creating can be as challenging and exciting to students at all levels as they were to Victor Frankenstein, even when their results are decidedly unlike his. Illustrating the novel's ability to speak to readers on many levels of reference and experience, one student in a Romantic poetry course saw in *Frankenstein* a forerunner of Ellison's *Invisible Man* and likened the Creature's fate to that of black Americans. An enduring literary achievement whose power continues to engage new generations of readers, *Frankenstein* is also an eminently "teachable" book that helps students to explore both their world and themselves.

SCB

Part One

MATERIALS

Stephen C. Behrendt

Editions

Teachers of *Frankenstein* face an initial decision of real consequence: whether to use the 1831 edition, which incorporates Mary Shelley's final revisions as well as the "Author's Introduction" that she added for that edition, or whether to opt instead for the novel as it first appeared, in the anonymously published text of 1818. Very significant differences separate the two texts, differences that affect the "worldview" that governs the novel and go beyond mere stylistic features to matters of philosophical import. Anne Mellor's essay on choosing a text argues that the earlier text is most perfectly representative of Mary Shelley's original vision. To choose the 1818 text, however, is to limit one's choice of a modern edition to the one prepared by James Rieger, originally published in 1974 by Bobbs-Merrill and now expensively reprinted in paperback—with a new two-page preface—by the University of Chicago Press. Most other paperback editions follow the 1831 text, which is also the preferred text for the vast majority of teachers who responded to the preliminary survey. As the survey clearly shows, however, these editions are usually chosen because of their comparatively low cost, and in fact many instructors may be unaware—like some Shelley scholarship—of the differences between the 1818 and 1831 texts.

The Bobbs-Merrill/Chicago edition reproduces the three-volume text of *Frankenstein* published in London by Lackington et al. in 1818, preserving not only the original volume and chapter designations but also all the original typographical errors. Three appendixes contain the 1831 "Author's Introduction"; a careful collation of the 1818 and 1831 texts; and the texts of the tales composed by Byron ("A Fragment") and his traveling companion John William Polidori ("The Vampyre; A Tale") as part of the famous ghost-story contest that took place in Switzerland in the summer of 1816 and of which *Frankenstein* was the most prodigious result. This edition is somewhat complicated by Rieger's decision to interpolate in the main text the autograph variants contained in the copy of the novel that the author gave to her acquaintance Mrs. Thomas in 1823. While there is probably no good way to handle these interpolations so that they do not interfere with reading, their treatment here is frequently intrusive and occasionally hard to decipher.

Rieger's introduction examines *Frankenstein*'s composition within the context of Mary Shelley's life and briefly traces the novel's place within the gothic tradition and the tradition to which it gave birth itself, the Frankenstein myth, whose clear outlines are visible in both "high art" and popular culture. The many teachers who object to the Rieger edition do so largely on the basis of the editor's introduction, which is frequently misleading and which significantly reduces Mary Shelley's role in composing her book. In his account of the text and of the novel's evolution (including the reading and correcting of proofs, which were in part carried out by Shelley's husband, Percy Bysshe Shelley, who made considerable emendations), Rieger tends to place Mary Shelley unfairly in her husband's shadow. This sort of misrepresentation of novel and author has been challenged increasingly by feminists and traditionalists alike in recent years, and particularly by the research of Betty T. Bennett on Shelley's letters, Paula Feldman and Diana Scott-Kilvert on her journals, and Anne K. Mellor on the text of *Frankenstein* itself.

Nevertheless, instructors interested in pursuing the evolution of the text and the effects of revision, as well as those teaching courses enrolling more advanced students, frequently characterize the Rieger edition as a "useful" resource. While 15% of those surveyed report that they use this edition in their classes—almost always because it presents both Shelley's "original vision" and the textual variants—fewer than 5% of instructors require it as their principal working text.

Of the paperbacks using the 1831 text, the clear leader is the Signet-NAL edition, edited by Harold Bloom, which was favored by 56% of those surveyed. The Chicago paperback is currently anywhere from three to five times as expensive as these editions. In addition, however, fully a third of those who use the Signet-NAL edition praise Bloom's "helpful" and "accessible" critical essay, "*Frankenstein*: Or, The New Prometheus," appended as an afterword and originally published in the *Partisan Review* in 1965. Most instructors appear to assign the essay to their students along with the novel, and one respondent offered the interesting comment that "the Bloom essay is useful if only to react against." Because of its wide usage, the Signet-NAL edition serves as the basis for page references in this volume.

The nearest competitor to the Signet-NAL edition and the choice of 14% of the respondents is the paperback published by Oxford. M. K. Joseph's introductory essay is praised particularly for its helpful discussion of the novel's narrative structure. Appended to this edition are excerpts from Mary Shelley's journal detailing her and Percy Shelley's Chamouni journey of July 1816 and textual materials that help to illustrate the relation of the novel's development to the author's direct experience of the environment.

Two other inexpensive paperback editions, each the choice of some 7% of the respondents, are the Bantam, edited by Diane Johnson, and the Penguin, edited by Maurice Hindle. Both editions contain critical introductions that attempt to locate the novel within biographical and a literary-historical contexts. Hindle's is perhaps the more ambitious of the two; its concluding section, "Science, Politics, and the 'Frankenstein Idea,'" explores in the context of the author's time and our own technological age the question of whether *Frankenstein* is the product of a radical or a reactionary consciousness and focuses, as Mary Shelley did, on the pressing need to consider the ethical alternatives implicit in any "great" enterprise.

Other paperback editions exist and will continue to appear: *Frankenstein*'s perennial appeal ensures that. Oxford has added to its World's Classics series an edition prepared by James Kinsley and M. K. Joseph, and Running Press (Philadelphia) has produced an edition that gathers excerpts relevant to *Frankenstein* from Robert Kiely's *Romantic Novel in England*, a reading that has been superseded to a considerable extent by more recent critical treatments. The University of California Press has published an edition that includes Barry Moser's fascinating illustrations. *The Annotated Frankenstein* is helpful in locating the novel within the contexts of its scientific background and of popular culture. These two illustrated editions were frequently mentioned by survey respondents as good secondary sources or as recommended reading.

The *Frankenstein* desiderata are brief but emphatic. Instructors feel acutely the need for a sound critical edition in the mold of the Norton Critical Editions—a project that was in the works at least once but, lamentably, has never been pursued to its completion. Second, those whose work with *Frankenstein* involves not only classroom teaching but also their own extended research remark on the need for a complete transcription and a decent-quality photoreproduction of the manuscript fragments in the Abinger Shelley collection at the Bodleian Library.

Other Works by Mary Shelley

1817: *History of a Six Weeks' Tour through a Part of France, Switzerland, Germany, and Holland: With Letters Descriptive of a Sail round the Lake of Geneva, and of the Glaciers of Chamouni.* With Percy Shelley. London: Hookham.

1823: *Valperga: Or, The Life and Adventures of Castruccio, Prince of Lucca.* London: Whittaker. Modern reprint edition, New York: AMS. A long novel of political ambition and its attendant moral and ethical corruption that examines within political and historical frameworks many of the issues treated in *Frankenstein.* In championing a heroism grounded in domestic virtue and an absence of self-aggrandizing ambition, *Valperga* proposes by analogy a counterexample to the then recent negative example of Napoleon.

1824: Editor, *Posthumous Poems of Percy Bysshe Shelley.*

1826: *The Last Man.* London: Colburn. An excellent modern edition is *The Last Man,* edited by Hugh J. Luke, Jr. (Lincoln: U of Nebraska P, 1965). A deeply pessimistic tale of the destruction of humanity by an incurable plague (and a dark analogy for the future of democratic idealism), set in the twenty-first century and centered on the virtuous Lionel Verney, the final survivor. The narrative framework draws on the familiar device of the editorial reconstruction, a convention of the gothic tale established by Horace Walpole's *Castle of Otranto* (1764) and employed by many, including Percy Shelley in his revolutionary *Swellfoot the Tyrant* (1820). A nameless editor informs the reader that the tale has been pieced together from bits of information written on leaves and bark and preserved in a cave.

1830: *The Fortunes of Perkin Warbeck.* London: Colburn. Modern reprint edition, Folcroft: Folcroft, 1975. Another historical novel, set in the years following the death of Richard III in 1485, centering on the conflicting impulses toward political ambition, personal virtue, and dignity. Articulates, again by analogy, the author's increasingly conservative, pragmatic view that social stability is ultimately more important in the modern world than determined (and costly) pursuit of heroic but outdated and impractical idealism.

1835: *Lodore.* Paris: Galignani. Modern reprint, New York: AMS. A sentimental and loosely autobiographical novel written, apparently, to illustrate, within the workings of a social circle that includes recognizable members of Mary Shelley's own set, the author's stated view that the primary value of human life is to be found in "the genuine affections of the heart."

1835:   *Lives of the Most Eminent Literary and Scientific Men of Italy, Spain, and Portugal.* Vols. 1 and 2. With James Montgomery. London: Longman. These and the related volumes listed below are part of Lardner's *Cabinet Cyclopedia.*

1836:   *Lives.* Vol. 3. London: Longman.

1837:   *Falkner.* London: Saunders. Modern reprint edition, Folcroft: Folcroft, 1975. Another illustration of the primacy of the affections of the heart, the novel traces the history of a would-be suicide and the six-year-old orphan girl who prevents his self-destruction through a series of adventures in which natural benevolence triumphs over personal guilt to lead to separate, but related, lives for both principal figures.

1838:   *Lives of the Most Eminent Literary and Scientific Men of France.* Vol. 1. London: Longman.

1839:   Editor, *The Poetical Works of Percy Bysshe Shelley.* London: Moxon. Mary Shelley's notes and comments are incorporated in the Oxford Standard Authors volume *Shelley: Poetical Works,* edited by Thomas Hutchinson and corrected by G. M. Matthews (Oxford: Oxford UP, 1971).

1839:   Editor, *Essays, Letters from Abroad, Translations and Fragments.* By Percy Bysshe Shelley. London: Moxon.

1839:   *Lives of the Most Eminent Literary and Scientific Men of France.* Vol. 2. London: Longman.

1844:   *Rambles in Germany and Italy, in 1840, 1842, and 1843.* London: Moxon. Modern reprint edition, Folcroft: Folcroft, 1975.

Beginning in 1824, Shelley also published some twenty-five tales and short stories, which have been collected, ably edited, and introduced by Charles E. Robinson in *Mary Shelley: Collected Tales and Stories* (Baltimore: Johns Hopkins UP, 1976). She also wrote two mythological dramas, *Proserpine* and *Midas,* both first published in 1922 and edited by A. Koszul (London: Milford; Rpt. Folcroft: Folcroft, 1974), as well as a novella, *Mathilda,* first published in 1959 and edited by Elizabeth Nitchie (Chapel Hill: U of North Carolina P, 1959; Rpt. Derby: Arden, 1983). Shelley was also the author of occasional poems, reviews, memoirs, and other literary notices.

The Instructor's Library

Because *Frankenstein* is taught in such a variety of classroom contexts, this checklist of recommended materials is necessarily highly selective, although its objectives are diverse. I include primary and secondary materials concerning Mary Shelley as well as other secondary materials that instructors have particularly recommended, either for their direct relevance to *Frankenstein* itself or for their insight into the milieu from which the novel emerged and those contexts in which it is now studied and taught. The listing makes no attempt to cover all the bases, but includes those materials identified by the survey respondents as the most immediately useful, stimulating, or controversial. I also attempt to suggest the diversity of available materials, which exists in direct proportion to the diversity of interests represented by the novel itself and by students and teachers of the novel.

As I have said, no teacher of *Frankenstein* can avoid the effect its various permutations have had on the public—representations ranging from stage productions (some dating from Shelley's own lifetime) to filmic versions to *The Munsters* television series and Frankenberry cereal. Appearing first as a literary work partaking of and contributing to established (albeit evolving) literary genres, Mary Shelley's novel, like the Creature who is often mistakenly saddled with his creator's name, has achieved in popular culture a virtually independent existence; this frequently extraliterary mythic dimension manages to address contemporary ideals and fears while retaining to a surprising degree the power that the novel bore for its original nineteenth-century audience. Both this part of the volume and the essays that follow attempt to provide useful suggestions for instructors who may themselves be products as much of the popular-culture versions of *Frankenstein* as of the literary source.

Reference Works

Recent years have seen the release of splendid new editions of Mary Shelley's letters and journals. *The Letters of Mary Wollstonecraft Shelley*, edited by Betty T. Bennett, collects in three volumes both the extant letters and a wealth of background material essential to the serious student of Shelley's life and works. Likewise, *The Journals of Mary Shelley*, edited by Paula Feldman and Diana Scott-Kilvert, presents with detailed biographical commentary in two volumes all surviving journal entries, a particularly valuable resource for contemporary details of external and internal landscapes that bear directly on the shape and composition of *Frankenstein*. An adequate, if occasionally inaccurate, modern biography is Jane Dunn's *Moon in Eclipse: A Life of Mary Shelley*, a much more ambitious undertaking than two earlier but nevertheless still valuable biographical and critical studies: Muriel Spark's *Child of Light: A Reassessment of Mary Wollstonecraft Shelley* (revised in 1987 as *Mary Shelley: A Biography*) and Elizabeth Nitchie's *Mary Shelley: Author of* Frankenstein, which offers perhaps the most insightful reading of the fiction Shelley composed after *Frankenstein*. Dunn's biography likewise supersedes Rosalie G. Grylls's *Mary Shelley: A Biography*, an excellent and judicious early assessment but one that newer research has now rendered outdated. A related study that many instructors find useful is Christopher Small's *Mary Shelley's* Frankenstein: *Tracing the Myth* (originally published as *Ariel like a Harpy*), which examines the reflections in *Frankenstein* of the relationship of Mary and Percy Shelley. The first biography, commissioned by Sir Percy and Lady Jane Shelley (Mary and Percy Shelley's son and daughter-in-law) and clearly bearing the latter's stamp, was Mrs. Julian Marshall's *Life and Letters of Mary Wollstonecraft Shelley* (1889). This idealized and idealizing study reveals perhaps as much about the late Victorian intellectual climate as it does about Mary Shelley. Given that *Frankenstein* is frequently included not just in English novel courses but also in courses in the Victorian novel, however, this study helps to shed light on the novel's appeal to the Victorians. Of great importance is Anne K. Mellor's *Mary Shelley: Her Life, Her Fiction, Her Monsters*, a reassessment of Mary Shelley's life and literary achievement that draws heavily on manuscript materials in the Bodleian Library. Still more recent is Emily Sunstein's *Mary Wollstonecraft Shelley: Romance and Reality.*

Instructors will undoubtedly find useful W. H. Lyles's *Mary Shelley: An Annotated Bibliography*, which provides a virtually complete and well-indexed guide to English and non-English materials about Mary Shelley and her works through 1975, with helpful annotations to most entries and appendixes of theatrical, film, and television versions of Shelley's works, also through 1975. Subsequent materials are best accessed through the MLA annual bibliographies and the *ELH* annual bibliography of Romantic studies, as well as through specialized publications like the *Keats-Shelley Journal* and the *Keats-Shelley Memorial Bulletin* (renamed the *Keats-Shelley Review* in 1986).

A valuable guide to Mary Shelley's literary milieu is *Shelley and His Circle*, now complete in eight volumes and edited by Kenneth Cameron and Donald Reiman. This meticulous descriptive catalog of materials in the Carl H. Pforzheimer Library (now relocated to the New York Public Library) spans the years 1773 to 1822 and includes, in addition to materials by and pertaining to Mary Shelley, manuscripts and other materials of her parents, Mary Wollstonecraft and William Godwin; her husband, Percy Bysshe Shelley; her stepsister, Clara Mary Jane (Claire) Clairmont; literary acquaintances like Byron, Leigh Hunt, and Thomas Love Peacock; and other members of this remarkable literary, social, and political circle. The volumes include transcriptions (and some photoreproductions) of manuscript materials, copious descriptive and background discussions, and introductions to each of the principal members of the circle. These introductory essays, which include Sylva Norman's witty but rather condescending essay on Mary Shelley, have been conveniently gathered in *Romantic Rebels: Essays on Shelley and His Circle* (ed. Cameron).

The matter of a "Shelley circle" poses something of a thorny issue, in that the achievements of Mary Shelley and other women have too often been accorded insufficient attention (and merit), at least partially as the unfortunate result of gender-oriented standards and preconceptions that have in the past gone largely unchallenged in critical and literary-historical inquiry. This trend has been ably—some would say controversially—countered in recent years by feminist theory and criticism. It is significant, indeed telling, that the original title of Christopher Small's popular study of Mary Shelley's best-known novel bears the subtitle *Shelley, Mary and Frankenstein*. Both the ordering of the names and the pointed handling of surname and Christian name illustrate a pattern all too familiar to those engaged in Mary Shelley studies. One hopes that the burst of enlightenment that led to the republication of *Ariel like a Harpy* under the title of *Mary Shelley's* Frankenstein: *Tracing the Myth* marks a significant critical and institutional divestiture of such implicit sexism.

That said, however, it must be noted that both the student and the teacher of *Frankenstein* will find much valuable background material, biographical and critical, in sources treating other members of Mary Shelley's circle, particularly her husband. The standard biography of Percy Bysshe Shelley is Newman Ivey White's *Shelley*; Richard Holmes's more recent *Shelley: The Pursuit* is less objective and less dependable, overall, though Holmes's discussion of Percy's relationship with Mary is often perceptive. Like Mrs. Marshall's biography of Mary Shelley, Edward Dowden's *Life of Percy Bysshe Shelley* (the "official" biography sponsored by Lady Shelley) offers an illuminating late-Victorian perspective on the poet and his circle. Especially revealing are Percy's letters to and about Mary, included by Frederick L. Jones in *The Letters of Percy Bysshe Shelley*. The letters trace the evolution of the Shelley's relationship from the early playfulness of genuine affection through the painful alienation that was the inevitable consequence of their difficult life-style and the enormous physical and emotional demands it placed particularly on Mary Shelley, who before she was twenty-three had endured four difficult pregnancies and the deaths of three of her children. Also valuable is *The Journals of Claire Clairmont*, which contains much information on the novelist's personal relationships, her reading, her opinions, and her health during the period most immediately relevant to *Frankenstein*.

Critical Works

A 1987 volume in Chelsea House's Modern Critical Interpretations series, *Mary Shelley's* Frankenstein, edited by Harold Bloom, conveniently assembles a number of previously published critical studies that instructors of *Frankenstein* will find helpful. The overwhelming favorite among instructors, however, both for their own use and for their students', is George Levine and U. C. Knoepflmacher's collection of critical essays, *The Endurance of* Frankenstein, which offers informative essays on the novel's scientific, literary, social, cultural, popular-cultural, and biographical backgrounds. Many teachers and scholars obviously agree with William Veeder, who deems this volume "a milestone in *Frankenstein* criticism" because "it shows that scholars have at last taken Mary Shelley seriously as an artist and have seen her candidly as a human being" (230). Among the book's excellent contributions is George Levine's "Ambiguous Heritage of *Frankenstein*," a useful overview of the varied literary and critical response to *Frankenstein*. Included also in the Levine-Knoepflmacher volume is Ellen Moers's "Female Gothic," excerpted from her *Literary Women*, itself an important and often recommended study. Moers examines Shelley's treatment of birth, which she views as gothic fantasy deeply rooted in the novelist's physical and psychological experience as "a woman who, as daughter, mistress, and mother, was a bearer of death" (98).

In this context the discussion of *Frankenstein* in Sandra M. Gilbert and Susan Gubar's *Madwoman in the Attic* is unquestionably central to feminist approaches to the novel and its author, as is Mary Poovey's chapter on the novel in *The Proper Lady and the Woman Writer*. Valuable here, too, is Barbara Johnson's "My Monster/My Self," which examines the interrelated themes of mothering, the woman writer, and autobiography. In *Bearing the Word*, Margaret Homans considers in the context of *Frankenstein* the situation of the woman writer whose creative activity is perceived as "literalization, as a form of mothering" by a male-dominated culture that devalues both these activities. Feminist criticism and the traditions of gothic art come together in interesting fashion in Mary K. Patterson Thornburg's *Monster in the Mirror*, which appeared too recently to be familiar to most survey respondents.

The context of the tradition of gothic art, which is of such import to *Frankenstein*, is examined in several other frequently recommended studies, including "Night Thoughts on the Gothic Novel" by Lowry Nelson, Jr. Interestingly, only one instructor mentioned as significant in this connection the two gothic romances Percy Shelley wrote before he met his future wife, perhaps because they have been much maligned by critics. These two novels, Zastrozzi and St. Irvyne, are now available in an Oxford World's Classics paperback, with a critical introduction by Stephen C. Behrendt. Two useful critical studies of the gothic in general are The Gothic Imagination: Essays in Dark Romanticism, edited by G. R. Thompson, and Devendra P. Varma's Gothic Flame. Ann B. Tracy's Gothic Novel: 1790–1830 combines critical and bibliographical resources.

In terms of the genre of the novel, some instructors recommend Robert Kiely's Romantic Novel in England, while others express reservations about the timeliness of its assumptions and conclusions. George Levine's "Frankenstein and the Tradition of Realism," like his Realistic Imagination, is also frequently cited for its usefulness to the beginning teacher of Frankenstein. An excellent recent study of Frankenstein's place in the context of monstrosity in nineteenth-century fiction is Chris Baldick's In Frankenstein's Shadow.

Harold Bloom's "Frankenstein: Or, The New Prometheus" remains a popular background essay, both because of its accessibility as the afterword to the Signet-NAL paperback edition and because of its incisive discussion of the novel as a counterstatement to Romantic doctrines of Prometheanism and hence to the Romantic mythology of the self. Also valuable for first-time instructors of Frankenstein is William Walling's Mary Shelley, which provides the introductory overview of biographical, textual, and critical matters that characterizes the Twayne English Author Series generally. This volume is currently being revised to take into account more fully the explosion of critical discussion since its first appearance in 1972.

The psychological dimension of Frankenstein has, of course, been the focus of many studies. Masao Miyoshi's Divided Self considers the doppelgänger (in both gothic literature and Frankenstein) within the context of post-Enlightenment dualisms of mind and material, and David Ketterer usefully explores the double in Frankenstein's Creation. Another excellent psychological study is Marc A. Rubenstein's " 'My Accursed Origin': The Search for the Mother in Frankenstein." Morton Kaplan and Robert Kloss, despite their seeming unwillingness to admit any but a Freudian reading of literature, nevertheless also write suggestively of Frankenstein in The Unspoken Motive. In Mary Shelley's Monster Martin Tropp investigates the novel in terms of dreams and dreaming, while Paul Sherwin's title, "Frankenstein: Creation as Catastrophe," indicates the thrust of this important article's internal and external concerns. Particularly stimulating is Mary Shelley and Frankenstein: The Fate of Androgny, in which William Veeder examines the phenomenon of Mary Shelley's simultaneously conservative and subversive vision within a novel in which biography, "self," and the literary work (including the author's subsequent writings) all participate in a complex and dynamic interrelation.

Several works defy clear categorization. A number of instructors recommend Radu Florescu's *In Search of* Frankenstein, which attempts to trace the historical origins of the characters and situation on which Mary Shelley's narrative is ostensibly based. Others find Donald Glut's *Frankenstein Legend* a useful—if occasionally overwhelming—guide to *Frankenstein*'s appearances in popular culture. Finally, and appropriately, the last word in popular-culture sourcebooks must inevitably belong to another production by Glut, whose own extended title says it all: *The* Frankenstein *Catalogue: Being a Comprehensive Listing of Novels, Translations, Adaptations, Stories, Critical Works, Popular Articles, Series, Fumetti, Verse, Stage Plays, Films, Cartoons, Puppetry, Radio and Television Programs, Comics, Satire and Humor, Spoken and Musical Recordings, Tapes, and Sheet Music Featuring Frankenstein's Monster and or Descended from Mary Shelley's Novel.*

Recommended Reading for Students

The works instructors recommend to their students depend, naturally, on the context in which *Frankenstein* is being taught and the readings that inform the instructor's approach. In courses in the novel, Robert Kiely's *Romantic Novel in England* is the most often recommended source, while students in a course in science fiction or fantasy may be directed to Eric S. Rabkin's *Fantastic in Literature*. The most frequently recommended feminist readings of the novel are found in Sandra M. Gilbert and Susan Gubar's *Madwoman in the Attic*, Mary Poovey's *Proper Lady and the Woman Writer*, and Ellen Moers's *Literary Women*. Too recent to have been mentioned in the survey are Anne K. Mellor's *Mary Shelley: Her Life, Her Fiction, Her Monsters*, the first full-length feminist study of Mary Shelley's life and works, and Emily Sunstein's *Mary Wollstonecraft Shelley: Romance and Reality*. For general background, many instructors recommend Christopher Small's *Mary Shelley's* Frankenstein: *Tracing the Myth* and Martin Tropp's *Mary Shelley's Monster*, as well as William Walling's *Mary Shelley* and Harold Bloom's "*Frankenstein*: Or, The New Prometheus." By far the greatest number of instructors, however, send their students to *The Endurance of* Frankenstein, the collection of essays edited by George Levine and U. C. Knoepflmacher. More than 60% of those instructors who recommend outside reading to their students cited this work as their principal choice. Finally, several instructors direct their students to Mary Shelley's journals and letters.

The literary works recommended by instructors also reflect the curricular environment in which *Frankenstein* is being taught, though most agree that students should read Coleridge's *Rime of the Ancient Mariner*. Other Romantic texts mentioned most frequently in this context are Percy Shelley's *Prometheus Unbound* and Byron's *Manfred*. One instructor reports that Percy Shelley's *Cenci* is helpful, since in that play and in Mary Shelley's novel alike potential goodness and love are turned to evil by the outrages of the parent and the hopelessness and helplessness of the child. Percy Shelley's *Alastor*, Byron's *Cain* and "Prometheus," Coleridge's "Christabel," Keats's "Lamia," Blake's *Book of Urizen*, and Goethe's *Faust* and *Sorrows of Young Werther* often supplement the study of *Frankenstein*. Surprisingly, only one respondent reports either suggesting or using any of Wordsworth's works, reflecting the general lack of attention to the strong (and after 1814 increasingly negative) formative influence exerted by Wordsworth and his works on the entire Shelley circle.

Other important literary texts that instructors recommend include Aeschylus's *Prometheus Bound*, Milton's *Paradise Lost*, and the Book of Genesis, as well as gothic novels like Matthew Lewis's *Monk*, Ann Radcliffe's *Mysteries of Udolpho*, and Volney's *Ruins of Empires*, which, like *Paradise Lost* and Coleridge's *Rime*, figures prominently in *Frankenstein*. Finally, instructors frequently recommend various writings of Mary Shelley's parents: Mary Wollstonecraft's *Maria: Or, The Wrongs of Woman* and *Vindication of the Rights of Woman* and William Godwin's *Caleb Williams, St. Leon*, and *Enquiry concerning Political Justice*.

It may be helpful to note here some of the novels with which *Frankenstein* is frequently linked in courses in English fiction. Most prominent are *Wuthering Heights, Great Expectations, Jane Eyre, Dr. Jekyll and Mr. Hyde, The Picture of Dorian Gray*, and James Hogg's *Private Memoirs and Confessions of a Justified Sinner*. Courses in gothic fiction commonly include some of the above, as well as Horace Walpole's *Castle of Otranto* (generally regarded as the first English gothic novel), William Beckford's *Vathek*, John William Polidori's "Vampyre," and Bram Stoker's *Dracula*. In such courses it is useful also to recommend Edmund Burke's *Philosophical Enquiry into the Origin of Our Ideas of the Sublime and Beautiful*, which greatly affected literary (and visual-arts) explorations of the sublime. Works most often mentioned for comparison with *Frankenstein* in the context of science fiction are Ursula Le Guin's *Left Hand of Darkness*, Fred Saberhagen's *Frankenstein Papers*, and Brian Aldiss's *Frankenstein Unbound*.

A Selected Filmography

This selective filmography lists some of the most important and influential, as well as the most accessible, cinematic versions of *Frankenstein*. For more detailed discussion of these and other films, see Wheeler Dixon's essay in this volume, as well as Albert J. La Valley's "Stage and Film Children of *Frankenstein*: A Survey."

Frankenstein. Dir. J. Searle Dawley. With Charles Ogle. Edison, 1910. Silent. 975 feet (approx. 11 min.).

Frankenstein. Dir. James Whale. Prod. Carl Laemmle, Jr. Adaptation by Robert Florey and John L. Balderston. Screenplay by Garrett Fort, Robert Florey, and Francis Edward Faragoh. Based on the play by Peggy Webling. With Boris Karloff, Colin Clive, and Mae Clarke. Universal, 1931. 71 min.

The Bride of Frankenstein. Dir. James Whale. Screenplay by William Hurlbut and John Balderston. With Boris Karloff, Colin Clive, Valerie Hobson, and Elsa Lanchester. Universal, 1935. 80 min.

Son of Frankenstein. Dir. and prod. Rowland V. Lee. Screenplay by Willis Cooper. With Bela Lugosi, Boris Karloff, Basil Rathbone, Lionel Atwill, and Josephine Hutchinson. Universal, 1939. 93 min.

The Ghost of Frankenstein. Dir. Erle C. Kenton. Prod. George Waggner. Screenplay by W. Scott Darling. Story by Eric Taylor. With Cedric Hardwicke, Lon Chaney, Jr., Ralph Bellamy, Evelyn Ankers, Lionel Atwill, and Bela Lugosi. Universal, 1942. 67 min.

Frankenstein Meets the Wolf Man. Dir. Roy William Neill. Prod. George Waggner. Screenplay by Curt Siodmak. With Lon Chaney, Jr., Bela Lugosi, Patric Knowles, Ilona Massey, and Lionel Atwill. Universal, 1943. 73 min.

House of Frankenstein. Dir. Erle C. Kenton. Screenplay by Edward T. Lowe. Story by Curt Siodmak. With Boris Karloff, Anne Gwynne, Lon Chaney, Jr., J. Carroll Naish, Elena Verdugo, John Carradine, and Lionel Atwill. Universal, 1944. 70 min.

House of Dracula. Dir. Erle C. Kenton. Prod. Paul Malvern. Screenplay by Edward T. Lowe. With Lon Chaney, Jr., John Carradine, Onslow Stevens, Ludwig Stossel, Jane Adams, and Lionel Atwill. Universal, 1945. 67 min.

Abbott and Costello Meet Frankenstein. Dir. Charles T. Barton. Screenplay by Robert Lees, Frederic Rinaldo, and John Grant. With Bud Abbott, Lou Costello, Bela Lugosi, Lon Chaney, Jr., Glenn Strange, and Lenore Aubert. Universal, 1948. 90 min.

The Curse of Frankenstein. Dir. Terence Fisher. Screenplay by James Sangster. With Christopher Lee, Peter Cushing, Hazel Court, and Valerie Gaunt. Warner Brothers/Hammer, 1957. Eastmancolor. 83 min.

The Revenge of Frankenstein. Dir. Terence Fisher. Screenplay by James Sangster. With Peter Cushing, Francis Matthews, Eunice Gayson, Michael Gwynn, and Lionel Jeffries. Columbia/Hammer, 1958. Technicolor. 91 min.

Frankenstein 1970. Dir. Howard W. Koch. Screenplay by George W. Yates and Richard Landau. Story by Aubrey Schenck and Charles A. Moses. With Boris Karloff, Don Barry, Jana Lund, and Charlotte Austin. Allied Artists, 1958. 83 min.

The Evil of Frankenstein. Dir. Freddie Francis. Prod. Anthony Hinds. Screenplay by John Elder. With Peter Cushing, Sandor Eles, Kiwi Kingston, Katy Wild, and Peter Woodthorpe. Universal/Hammer, 1964. Eastmancolor. 87 min.

Frankenstein Created Woman. Dir. Terence Fisher. Screenplay by John Elder. With Peter Cushing, Susan Denberg, and Thorley Walters. Fox/7A-Hammer, 1966. Color. 92 min.

Frankenstein Must Be Destroyed. Dir. Terence Fisher. Prod. Anthony Nelson-Keys. Screenplay by Bert Batt. With Peter Cushing, Simon Ward, Veronica Carlson, and Freddie Jones. Warner Brothers/Hammer, 1969. Eastmancolor. 97 min.

Frankenstein and the Monster from Hell. Dir. Terence Fisher. Prod. Roy Skeggs. Screenplay by John Elder. With Peter Cushing, Shane Briant, David Prowse, Bernard Lee, and Madeline Smith. Paramount/Hammer, 1973. Eastmancolor. 94 min.

Young Frankenstein. Dir. Mel Brooks. With Gene Wilder, Peter Boyle, Madeline Kahn, Cloris Leachman, and Marty Feldman. Fox, 1974. Black and white.

Terror of Frankenstein (Victor Frankenstein). Prod. and dir. Calvin Floyd. Screenplay by Yvonne and Calvin Floyd. With Leon Vitali, Per Oscarsson, Nicholas Clay, and Stacey Dorning. Aspekt Film/Independent International, 1976. Color. 93 min.

The Bride. Dir. Franc Roddam. Prod. Victor Drai. Screenplay by Lloyd Fonvielle. With Sting, Jennifer Beals, Anthony Higgins, and Clancy Brown. Columbia, 1986. 118 min.

Gothic. Dir. Ken Russell. Prod. Penny Corke. Screenplay by Stephen Volk. With Natasha Richardson, Julian Sands, Gabriel Byrne, Myriam Cyr, and Timothy Spall. Vestron, 1987. 90 min.

A Note on Rentals

Most of these films are available either on videocassette (VHS or Beta format) or on 16mm film for nontheatrical rental. For information, consult the latest edition of James L. Limbacher's *Guide to Rental Films in 16mm* (R. R. Bowker) or either of the following:

Films Incorporated
440 Park Avenue South
New York, NY 10016
212 889-7910

Swank Motion Pictures
393 Front Street
Hempstead, NY 11550
516 538-6500

For *The Terror of Frankenstein (Victor Frankenstein):*

Independent-International Pictures
223 State Highway 18
East Brunswick, NJ 08901
201 249-8982

Part Two

APPROACHES

INTRODUCTION

The following essays reflect the wide range of contexts and institutions in which *Frankenstein* is taught as well as the individual interests of the instructors who teach it. While a work as multifaceted as *Frankenstein* is unlikely to yield a unanimity of approach or interpretation, these essays respond to key issues that surface repeatedly in discussions of the novel. The essays address a variety of classroom situations, from the introductory to the very advanced, both within and outside the parameters of traditional "English" courses.

Many points of critical and pedagogical intersection inform these essays, but I have made no attempt to minimize the differences of interpretation and, occasionally, of politics that occur. Although unsettling to students who long for the security of critical unanimity, such differences are the lifeblood of critical inquiry. Moreover, they testify to the capacity of Mary Shelley's novel to stimulate continuing discussion of complex issues. Indeed, the present volume kindled warm debate among its contributors and reviewers as it progressed, both over the subjects it addresses and the manner in which they are pursued. One reviewer observed that, since Shelley's novel deals with "monstrous reflections," the conflicting readings and pedagogies it generates should come as little surprise. *Frankenstein* draws heat and intellectual vigor from the collision of diverse ideologies in its pages; students may be intrigued—and perhaps both emboldened and empowered—to discover the passionate debate it ignites among teachers and specialists.

The essays included here constitute only a portion of the intellectual and pedagogical approaches to *Frankenstein;* they are not intended to appear either exclusive or exhaustive. Rather, these essays are most properly regarded as contributions to an ongoing critical, intellectual, and pedagogical discussion. I encourage the readers of this volume to study, to compare, and to join in the dialogue.

The first section of essays deals with general issues involved in teaching the novel. As I observe in the "Materials" section of this volume, choosing a text of *Frankenstein* to teach is an important decision. Anne K. Mellor discusses the significant differences between the 1818 and the 1831 texts as well as their implications for reading, comprehending, interpreting, and teaching the novel. Her essay underscores the urgent need for a reasonably priced and widely available edition of the earlier text.

William Veeder's essay describes a structural approach to *Frankenstein* that takes into account the narrative frames and their function. American feminist literary criticism has recently examined the concept of gender as a manifestation of particular historical moments, classes, and cultures. This complex matter holds special relevance in Veeder's essay, which emphasizes gender relations and the human motivations that various characters in *Frankenstein* attempt to hide, both from themselves and from others.

The essay by Susan J. Wolfson explores the field of feminist inquiry as it relates to the curricular contexts within which *Frankenstein* is currently taught. Using the novel to raise questions about the ideology of gender-endorsed behavior, Wolfson details a strategy to examine Shelley's characters as "extremes"—egoists, repressors, self-sacrificers—or as "balanced," equilibrious nurturers. This approach reveals that the Creature has many "feminine" traits that place him in inevitable opposition to the novel's prevailing masculinist power structures.

Drawing on narrative theory, Syndy M. Conger emphasizes the ways in which Shelley's novel forces readers to alter their customary responses to fiction, particularly gothic fiction. Readers become active participants in evaluating the novel because it denies them the familiar reliable narrator and the traditional naive reader responses of unmixed sympathy for the protagonist and disgust at the antagonist.

The essay by Paula R. Feldman examines the psychology of *Frankenstein*. Feldman's principal concerns are the recurrent dream of resurrecting the dead; the themes of creation and destruction, acceptance and rejection; and Shelley's ambivalence about being both writer (creator) and mother (procreator). Concluding this section is my essay on the complex language and style of *Frankenstein*, perhaps the single most frustrating and alienating aspect of the novel for student readers. The essay suggests strategies to help students appreciate the intentional authorial choices that underlie the work's challenging diction and syntax.

The second group of essays offers a number of significant contexts for studying *Frankenstein*. Like many instructors, Betty T. Bennett devotes considerable classroom time to the biographical details of Mary Shelley's life. Bennett's approach familiarizes more advanced students with Shelley's letters and journals and explores particular passages (such as those singled out in the introductions to Bennett's edition of Shelley's letters) to investigate the extent to which the novel is grounded in biography.

Elsie B. Michie applies a Marxist approach to Shelley's novel. Michie views Shelley's characterization of the Creature less as creation than as "product," a characterization that anticipates Marx's theory of the alienation between workers and their products. Within the context of a course in Romantic literature and aesthetic theory, a second essay by Anne Mellor considers the novel's relation to the views of Edmund Burke and Immanuel Kant on the nature of the sublime and the beautiful, demonstrating affinities between the novel's treatment of the sublime and a semiotic reading of nature. William Walling's essay also approaches *Frankenstein* in terms of analogous Romantic literary works.

The next group of essays describes approaches to teaching *Frankenstein* within specific course settings. In science fiction courses, for example, the novel is often taught to students whose concept of "science" is somewhat fuzzy. Terrence Holt suggests a method to show students in science fiction courses the sophisticated literary techniques Shelley uses to distract the reader from—and indeed to supersede—the empirical detail required in writing about science. Evident (or implied) in Holt's essay and in many of the others in this volume is the need for instructors to anticipate variations in student backgrounds and expectations when they prepare to shift from one course or context to another.

In a course in women's literature, Marcia Aldrich and Richard Isomaki focus on *Frankenstein* as a means to explore the notion of the woman writer's creation as "hideous" within the context of other creation myths like *Paradise Lost* and Sylvia Plath's *Ariel*. Their essay discusses ways to examine Shelley and the Creature as figures denied social legitimacy because of their troubled parentage. The matter of real and perceived marginality in *Frankenstein* is taken up in the essay by Paul A. Cantor and Michael Valdez Moses. In their literature survey courses, Cantor and Moses emphasize the Creature's narrative account of life on the margins of society, relating it to Rousseau's views on education and to the lower educational status of women in Shelley's time (see also Vlasopolos, "Mask of Reason").

Mary K. Thornburg describes a method for teaching the novel to lower-division nonmajors in a required literature course. Her essay focuses on the distinctive thematic and rhetorical patterns that a structural approach to *Frankenstein* can reveal, particularly to unsophisticated readers. Similarly, Donovan Johnson and Linda Georgianna teach the novel in a large lower-division interdisciplinary humanities course, whose enrollment comprises students with varied majors and career interests. Linking *Frankenstein* to a surprising companion text, these authors attempt to address both the desire for curricular breadth and the emphasis on student writing that are typical objectives of such courses.

In her essay, Sylvia Bowerbank invokes the context of science and empirical analysis to assess Victor Frankenstein in terms of the contrasting perspectives of science and sentiment. Bowerbank's essay shows how Shelley deliberately places the burden of judging on the reader, despite the novel's emphasis on abdication of moral authority. Concluding this section, Art Young describes the pedagogy of writing across the curriculum and details effective assignments and the type of student-teacher interaction such assignments can produce.

Two essays on the filmic versions of *Frankenstein* complete the collection. Harriet E. Margolis discusses the typical cinematic simplifications of the novel and uses them to explore ways in which the various adaptations can help, rather than hinder, students' understanding of *Frankenstein*.

Wheeler Winston Dixon's essay is both longer than and pedagogically different from the other essays. Because the filmic versions of *Frankenstein* strongly influence students' preconceptions of the novel and affect the teaching process itself, a historical and critical survey of that cinematic tradition seems appropriate. Dixon's essay highlights the aesthetic, historical, and economic factors involved in the making of some of these films and considers the implications—for the film industry and for our culture—of the evolution of the celluloid Creature.

In the essays that follow, parenthetical page numbers refer to the Signet-NAL edition of *Frankenstein*, edited by Harold Bloom, unless otherwise indicated. References to the Rieger edition of the 1818 text are identified parenthetically as "Rieger."

GENERAL ISSUES

Choosing a Text of *Frankenstein* to Teach

Anne K. Mellor

Which edition of *Frankenstein* should I teach? This question is more complicated than it might at first appear. There are critically significant differences among the manuscript of *Frankenstein* in the Bodleian Library, the first edition of the novel in 1818, and the second and heavily revised edition of 1831. Since current text-editing theory and practice no longer assume that the author's final word is definitive, we cannot select the final edition for that reason alone. Nor should we be unduly swayed by the fact that the 1831 edition in the Signet-NAL paperback costs less than two dollars.

I strongly believe that the text of preference should be the 1818 edition, for the same reasons that students of Romanticism prefer the 1805 edition of Wordsworth's *Prelude* to the final 1850 edition. The first completed versions of both works have greater internal philosophical coherence, are closest to the authors' original conceptions, and are more convincingly related to their historical contexts. In *Frankenstein*, these contexts are biographical (the recent death of Mary Shelley's first baby and her dissatisfactions with Percy Shelley's Romantic ideology), political (her observations of the aftermath of the French Revolution in 1814–16), and scientific (the experiments with galvanic electricity in the first decade of the nineteenth century).

The most striking thematic differences between the two published versions of the novel concern the role of fate, the degree of Frankenstein's responsibility for his actions, the representation of nature, the role of

Clerval, and the representation of the family. I discuss these issues in more detail later in this essay, but here I must make two preliminary observations. Even the first published text of *Frankenstein* has moved away from Mary Shelley's original style and conception, insofar as we can determine these from the surviving sections of the manuscript in the Abinger Shelley Collection in the Bodleian Library (these sections constitute page 30, line 13, through page 109, line 9, plus page 117, line 17, to page 221, line 12, in the Rieger edition of the 1818 text). Furthermore, the account given of this manuscript by James Rieger, the editor of the only available reprint of the 1818 text of *Frankenstein*, is so inaccurate and so prejudiced in favor of Percy Shelley that students must be warned against its misleading combination of truths, half-truths, and unwarranted speculations.

As Mary Shelley wrote her story of Frankenstein, she gave it to her husband to edit. She rightly claimed that she "did not owe the suggestion of one incident, nor scarcely of one train of feeling" to Percy Shelley (Rieger 229), with one minor exception: it was Percy who suggested that Frankenstein's trip to England be proposed by Victor himself, rather than by his father. Yet Percy Shelley made numerous corrections, about a thousand in all, on the surviving manuscript pages, almost all of which Mary Shelley accepted.

James Rieger credits Percy Shelley with wording the descriptions of contrasts between the personalities of Frankenstein and Elizabeth and between the governments of the Swiss republic and less fortunate nations, with coining the metaphoric description of the power within Mont Blanc, with conceiving the "idea that Frankenstein journey to England for the purpose of creating a female Monster," with making the "final revisions" of the last pages, and with correcting Mary Shelley's "frequent grammatical solecisms, her spelling, and her awkward phrasing." He then concludes that Percy Shelley's "assistance at every point in the book's manufacture was so extensive that one hardly knows whether to regard him as editor or minor collaborator" (Rieger xviii).

Close examination of the surviving manuscript fragments shows that Percy Shelley's numerous revisions of Mary's original text damaged as well as improved it. To dispose of Rieger's misinformation, Percy did expand, although he did not initiate, the comparison of Elizabeth's character to Victor Frankenstein's; and he did interpolate a favorable comparison of Switzerland's republicanism with the tyranny of other nations. However, the descriptions of Mont Blanc and the Mer de Glace in the novel are based primarily on Mary Shelley's own observations, which she made in July 1816 and recorded both in her journal entries for 22–26 July and in her letters to Fanny Imlay; these letters were later published in her *History of a Six Weeks' Tour* (1817). As already noted, Percy suggested merely that

Victor rather than Alphonse Frankenstein propose the trip to England. We might pass over Rieger's annoying habit of referring to Percy Shelley only by his last name and to Mary Shelley by her first, or his failure to acknowledge, in his assertion that Percy corrected "her frequent grammatical solecisms, her spelling, and her awkward phrasing," that Mary's grammatical errors or misspellings were infrequent, while her phrasings were often more graceful than her husband's revised versions. Rieger's concluding suggestion that Percy Shelley can be regarded as a "minor collaborator" or even as one of the two authors of the novel (xliv) is not only unjustified by the evidence. It is also, as we can now recognize, explicitly sexist, since it implies that Mary Shelley could not have created her story alone. Rieger thus does a great disservice to Mary Shelley's genius.

Percy Shelley did improve the manuscript of *Frankenstein* in several minor ways: he corrected three factual errors, eliminated a few grammatical mistakes, occasionally clarified the text, substituted more precise technical terms for Mary's cruder ones, smoothed out a few paragraph transitions, and enriched the thematic resonance of the text. But Percy Shelley misunderstood his wife's intentions. He tended to see the Creature as more monstrous and less human than Mary did, and he frequently underestimated the flaws in Victor Frankenstein's personality. Furthermore, he introduced into the text his own philosophical and political opinions, opinions that were often at variance with his wife's beliefs. For instance, throughout her manuscript Mary assumes the existence of a sacred animating principle, call it Nature or Life or God, which Frankenstein usurps at his peril. But Percy undermined her notion that Frankenstein's pursuit of his Creature was "a task enjoined by heaven" by adding his atheistic concept of a universe mechanistically determined by necessity or power, "the mechanical impulse of some power of which I was unconscious" (Rieger 202). Percy also introduced all the references to Victor Frankenstein as the "author" of the Creature (see Reiger 87, 96) and thus may be largely responsible for recent discussions of Mary Shelley's anxiety of authorship (see Gilbert and Gubar 49; Poovey, chs. 4 and 5).

More important, Percy changed the last line of the novel in a way that potentially alters its meaning. Mary had penned Walton's final vision of the Creature thus:

> He sprung from the cabin window as he said this upon an ice raft that lay close to the vessel & pushing himself off he was carried away by the waves and I soon lost sight of him in the darkness and distance.

But Percy changed this to

> He sprung from the cabin-window, as he said this, upon the ice-raft which lay close to the vessel. He was soon borne away by the waves, and lost in darkness and distance.   (Rieger 221)

Mary's version, by suggesting that Walton has only lost sight of the Creature, leaves open the troubling possibility that the Creature may still be alive, while Percy's flat assertion that the Creature is lost provides the reader a more comforting closure of the novel's monstrous threats.

By far the largest number of Percy's revisions were stylistic. He typically changed Mary's simple, Anglo-Saxon diction and straightforward or colloquial sentence structures into more refined, complex, and Latinate equivalents. He is thus largely responsible for the stilted, ornate, putatively Ciceronian prose style about which so many students complain. Mary's voice tended to utter a sentimental, rather abstract, and generalized rhetoric, typically energized with a brisk stylistic rhythm. Here, for instance, is Mary on Frankenstein's fascination with supernatural phenomena:

> Nor were these my only visions. The raising of ghosts or devils was also a favorite pursuit and if I never saw any I attributed it rather to my own inexperience and mistakes than want of skill in my instructors.

And here is Percy's revision:

> Nor were these my only visions. The raising of ghosts or devils was a promise liberally accorded by my favourite authors, the fulfillment of which I most eagerly sought; and if my incantations were always unsuccessful, I attributed the failure rather to my own inexperience and mistakes, than to a want of skill or fidelity in my instructors. (Rieger 34)

Percy's preference for more learned, polysyllabic terms was obsessive; in addition, he rigorously eliminated Mary's colloquial phrases, as the following lists indicate.

Mary Shelley's manuscript	*Percy Shelley's revision*
have	possess
wish	desire, purpose
caused	derive their origin from
a painting	a representation
place	station
plenty of	sufficient

Mary Shelley's manuscript	Percy Shelley's revision
time	period
felt	endured
hope	confidence
had	experienced
stay	remain
took away	extinguish
talked	conversed
hot	inflamed
smallness	minuteness
end	extinction
inside	within
tired	fatigued
die	perish
leave out	omit
add to	augment
poverty	penury
mind	understanding
ghost-story	a tale of superstition
about on a par	of nearly equal interest and utility
we were all equal	neither of us possessed the slightest pre-eminence over the other
it was safe	the danger of infection was past
bear to part	be persuaded to part
the use I should make of it	the manner in which I should employ it
eyes were shut to	eyes were insensible to
do not wish to hate you	will not be tempted to set myself in opposition to thee
wrapping the rest	depositing the remains
it was a long time	a considerable period elapsed
had a means	possessed a method
how my disposition and habits were altered	the alteration perceptible in my disposition and habits
whatever I should afterwards think it right to do	whatever course of conduct I might hereafter think it right to pursue
what to say	what manner to commence the interview

I wish to claim not that Mary Shelley is a great prose stylist but only that her language, despite its tendency toward the abstract, sentimental, and even banal, is more direct and forceful than her husband's. (For a more detailed discussion of Percy Shelley's revisions of the manuscript of *Frankenstein*, see Mellor, *Mary Shelley*, ch. 3 and app.)

Turning now to the differences between the first and second published editions of *Frankenstein*, we must recognize that between 1818 and 1831, Mary Shelley's philosophical views changed radically, primarily as a result of the pessimism generated by the deaths of Clara, William, and Percy Shelley; by the betrayals of Byron and Jane Williams; and by her severely straitened economic circumstances. These events convinced Mary Shelley that human events are decided not by personal choice or free will but by an indifferent destiny or fate. The values implicitly espoused in the first edition of *Frankenstein*—that nature is a nurturing and benevolent life force that punishes only those who transgress against its sacred rights, that Victor is morally responsible for his acts, that the Creature is potentially good but driven to evil by social and parental neglect, that a family like the De Laceys that loves all its children equally offers the best hope for human happiness, and that human egotism causes the greatest suffering in the world—are all rejected in the 1831 revisions.

In the 1818 version, Victor Frankenstein possessed free will: he could have abandoned his quest for the "principle of life," he could have cared for his Creature, he could have protected Elizabeth. But in the 1831 edition, he is the pawn of forces beyond his knowledge or control. As he comments, "Destiny was too potent, and her immutable laws had decreed my utter and terrible destruction" (Rieger, app. 239). Elizabeth also subscribes to this rhetoric of fatalism: "I think our placid home, and our contented hearts are regulated by the same immutable laws" (Rieger, app. 243).

In the 1831 edition, Mary Shelley replaces her earlier organic conception of nature with a mechanistic one. She now portrays nature as a mighty machine, a juggernaut, an "imperial" tyrant (Rieger, app. 249). Since human beings are now but puppets ("one by one the various keys were touched which formed the mechanism of my being," says Victor [Rieger, app. 241]), Victor's downfall is caused not so much by his egotistical "presumption and rash ignorance" as by bad influences, whether his father's ignorance or Professor Waldman's Mephistophelian manipulations. Victor's only sin is not his failure to love and care for his Creature but his original decision to construct a human being. His scientific experiments themselves are now described as "unhallowed arts" (Rieger, app. 247).

Not only is Frankenstein portrayed in 1831 as a victim rather than an originator of evil, but Clerval—who had functioned in the first edition as the touchstone of moral virtue against which Victor's fall was measured—is now portrayed as equally ambitious of fame and power, as a future colonial imperialist who will use his "mastery" of Oriental languages to exploit the natural resources of the East (Rieger, app. 243, 253). Furthermore, the ideology of the egalitarian and loving bourgeois family that Mary Shelley had inherited from her mother's writings and that sustained the first edition of *Frankenstein* is now undercut. Maternal love is identified with self-destruction when Caroline Beaufort deliberately sacrifices her life to nurse Elizabeth. And Elizabeth Lavenza has become a passive "angel in the house," no longer able to speak out in the law courts against Justine's execution.

By coming to construe nature in the 1831 edition as only Waldman and Frankenstein had done in the first edition, as a mighty and amoral machine, Mary Shelley significantly decreased the critical distance between herself and her protagonist. In the "Author's Introduction" added to the novel in 1831, Mary Shelley presents herself as she now represents Frankenstein, as a victim of destiny. She is "compelled" to write (Rieger 222); her imagination "unbidden" possessed and guided her (Rieger 227). She ends with a defensive lie: "I have changed no portion of the story, nor introduced any new ideas or circumstances" (Rieger 229). Thus in the final version of her novel, Mary Shelley disclaims responsibility for her hideous progeny and at the same time insists that she has remained passive before it, "leaving the core and substance of it untouched" (Rieger 229). For invention "can give form to dark, shapeless substances, but cannot bring into being the substance itself" (Rieger 226). Imperial nature, the thing-in-itself, is now triumphant. Before it, Mary Shelley's human imagination can only mold shapeless darkness into a hideous monster. Like Victor Frankenstein, she has become the unwilling "author of unalterable evils." (For a more detailed description of Mary Shelley's revisions of *Frankenstein* in 1831, see Mellor, *Mary Shelley*, ch. 9.)

The remarkable shifts in both diction and philosophical conception between the three versions of *Frankenstein*—the manuscript, the 1818 edition, and the 1831 edition—make this an ideal text for use in courses in either text editing or the theory of the text itself. From the perspective of deconstructive literary criticism, *Frankenstein* exemplifies what Julia Kristeva has called "the questionable subject-in-process," both a text and an author without stable boundaries. For students who have time to consult only one text, the 1818 text alone presents a stable and coherent conception of the character of Victor Frankenstein and of Mary Shelley's political and moral ideology. It is a pity that the significantly higher price of the Rieger edition often proves decisive in persuading teachers to opt for the cheaper editions of the revised 1831 *Frankenstein*, editions that cannot do justice to Mary Shelley's powerful originating vision.

Gender and Pedagogy:
The Questions of *Frankenstein*

William Veeder

Great texts are always braver than their readers, more daring and resolute and honest. What I try above all to convey to my students is the probity of John Keats's commitment to "*Negative Capability*, that is when man is capable of being in uncertainties, Mysteries, doubts, without any irritable reaching after fact & reason." The chief danger in reading is not (as we tend to fear) that we will not find meaning but that we will find it too soon, that irritably we will reach after and find, insist on and settle for, that fraction of the text that fits most conveniently into our biases. What I principally urge my students to do, therefore, is to trust themselves with the text by entrusting themselves to the text. I ask not what is going on but how much is; not what might be there but what might not be.

With *Frankenstein*, my overall concern is with what I take to be Mary Shelley's central preoccupation—gender. To generate aggressive discussion of the vexed intricacies of this issue, I ask the class to focus on the basic techniques of fiction: point of view, characterization, and plot, and style as it participates in all three. (In the process I confront the students both with the original 1818 edition of the novel when it diverges interestingly from the 1831 text and with the methodological implications of such textual interplay.) From close analysis will emerge a consistent concern with the man-woman relations that obsess Mary Shelley.

Before I go on to these issues, I want to add a caveat more important than anything that follows. Believing in the value of each student's experience of the text, I cannot believe less in each teacher's comparable experience. I cannot, therefore, offer my experience as a blueprint for reading and teaching *Frankenstein*. What I have called Mary Shelley's vision, for example, is nothing more than my version of that vision. What I offer in this essay is, necessarily, more a way of asking questions than a setting forth of answers, more an approach than an arrival. When I began teaching, I was forever asking myself whether a particular question was a good one; now I find myself asking the class, How do you know what a good question is?

Beginning with Point of View: The Opening Frame

Why does Mary Shelley frame the story of Victor Frankenstein with the letters of Robert Walton? Students will suggest several answers readily enough. Robert provides credibility for Victor both because Walton undertakes the same type of quest and because he believes a story as unlikely as

Frankenstein's; Robert at the same time provides us with an evaluative distance on Victor that we could not have if the novel were narrated by the protagonist in the first person; Robert also prepares us for Victor's personality (both men are failed Promethean questors, ambitious, lonely, willing to sacrifice other people despite claims of philanthropic idealism), while he emphasizes Victor's superior stature. What usually does not occur to the class immediately is the gender aspects of the frame narration. Why are Robert's letters written to a woman rather than a man, why to a sister rather than a fiancée, and why to a married woman?

I begin the discussion of gender simply: how to characterize Robert's relationship with Margaret? The obviously benign aspects are what students usually mention first—Margaret's evident concern for Robert's safety, his stated worry about worrying her. The darker aspects of the relationship can be reached by an apparently oblique move to the sister's initials: why M. S.? Quickly some students will see Mary Shelley's own initials here. Is Margaret Mary's spokeswoman? One recourse here is the Bible, where Margaret and Mary are kinswomen. Another recourse, more problematic but also more interesting methodologically, is to examine the differences between the names Mrs. Margaret Saville and Mrs. Mary W. Shelley. Since Mary affirms her Wollstonecraft heritage by using the middle initial W, rather than the expectable G for Godwin, she is all the more associated with Margaret, whose maiden name of Walton gives her too the middle initial W. Why then does Mary omit the W from Margaret's name? One explanation relates to why Mary chooses the name Walton in the first place. "Walton" as "walledtown" suggests the isolation inevitable to Prometheans like Robert and Professor "Waldman." Only by leaving Robert's unmarried realm behind—without even the trace of a middle initial—can Margaret Saville reach *sa ville*, that communal state which is the union of male with female and the ideal of *Frankenstein*.

That the novel opens with a male crew entirely isolated from women suggests the separation of the sexes that will recur throughout *Frankenstein*. Robert tries to bridge the gap by writing to Margaret, but the fact that he is seeking to bond with another man and that she is already married presages the fate of relations in the novel. Prometheans war with women. Margaret as the embodiment of Mary's values cannot empathize with Promethean drives. And Robert knows it:

> Do you [Margaret] understand this feeling? . . . I cannot describe to you my sensations. . . . It is impossible to communicate to you a conception of the trembling sensation. . . . Will you smile at the enthusiasm I express? (15, 20, 27)

Man and woman disagree in the very first sentence of *Frankenstein*: ". . . an enterprise which you have regarded with such evil forebodings" (15). By phrasing it this way, Robert says more than that Margaret has foreseen trouble: "evil forebodings" indicates that foreseeing trouble seems evil, disloyal to him. He counterattacks in a characteristically male way. Defending against Margaret's skepticism his pet belief that the poles are ice-free, Robert trusts male expertise over female intuition: "With your leave, my sister, I will put some trust in preceding navigators" (15). The men are of course wrong, and the woman is right. Cold increases as *sa ville* recedes. At issue are differences as basic as gender itself: the sensible versus the fanciful viewpoint, the warm versus the cold heart. By incorporating gender disagreement in the frame of *Frankenstein*, Mary Shelley prepares for Frankenstein's fundamental incompatibility with women.

The Middle Section of Frankenstein: *Characterization and Plot*

Even more than Robert, Victor feels toward woman an antagonism particularly dangerous because largely unconscious. The 1818 edition locates trouble early, as Victor's ostensible testament to complimentarity with Elizabeth is sown with condescension:

> Although there was a great dissimiltude in our characters, there was an harmony in that very dissimilitude. I was more calm and philosophical than my companion; yet my temper was not so yielding. My application was of longer endurance; but it was not so severe whilst it endured. I delighted in investigating the facts relative to the actual world; she busied herself in following the aerial creations of the poets.   (Rieger 30)

Victor defines his forte as active "investigating," whereas Elizabeth's is only devoted "following"; her poetry is merely "aerial," whereas his science deals with "facts"; "busied herself" suggests dalliance, whereas Victor grapples with "the actual world." Condescension is not the worst of it, moreover. Victor calls Elizabeth "gay and playful as a summer insect." He then goes on, amazingly, "I loved to tend on her, as I should on a favourite animal" (Rieger 29, 30).

Frankenstein is reflecting here what he enacts throughout both the 1818 and 1831 editions of the novel: his culture's divided view of woman. With her polarized into angel and whore, the demeaned aspect is traditionally depicted in animal imagery—pig, bitch, birdbrain. More interesting than the disease is the cure implied in Victor's reference to Elizabeth as a "summer" bug. Woman is ephemeral, or at least can be made so. Victor proceeds to enact the ephemeralization of Elizabeth by murdering her twice—in his nightmare and on his wedding night:

> I thought I saw Elizabeth, in the bloom of health, walking in the streets of Ingolstadt. Delighted and surprised, I embraced her; but as I imprinted the first kiss on her lips, they became livid with the hue of death; her features appeared to change, and I thought that I held the corpse of my dead mother in my arms; a shroud enveloped her form, and I saw the grave-worms crawling in the folds of the flannel. I started from my sleep with horror . . . I beheld the wretch—the miserable monster whom I had created. (57)

Why does Victor kill Elizabeth with a kiss? Is he a Judas whose bad heart betrays the person he purports to love? Does he fear that the conjugal sexuality inevitable if he marries Elizabeth will bring about death? (I ask the class at this point why Victor views marriage to Elizabeth with "horror and dismay" [145]. Can revulsion this extreme possibly be accounted for by his explanation—that he had promised to make the female creature first?) Why, moreover, does Elizabeth in death turn into Victor's mother, Caroline?

Victor feels himself failed by women on every side. Elizabeth has killed his mother. Why does Mary Shelley choose for the lethal disease not small pox or some other traditional childhood malady but scarlet fever? Elizabeth is bound to Victor so affectionately as "sister" that some tension between her and his adoring mother is virtually inevitable, but the rivalry becomes particularly intense once the sister-daughter becomes the fiancée. In this context, the sexual connotations of a scarlet fever are crucial. Victor sees the daughter-as-future-wife destroying the older mother-as-rival in order to possess him exclusively. His response to such predatory sexuality is reflected in his nightmare diction: "in the streets," Elizabeth is angel turned whore.

Worse still, not only has Elizabeth both killed his mother and presumed to replace her, but Caroline has—by Victor's lights—abetted in the replacement. Having first displaced Victor by introducing the interloper Elizabeth (whom he calls his mother's "favourite" [42] at the very moment when Caroline contracts her lethal fever), his mother has joined him incestuously to a sister whose role as surrogate mother means that Caroline has wed her son to herself. To such failures of the womanly ideal Victor responds murderously. His nightmare kiss dispatches Elizabeth to Caroline's grave, where both women can be finished off by the phallic worms.

When Elizabeth actually dies, the timing—her wedding night—and the location—her "bridal bier" (186)—indicate that conjunction of sex and death that Victor feared so flagrantly in his nightmare. To what extent can the murder of Elizabeth be seen as an expression of his homicidal drives? This question posed to the class will echo questions raised by the text itself, questions designed to generate in readers the same skepticism about Victor's self-proclaimed purity of motive that I try to generate in students.

Victor's questions—"Why am I here to relate the destruction. . . . Could I behold this and live? (186)—encourage us to question many of his acts. Why, for example, does Victor not thwart the monster beforehand, either by destroying it outright or by understanding its threat? Destroying the monster is definitely possible: "I would have seized him; but he eluded me" (161). Victor then asks our question: "Why had I not followed him, and closed with him in mortal strife?" (161). One possible answer, fear of physical harm, is contradicted by the fact of Victor's fearlessness before the huge Creature. An answer in terms of the unconscious—that Victor "had suffered him to depart" (161) because Frankenstein did not really want him stopped—seems confirmed after Elizabeth's murder when the Creature again "eluded" Victor (187). The repetition of "eluded me" emphasizes how little has changed in the elusive relation of creator and Creature. The monster escapes both times because he effects what Victor wants each time. This is also why Victor fails to understand the monster's threat: "*I will be with you on your wedding-night!*" (179). The sentence against Victor as bridegroom is pronounced by Victor as monster. The actual meaning of the threat becomes clear to Frankenstein too late (186). Only after the fact can he do what he should have done earlier, because only now is the failure ensured that is Victor-y.

The monster's threat indicates how Mary Shelley uses formal elements to reveal Victor's murderous will on the wedding night. As the threat is open to two interpretations and as Victor is operating on both conscious and unconscious levels, she provides a second, subversive layer to language also: "[I resolved] not to join her until I had obtained some knowledge as to the situation of my enemy. She . . ." (186). By "enemy" Victor consciously means the monster, of course. But "my enemy. She" suggests that the real enemy is Elizabeth. (How legitimate it is to read over punctuation [granting Freud's imprimatur] is a methodological point I raise with the class at this point.) A similar use of language has occurred a few lines earlier: "I resolved . . . not [to] shrink from the conflict until my own life or that of my adversary was extinguished. Elizabeth . . ." (185). What will end Victor's dilemma is "extinguished Elizabeth." In this battle of the sexes, Victor "reflected how fearful the combat . . . would be" to his wife (185). He means that Elizabeth would be frightened by his battling a monster, but unconsciously he know how much more fearful she will be when her own battle with the monster begins.

Victor also knows how fearful he is until then. "A thousand fears," "anxious," "watchful," "terrified," "agitation," "agitates," "dreadful," and "fear" reverberate throughout the passage (185). The sexual sources of this fear, the issue of manliness implicit in his diction of fear, is foregrounded in the original text. "Thoughts of mischance" seem to Victor "unmanly." Especially with Elizabeth "fearless," he is "half ashamed" of his fears (Rieger 190, 191). In both editions, Victor seems anything but effective when his "right hand grasped a pistol which was hidden in [his] bosom; every sound terrified" him (185). The gesture of phallic uncertainty here and the unwitting association of Victor with the female ("bosom") are as ludicrous as his misconception of the whole situation is: "I resolved that I would sell my life dearly" (185). Since we know that Victor's life is not in danger, his bravado here makes him seem less like a heroic bridegroom than like a pander selling "dearly" the love of his life. " 'Oh! Peace, peace, my love,' replied I; 'this night, and all will be safe' " (185) sounds like the bridegroom's loving assurance to his anxious bride that the difficulties of the first night will give way to the pleasures of a lifetime. But the decency of such an admonition contrasts with Victor's unconscious meaning—that he will be safe after tonight because Elizabeth will threaten him no more.

Victor's wedding night is a pyrrhic victory. It does end the anguishing struggle to separate mother-sister-wife. All Frankenstein women are now dead, so there can be no separate female roles and no positive potential for sexuality. But Victor's victory over moribund flesh is pyrrhic because banishing the woman to figurative or literal death leaves the man finally moribund and useless too. At Elizabeth's wedding-night scream, "my arms dropped" (186). Impotence characterizes Victor now (he can't fire his pistol effectively). Effeminacy is then confirmed by his last act in the scene: "I fell senseless on the ground" (186).

The act of a man fainting makes a nice, if intricate, transition to the question that every reading of *Frankenstein* must face: why does Victor create the monster? Since this is the most overdetermined act of his life, many answers are possible. A rich discussion can be generated by restating the question in terms of gender: how does the monster's creation relate to Frankenstein's misogyny? The emasculation evident in fainting appears first when the male protagonist attempts to usurp woman's place and produce an offspring parthenogenetically. Rather than woman's fecundity, what we see is a physical debility ("my person had become emaciated" [53]) that has a decidedly sexual aspect: "My candle was nearly burnt out" (56); after the creation, "I was lifeless" (60). Impotence marks Victor long before his wedding night. The gender-role reversal implicit in Victor's statement, "the bolt has entered my soul" (153), is confirmed by the monster's threat: "the bolt will . . . ravish from you your happiness" (160). (Indeed, in the 1818 text, Victor during his emaciating labors on the Creature admits that he "became as timid as a love-sick girl" [Rieger, 51]). To indicate what has happened in this act of creation, I ask the students to discuss the puns in Victor's description of the gestation process. In the laboratory, he longs for the time when his "creation should be complete" (55); later he defines the monster's awakening as the moment from which he "dated [his] creation" (74). A new creator as well as a new creation is produced. What Mary Shelley is dramatizing here is projective narcissism, male self-love. In creating the monster, Victor projects outward the "male" half of his psyche: he then becomes "female." The rest of the novel dramatizes his pursuit of the monster, as Victor seeks the narcissistic victory of rejoining the riven halves of his psyche in a solipsistic embrace that will thwart death—both by avoiding the fatality of union with woman and by healing the split in the self that various myths associate with humanity's initial fall into mortality.

Since many critics see the monster as "female," I encourage the class to find all the evidence against my interpretation; I read both from Muriel Spark's argument that the monster is associated with the female heart rather than the male head and from much stronger feminist arguments that the monster expresses Mary Shelley's own feelings of abandonment and rage. Eventually we reach something of a compromise. The Creature, as a character in his own right, has many traditionally feminine traits because he is the most ideally androgynous character in the novel; but, the Creature as a projection of Victor is emphatically male in gender and prowess. He displays, for example, physical features conventional with the ravisher: "[H]is hair was of a lustrous black, and flowing; his teeth of a pearly whiteness" (56). The monster's first conscious act is straight out of seduction stories. He enters the sleeper's chamber, draws aside the bed curtains, and, with a smile and murmured words, reaches out his hand. Horrified into the conventional flight, the sleeper reacts revealingly: "Sometimes my pulse beat so quickly and hardly, that I felt the palpitation of every artery; at others, I nearly sank to the ground through languor and extreme weakness" (57). By attributing to a male the "palpitation" and "languor" traditional with female passion and its aftermath, Mary Shelley is suggesting a complex reversal of roles. As the monster bodies forth Victor's male self, Frankenstein becomes the effeminate beloved who like a lovesick girl awaits the ravishing bolt.

An End: The Closing Frame

The immediate consequences of self-pursuit—the death of Elizabeth and the fainting of Victor—do not establish the final consequences of such pursuit. What does the end of *Frankenstein* say about Mary Shelley's vision of human experience? By focusing on critics' claims that Victor is finally "heroic" and that Robert is ultimately "redeemed," I can ask the class what features of the closing frame militate against and support an ultimately benign reading of the novel.

I begin the discussion of Victor's heroism by quoting Robert Kiely's claim that "though a good and gifted person before his 'ruin,' it is really afterward, by means of the uniqueness and depth of his suffering, that Frankenstein achieves superiority over other men" (158). After the class registers its reactions (usually more con than pro), I quote Mary Shelley's insistence that "he who conquers himself is, in my eyes, the only true hero" (*Falkner* 2: 6) and then offer the following proposition: Since Frankenstein cannot undo the horrors perpetrated by his monster, his hope for heroic status lies in self-knowledge, in an increased awareness of his unconscious rage. How self-aware is he during his arctic pursuit of the monster and then aboard Robert's ship? Take, for example, the food that Victor keeps finding in the arctic. After he indicates what he imagines is the source of the food ("a spirit of good followed and directed my steps. . . . I will not doubt that it [food] was set there by the spirits that I had invoked to aid me" [194]), the monster defines the real situation: "My power is complete. Follow me. . . . You will find near this place, if you follow not too tardily, a dead hare; eat, and be refreshed" (195). The undercutting here, which Victor misses, is especially obvious to the students who remember that the Creature has already proclaimed the absurdity of Promethean pretentions:

> I [Frankenstein] call on you, spirits of the dead, and on you, wandering ministers of vengeance, to aid and conduct me in my work. . . . I was answered through the stillness of night by a loud and fiendish laugh.   (193)

Does light dawn for benighted Victor? Does he know himself, or at least know doubt? "Surely in that moment I should have been possessed by phrenzy, and have destroyed my miserable existence, but. . . ." There is always a "but" for Victor, always a self-justifying rationale for ignoring the truths about himself that have momentarily surfaced: ". . . but that my vow was heard and that I was reserved for vengeance" (193). How does Victor know that his vow was heard? Instead of corroborating his claim existentially, Mary Shelley undercuts it stylistically with the pun in "reserved for vengeance," which I ask the class to unpack. While Victor imagines himself an agent of heavenly wrath, we see the limits to wrath. Men who ask to wreak vengeance are "reserved for" it, are set aside to receive it. The death that Victor plans for the Creature is reserved for him as Mary takes her revenge on vengeful males.

Aboard ship, Victor has several opportunities to show increased self-awareness. Does he accept responsibility for the mayhem? No: "I have been . . . examining my past conduct; nor do I find it blameable" (206). Does he in particular see the error of denying the Creature a mate? No: "she might become ten thousand times more malignant than her mate" (158). Victor still has one last chance; his final words will indicate what he has learned. I prime the pump by quoting various critics: Small maintains that the "last speech . . . leaves everything unresolved" (188); Levine, that "the novel will not resolve the issue" ("Ambiguous Heritage" 10); Dussinger, that "in his last breath he urges Walton contradictorily" (53); Swingle, that "at the last moment he admits that Walton had best think through the evidence for himself" (54–55). What does Victor actually say?

> Seek happiness in tranquillity and avoid ambition, even if it be only the apparently innocent one of distinguishing yourself in science and discoveries. Yet why do I say this? I have myself been blasted in these hopes, yet another may succeed.   (206)

The domestic ideal of "tranquillity" and the Promethean goal of victory are initially juxtaposed, but the final words of Frankenstein are not ambiguous. If he had died after "ambition" or even "discoveries," he would have sided with Mary. But he goes on to pledge allegiance to Prometheanism. "I have myself been blasted in these hopes" is very different from "I have blasted myself in these hopes" or "my hopes have blasted me." Victor's "blasted" is in the passive voice because he persists in seeing himself victimized by external forces. Personal responsibility, like self-knowledge, remains largely absent. "Another may succeed" indicates Victor's inability to learn the general lesson of his life. He admits only that he was inadequate to his dream: he sees nothing inherently fatal and thus vicious in the dream itself. Frankenstein has missed the point of *Frankenstein*.

What about Robert Walton? Is he "redeemed"? The question is important because if Robert can learn what Frankenstein has not, there may yet be hope for Prometheans. Walton unlike Victor does turn south toward warmth. But this physical motion must have a psychological counterpart before he can actually practice true love of neighbor. Again I read to the class from the critics: from Knoepflmacher, that Walton "refuses to bring death to his crew" (107); from Tropp, that he learns that "exploration must begin with true concern for his fellow men" (82); from Hill, that he "heeds" his crew and "consents" (356). But is this so? Robert admits that he turns back because he is forced to: "the fears [he] entertained of a mutiny" (203) are realized, and Robert yields to intimidation. Such weakness continues to foster the macho compensations that have marked Robert's whole life. He resentfully sees his crew as unmanly, as "unsupported by ideas of glory and honour" (204). What we see, I believe, is a maturity that allows the crew members who initially shared his adolescent enthusiasm to achieve Margaret-Mary's perspective on Promethean pursuits.

The persistence of machismo and self-pity in Robert signals a continuing disaffiliation from women. In the last paragraph addressed directly to Margaret, Robert repeats his earlier insistence on the limits of heterosexual communion. "What can I say that will enable you to understand the depth of my sorrow?" (207). The continuing gap between Robert and woman is not closed by his movement south. He is paralleling Frankenstein geographically and psychologically. Victor came south from Ireland to wed Elizabeth, but emotionally he never left the north. Destroying the monster's mate kept Victor bound to the monster. The monster's following him south indicated the tenacity of their male bond, the impossibility of any real union between Promethean and woman. Thus Victor's honeymoon trip south from Geneva to Lake Como began with the newly weds going north to Evian. (I ask how many of the students had got out maps and charted an action set in obviously recognizable locales.) Elizabeth died without ever turning south because Victor had been heading north all along—first to Ingolstadt, then to Britain, and finally to the pole. Robert Walton's move south remains only geographical because he too leaves unfinished business in the north. His bond with Victor is sealed by death, in the same way that destruction of the monster's mate sealed Victor's union with the monster. This Creature remains alive at the end of Walton's narrative (I challenge the class to find any textual warrant for the widespead assumption of the monster's death), as he did after his mate's destruction, to indicate the persistence of male forces that cannot be satisfied by southerly motions toward women. Such journeys are no more part of Robert's true psychological orientation than they were of Victor's: Walton too has been heading north all along in his own three-stage progression. First he went with "whale-fishers on several expeditions to the North Sea" (16), then by himself to Saint Petersburg and Archangel, and finally with his crew to the pole. From that undiscovered country no Promethean ever returns.

So dark a view of the end of *Frankenstein*, and thus so dark a view of Mary Shelley's vision of gender relations, needs to be checked against many other aspects of the novel. As time permits, I ask the students to consider the following questions: How should we relate the happiness of the De Lacey family to the unhappiness of the Frankensteins? Why of all the Frankensteins is Ernest (remember him?) left alive at the end? Why is Ernest in the novel at all? To what extent are the women of *Frankenstein* more intricate and even subversive than their True Womanly appearances suggest (here I direct attention to the peculiarities in Elizabeth's courtroom "defense" of Justine and in her letters to Victor and to the misogyny in Caroline's presentation of Elizabeth to Victor)? What part does Alphonse Frankenstein play in his son's disastrous turn to science—to what extent, that is, does Victor (again) try to escape responsibility by blaming his disasters on someone else? Does the fact that Alphonse is the last of Victor's family to die mean that there is a sequence, a trajectory, to the killings that makes him and not Elizabeth the ultimate target of Victor's unconscious wrath?

Finally, I attempt to relate Mary Shelley's anti-Prometheanism to the larger issue of the Romantic male. Self-division and self-pursuit are essential motions in Percy Shelley's work (*Alastor* is particularly relevant here), as well as in the works of Byron, Blake, James Hogg, and Charles Robert Maturin. Mary's espousal of domesticity shows forth at its bravest and angriest against the full backdrop of the era she called, futilely, to account. *Frankenstein* is nowhere more a woman's book than in its frustration. Margaret Saville is the emblem of this frustration: she never appears in the novel. She fails to get into the action—into the plot or into Robert's adult life—not because the domestic virtues thwart women but because Promethean males are incorrigible. Robert would not heed her before he left, and he will listen still less on a return that proves her right all along. Mary was equally helpless with Godwin and Percy whenever it really mattered. By 1816 when she is staying with Percy, Byron, and John William Polidori in Switzerland, she is analyzing, judging every minute, but she is still the silent figure who as a little girl watched from the silent corner of her father's living room as Samuel Taylor Coleridge read *The Rime of the Ancient Mariner*. In 1816 she still can only look powerlessly on as the precocious males of Diodati leave the ghost-story project unfinished and die by drowning, fever, and suicide within a decade.

Mary's men flee from her into the wild abandonment of ego and the inevitable collapse of prowess. She can rail inwardly at these men, but she cannot change them. And so she takes her only way out—she tells the story of her generation. In a widening gyre she moves out from Percy and Godwin as husband and father, to Percy, Godwin, and Byron as Prometheans, to all Romantic males, to almost all men as Romantics. *Frankenstein* raises the issue of "our infantine dispositions, which, however they may afterwards be modified, are never eradicated" (201) because regression, or rather the failure to mature, is Mary's theme. Men are too death-obsessed to escape tangled feelings for mother and father; they attempt to escape through Promethean fantasies boyish and impracticable.

Doubly shut off from reality and community, the overaspiring male finds community particularly difficult in Mary's era, when the career of Byron and the general thrust of Romanticism have written Prometheus across the sky. Can males caught between heaven and death mature into useful citizens and happy husbands? Can they grow up by coming down from adolescent reveries—without falling too far?

Feminist Inquiry and *Frankenstein*

Susan J. Wolfson

Frankenstein has long had a place in courses in English Romanticism, both as a Romantic reading of *Paradise Lost* and as a critical comment on the conception of male Prometheanism—brilliant, isolated, transgressive, guilt-ridden—advanced in the poetry of Mary Shelley's contemporaries Percy Shelley and Lord Byron. Since the early 1970s the novel has assumed another kind of importance, as a locus of feminist inquiry and, for some, as an instance of feminist critique. This new significance has emerged because Shelley (often the only woman read in courses on Romanticism) is the daughter of the most prominent feminist of the immediate postrevolutionary era and because her novel makes visible an ideology of gender through the psychological orientation and social behavior of its characters. With appropriate adjustments for the experience of the students involved, teaching *Frankenstein* in relation to these issues works as well in introductory literature classes as in specialized courses in Romanticism or gender studies. My discussion draws on many provocative essays that have appeared in recent years, especially by readers specifically concerned with gender: Kate Ellis, Sandra Gilbert and Susan Gubar, Margaret Homans, Barbara Johnson, U. C. Knoepflmacher, Anne Mellor, Ellen Moers, Mary Poovey, and William Veeder. My purpose is not to submit *Frankenstein* to single-minded distinctions and definitions but to show how attention to Shelley's representations of gender can open up the complexities of her text to further, productive inquiry.

Students might find this approach somewhat mysterious at first because its signposts are more implicit that explicit: the actual vocabulary of gender—"masculine," "manly," "feminine," "womanly"—appears less often than one might suppose. Moreover, as Johnson notes, *Frankenstein* seems

> much more striking for its avoidance of the question of femininity than for its insight into it. All the interesting, complex characters in the book are male, and their deepest attachments are to other males. The females, on the other hand, are beautiful, gentle, selfless, boring nurturers and victims who never experience inner conflict or true desire. (7)

(Veeder is alone, I think, in making a case for the complexity of Elizabeth Lavenza, but the extreme ingenuity of his readings underscores Johnson's point.) Most students will be able to supply examples for the paradigm Johnson sketches: Robert Walton, Victor Frankenstein, and his Creature are Shelley's most psychologically complex, internally divided characters, while Caroline Beaufort-Frankenstein, Elizabeth, and Justine fulfill culturally endorsed definitions of femininity: nurturing, devoted to home and family, self-sacrificing to the point of death. Teachers can also ask students to consider an interesting corollary, that the deepest emotional ties in the novel are those between Victor and other men—Clerval, Walton, the Creature—relations that often seem to parody the eroticism of heterosexual passion. Moreover, as Knoepflmacher notes, "*Frankenstein* is a novel of omnipresent fathers and absent mothers" (90).

I ask students whether, in view of such evidence, they think the male-centeredness of Shelley's tale is equivalent to an endorsement of traditional masculine ideology—especially as it is manifested in Victor's bold alignment with patriarchal creation, in which he both competes with the male god and circumvents, or usurps, the woman's part. Gilbert and Gubar argue that the novel constitutes a critical reading of "the male cultural myth" represented and promoted by *Paradise Lost*, "Milton's patriarchal epic" (220, 225). Students can be prompted to consider this issue in the way Shelley encodes the pride of patriarchal authority into Victor's transgression: "No father could claim the gratitude of his child so completely as I should deserve theirs," Victor surmises of the race he means to engender (52). We can then turn to Walton's letter of 5 September, in which Shelley reveals the social consequences of this male pride with particular force. Students should pay close attention to Victor's vehement response when Walton's crew demands to abort their northward mission should the ice break. Reminding the crew of their "glorious expedition," Victor goads them in terms calculated to stake their decision on their manhood:

> You were hereafter to be hailed as the benefactors of your species, your names adored as belonging to brave men who encountered death for honour and the benefit of mankind. And now, behold, with the first imagination of danger, or if you will, the first mighty and terrific trial of your courage, you shrink away and are content to be handed down as men who had not strength enough to endure. . . . Oh! Be men, or be more than men. Be steady to your purposes and firm as a rock. This ice is not made of such stuff as your hearts may be. . . . Do not return to your families with the stigma of disgrace marked on your brows. Return as heroes who have fought and conquered and who know not what it is to turn their backs on the foe. (203–04)

Students will be able to identify the terms important to this code: benefit to the species is the rationale, but the emphasis is on the glory, reputation, and honor attached to one's name, and the threat is the stigma of humiliation, disgrace, and shame. To be a man is to align oneself with the former and shun the latter. It is important to call attention to the psychological orientation that Victor registers in this version of manhood: a rocklike will, an icy heart, and an implied willingness to die rather than return home with anything less than victory.

Walton himself shares these values: "I had rather die than return shamefully, my purpose unfulfilled," he writes to his sister in the same letter; two days later, when he gives in to his crew, he reports, "[M]y hopes [are] blasted by cowardice and indecision; I come back ignorant and disappointed. It requires more philosophy than I possess to bear this injustice with patience" (204). Teachers can help students see that the complications Shelley adds have the effect of supplying the philosophy Walton lacks. First, she lets Victor's motives remain deeply ambiguous: true, he seems to revert to the Promethean glory against which he has lectured, but he also seems interested in keeping Walton's ship on the northward course he believes will converge on the Creature's path. Second, his exhortation to the men to "be more than men" carries a darkly ironic reminder of the motivation that led him to "make [a] being of a gigantic stature" (52). These critical perspectives bring into focus the egotism that impels this particular idea of manhood and the masculine self-assertion that propels Promethean designs.

One can help explain Shelley's coordination of these conflicting values by detailing the phallic language she gives to Victor's intellectual enthusiasms: Walton notes Victor's capacity for "penetration into the causes of things" (28); Victor describes himself "as always having been imbued with a fervent longing to penetrate the secrets of nature" and eager to become the "disciple" of "men who had penetrated deeper and knew more" (39). This masculine aggression is enhanced by the gendering of nature as its feminine object: from Waldman Victor learns that the "masters" of science "penetrate into the recesses of nature and show how she works in her hiding-places" (47), and he echoes this language as he describes his activities in his "workshop of filthy creation": "I pursued nature to her hiding-places" (53).

Poovey's analysis of this aspect of Victor's imagination offers a helpful transition to another, clearly related issue: the domestic sphere. Like nature, this realm is represented as female and proves vulnerable, or at the very least opposed, to the ambitions of male intellect: "in aiding and abetting the ego," Poovey argues, this mode of "imagination expands the individual's self-absorption to fill the entire universe, and . . . murders everyone in its path" (126). But if the domestic sphere falls victim to this egotism, it is also the case that the domestic sphere itself figuratively murders by rejecting or repressing its alien figures: Victor flees from the monstrous child that disappoints his hopes, and Felix expels the Creature who had served his family's needs and hoped to claim their protection. Domestic affection never extends to the Creature.

Referring to this opposition, I ask students to think about murder, both real and figurative, and homebound values. Is Victor's claim that it would be better to die than return home with aspirations unfulfilled perhaps another way of saying that home is fatal to male ambition or that men in the novel sense all too keenly the paradigm of self-sacrifice that guides the ideal of female domesticity? One may recall an earlier statement by Walton that anticipates the terms of Victor's exhortation to the crew: "I will be cool, persevering, and prudent. But success *shall* crown my endeavours," Walton writes to his sister; "What can stop the determined heart and resolved will of man?" The answer to this question turns out to be, in effect, "woman." Not coincidentally, his pledge begins with his bidding "adieu" to his "dear Margaret," his "beloved sister" (22), whose very name, Mrs. Saville, conveys domestic obligations and civilized values and whose bonds of tender love and affection represent for her brother terms of restraint as well as of ethical foundation. Although Walton credits Margaret's "gentle and feminine fosterage" for refining the "groundwork of [his] character" (19), Shelley repeatedly has his letters note the divergence of brother and sister—"You have been tutored and refined by books and retirement from the world" (27)—and has Walton repeatedly test and tempt her judgment. His first letter opens by mocking his sister's "evil forebodings" about his "enterprise," attempting to allay her disapproval with the positive Prometheanism of his undertaking—"you cannot contest the inestimable benefit which I shall confer on all mankind, to the last generation" (16)— and entreating her consent: "dear Margaret, do I not deserve to accomplish some great purpose?" (17). Feminist critics read the perversion of such great purposes as a specifically male event: Veeder, for instance, sees the Creature embodying Victor's "phallic drives" (246n8), and the novel's scheme makes it evident that Victor's bond to the Creature constitutes a hidden first marriage, implicitly in competition with the dream of domesticity represented by his wedding Elizabeth. Mellor argues not only that the "destruction of the female" is implicit in Victor's "usurpation of the natural mode of human reproduction" but that it "symbolically erupts" in his subsequent nightmare, "in which his bride-to-be is transformed in his arms into the corpse of his dead mother" ("Possessing Nature" 220; see also Homans).

Some students may want to suggest that, Victor's transgressions notwithstanding, the domestic sphere defined by the women in *Frankenstein* bears Shelley's moral approval: it keeps men human, fosters their capacities for tenderness and affection, and restrains the excesses of their ambition—specifically, given Shelley's subtitle, their tendency to self-mythologizing Promethean transgression and isolation. Most students will sense that, despite Victor's alternately self-lacerating and self-aggrandizing rhetoric, the novel does not indict him so much for violating the boundaries of life and death as for abdicating parental responsibility for the life he has created. One may extend this view by considering all the caregivers in the novel and their recipients: students will observe that while some characters are both, Victor is always a recipient and never a giver, and the Creature (before he is embittered) is always a giver and never a recipient (even in their final chase, the Creature leaves food for his pursuer). Equally notable are the instances of men who feed, warm, protect, rescue, nurse, or nurture those needing their care and remain generously devoted to the welfare of others: Walton, his shipmaster, Alphonse, Clerval, Felix, Kerwin, the Creature.

Feminist readers often note this expansion of male capacity into traditionally female exercises: Poovey sees Walton as an example of the domestic male, "the alternative" to Victor's "antisocial ambition" (131–32); Veeder is willing to see even in Victor the admirable balance of "gender traits" that both he and Poovey read in Walton: "Their 'manly' qualities—ambition, daring, scientific intelligence, physical hardihood—are tempered by a sympathetic love of neighbor which manifests itself publicly in concern for human welfare and privately in affection." The balance fails only when the "masculine and feminine traits in their psyches polarize into willfulness and weakness" (81). Victor never personalizes his deficiency this way; as close as he gets is a kind of general pastoral formulation:

> [I]f no man allowed any pursuit whatsoever to interfere with the tranquillity of his domestic affections, Greece had not been enslaved, Caesar would have spared his country, America would have been discovered more gradually, and the empires of Mexico and Peru had not been destroyed.   (54)

This assessment is congruent with some feminist perspectives. Poovey argues, for instance, that the novel reveals Victor's

> imagination as an appetite that can and must be regulated—specifically by the give-and-take of domestic relationships. If it is aroused but is not controlled by human society, it will project itself into the natural world, becoming voracious in its search for objects to conquer and consume.   (123)

The total effect of the novel, however, is not as prescriptive as Poovey's "must be" implies, especially since, as students remark, the work seems more devoted to the destruction of domestic relationships than to their preservation. One may complicate things further by asking whether women's prescribed role in these relationships, even if it does not entail the radical self-sacrifice of death, has any liabilities. Two instances are especially worth attention. The first is the history of his mother, Caroline, that Victor gives at the beginning of his narrative. Her father, a man "of a proud and unbending disposition," subscribes to the cultural equation of manhood with financial power and with pride that resists accommodation. Ruined financially, he "could not bear to live in poverty and oblivion in the same country where he had formerly been distinguished for his rank and magnificence" (31) and so retreats into obscurity and declines into virtual impotence, "incapable of any exertion." His daughter, not incapacitated by pride, willingly abases herself to enter the lowest rank of the wage economy, contriving "to earn a pittance scarcely sufficient to support life" (32). Victor's narrative begins, then, with contrasting accounts of male pride acting against domestic integrity and life itself and of female self-sacrifice as the support of life. It is significant that Caroline's devotion to her father wins the admiration and reverence of Alphonse, who appears as a second father—"a protecting spirit" (32), considerably older—before he becomes a husband; indeed Alphonse creates an icon of the event by commissioning a "historical" painting of Caroline weeping over her father's coffin.

A second instance of the liability inherent in women's domestic role concerns Caroline's "favourite" (42), Elizabeth, an alter ego also left "an orphan and a beggar" whom she presents to Victor as a "gift" to "protect, love, and cherish" (34, 35). Elizabeth's role in relation to Victor and Henry is especially revealing. Victor is occupied by "the inner spirit of nature and the mysterious soul of man"; Henry is concerned with "the busy stage of life, the virtues of heroes, and the actions of men" (37); and Elizabeth is the unbusy, serene servant of both. Her

> saintly soul . . . shone like a shrine-dedicated lamp on our peaceful home. Her sympathy was ours; her smile, her soft voice, the sweet glance of her celestial eyes, were ever there to bless and animate us. . . . I might have become sullen in my study . . . but that she was there to subdue me to a semblance of her own gentleness. And Clerval . . . might not have been so perfectly humane, so thoughtful in his generosity, so full of kindness and tenderness amidst his passion for adventurous exploit, had she not unfolded to him the real loveliness of beneficence and made the doing good the end and aim of his soaring ambition. (37–38)

Elizabeth has no function that is not directed toward her male companions. One possible exception to this company of adventurous men and homebound women is Felix's fiancée, Safie, whose mother, "born in freedom, spurned the bondage" to which she was "reduced" by her necessary marriage to the Turkish merchant who redeemed her from slavery. Because the mother "instructed her daughter in the tenets of her [Christian] religion to aspire to higher powers of intellect and an independence of spirit forbidden to the female followers of Muhammad," Safie sickens

> at the prospect of again returning to Asia and being immured within the walls of a harem, allowed only to occupy herself with infantile amusements, ill-suited to the temper of her soul, now accustomed to grand ideas and a noble emulation for virtue. The prospect of marrying a Christian and remaining in a country where women were allowed to take a rank in society was enchanting to her.   (118–19)

We can note how Safie applies these lessons when, rebelling against her father's instruction, she schemes to travel from Leghorn to the De Laceys' impoverished residence in Germany, accompanied only by a young girl, who dies en route. Safie is an interesting case of female strength in the Wollstonecraft mode; indeed, Mellor, who is also reminded of Wollstonecraft, sees Safie as "the novel's only alternative to a rigidly patriarchal construction of gender and sex roles" and views her disappearance from the novel as a reflection of how Wollstonecraft's death deprived her daughter of "a feminist role model" ("Possessing Nature" 223). Even before Safie's departure from the novel, her presence is quite peripheral; Shelley dilutes its potential as ideological critique by attributing the specter of female bondage entirely to the oppression of Eastern religious ideologies, while avoiding any focus on the way in which the Western Christian idealization of woman also imposes certain restrictions. Moreover, despite the interlude of adventure and learning, Safie is clearly destined for domestic life.

Students may find it interesting in this respect that the most forceful articulation of the domestic ideal, apart from Victor's rueful nostalgia, appears in another male voice, namely the preface Percy ventriloquized for his wife: "my chief concern," this voice claims, "has been . . . the exhibition of the amiableness of domestic affection, and the excellence of universal virtue" (xiv). Mary's preface, we shall see, has other subjects to discuss, and within the novel Victor's articulation of the value of domestic life is intermittent at best. In the preface, quoted above, the brief for domestic affection is a digression; in Victor's narrative it is an irritating delay in the more captivating story of his transgression: "But I forget that I am moralizing in the most interesting part of my tale [his resistless and almost frantic impulse to create life], and," Victor says, acknowledging Walton's complicity, "your looks remind me to proceed" (54). That students, too, want him to proceed is telling: however culpable male appetite is, the story it generates excites a stronger imaginative interest than examples of "domestic relationships" do. If the world of male ambition breeds monsters, it also stimulates education, discovery, and the intellect. Shelley makes it clear that the domestic sphere not only constricts the energies of Victor's intelligence but also leaves Walton and Clerval dissatisfied. For that matter, even Alphonse becomes "a husband and the father of a family" only after he retires from a life of "indefatigable attention to public business," occupied by the "several public situations" he filled "with honour and reputation . . . respected by all" (31).

At the center of all these concerns with gender and behavior is Shelley's characterization of the Creature. For some readers, he bears the repressed phallic aggression of his creator: he is Victor's agent of violence against the constraints of domesticity or the expression of Victor's jealous anger at the family "darling," William, and his mother's "favourite" (42), Elizabeth. Others, however, see the Creature, especially in his status as an object of male creation, as an inscription of the feminine. As a "victim of both the symbolic and the literal," Poovey suggests, he is "doubly like a woman in patriarchal society—forced to be a symbol of (and vehicle for) someone else's desire, yet exposed (and exiled) as the deadly essence of passion itself" (128). Gilbert and Gubar find it significant that when the Creature reads *Paradise Lost*, he suppresses identification with his most obvious counterpart, Eve, who, like him and like Satan's self-begot offspring, Sin, is "defective," a "deformity," and hence monstrous in the male world of the poem (244). One can also discuss the personally traumatic resonance of this identification for Shelley: if Sin begets "the Monster" Death (*PL* 2.674), Shelley may have felt monstrous in learning that her birth was the cause of her own mother's death and the source of a lifelong tension between her and her father. Knoepflmacher gives this connection a full and searching treatment. For Gilbert and Gubar, the novel so emphatically writes "femaleness" as "the gender definition of mothers and daughters, orphans and beggars, monster and false begetters"—all disenfranchised by and alienated from the patriarchal order (232)—that they are willing to view even Victor as feminine: "Victor as Satan . . . was never really the masculine, Byronic Satan of the first book of *Paradise Lost*, but always, instead, the curiously female, outcast Satan who gave birth to Sin" (233). A related issue, of course, is Victor's abortion of the female monster. Johnson offers the assessment that "[m]onstrousness is so incompatible with femininity that Frankenstein cannot even complete the female companion that his creature so eagerly awaits" (7). But might one suggest the opposite—that feminine monstrosity is suppressed because it is too potent, immune to all regulation and control?

The other crux for feminist interpretation, and one related to the situation of the Creature, is Shelley's introduction to the 1831 edition—a document, not coincidentally, that explores the status of the novel as the hideous progeny of a woman's imagination. As Poovey remarks, Shelley's account shows traditional feminine restraint, anticipating the way "*Frankenstein* calls into question, not the social conventions that inhibit creativity, but rather the egotism that [she] associates with the artist's monstrous self-assertion" (122). The introduction also indicates, as Veeder observes, that Shelley's feminism consists chiefly of a desire "to improve woman's lot by both curbing male extremism and confirming female otherness" without transcending her "desire to please dominating males" (12–13). Raising the question of how she, as "a young girl, came to think of and to dilate upon so very hideous an idea," Shelley adopts an almost embarrassed tone that reflects commitment to codes of feminine modesty. Insisting that she is "very averse to bringing [herself] forward in print" and concerned to deflect any potential accusations of "personal intrusion" (vii), she attributes her forwardness to her husband: he "was from the first very anxious that I should prove myself worthy of my parentage and enrol myself on the page of fame. He was forever inciting me to obtain literary reputation." Although she says she is now "infinitely indifferent" (viii) to literary achievement, Percy "urged [her] to develop" her "idea" from the start, and "but for his incitement it would never have taken the form in which it was presented to the world" (xi). She represents even that idea as something before which she is helpless and for which she is scarcely responsible: "My imagination, unbidden, possessed and guided me, gifting the successive images that arose in my mind. . . . I saw . . . I saw. . . . I saw. . . . The idea . . . possessed my mind" (x–xi). This stance of passivity marks a kind of proper feminine withdrawal from the act of moral transgression defining this "idea." "Shelley's book is most interesting, most powerful, and most feminine," argues Moers, in its elaboration of "the motif of revulsion against newborn life, and the drama of guilt, dread, and flight surrounding birth and its consequences." In this respect, *Frankenstein* is "distinctly a *woman's* mythmaking on the subject of birth" ("Female Gothic" 81).

These readings of the novel in the perspective of feminine propriety are important and suggestive, but I think it is also important to direct students' attention to Shelley's obvious fascination in detailing Victor's transgressive discovery and its potent issue. Gilbert and Gubar claim that Victor's desire to investigate origins is "in some sense female" (225); I find the gender of that desire more difficult to categorize, especially because Shelley's introduction affiliates her creative energy with his in ways that challenge conventional notions of the feminine. I ask students to ponder a set of compelling parallels. Like Victor assembling the Creature's body from other parts, Shelley represents herself as assembling parts of other tales to fashion her story. She needs "to invent the machinery of a story" (ix), a task that "consists in . . . the power of moulding and fashioning" one's materials (x); the "artist" in her originating vision is employed with the "working of some powerful engine," in mockery of the "mechanism of the Creator" to "communicate" life to dead matter. Eager to "rival" literary precedent (ix), she struggles to reverse the "mortifying negative" of inspiration with the "progeny" or "offspring" of imagination (xii). She has her protagonist describe the sensation of discovering how to cross the boundary from "death to life" in terms that echo her own moment of inspiration: Victor reports, "[F]rom the midst of this darkness a sudden light broke in upon me—a light so brilliant and wondrous, yet so simple that . . . I became dizzy with the immensity of the prospect" (51); Shelley says, "[S]wift as light and cheering was the idea that broke in upon me" (xi).

It is also significant that both Shelley and Victor are credited with being "authors," although with a difference. Shelley remarks that "the blank incapability of invention . . . is the greatest misery of authorship" (x); that misery overcome, she is pleased to write the "Author's Introduction" to a tale in which authorship proves a misery to her protagonist: "I had been the author of unalterable evils" (87), their "miserable origin and author" (96). With the material of fiction, Shelley seems rather to enjoy generating monsters: "If I could only contrive [a story] which would frighten my reader as I myself had been frightened that night" by "my hideous phantom"; "What terrified me will terrify others" (xi). Unlike her protagonist, Shelley does not repent; in 1831 she melodramatically concludes her story of creation with a theatrical envoi: "And now, once again, I bid my hideous progeny go forth and prosper. I have an affection for" this "offspring of happy days" (xii). As Mellor points out (see *Mary Shelley* 54), Shelley even insinuates herself into her novel as the enabling auditor: the whole story is delivered to Margaret Walton Saville, whose name shares its initials with Mary Wollstonecraft Shelley. Like the unorthodox Safie, this "author" is a peripheral figure, but because the terms, and indeed the informing events, of her introductory tale of origins are repeated and echoed in her novel, the account is not so much marginal as it is contextual or metatextual. The questions it raises—Is female authorship exciting, improper, or monstrous? Is monster making fascinating and dramatically compelling or is it a subject for moral judgment? Is the domestic sphere salvation or constriction? Is monstrosity male or female?—are ultimately not settled. But Shelley's ability to give compelling representation to these dilemmas and to associate them with the ideologies of gender by which she was influenced animates the text of *Frankenstein* in ways that can continue to animate our students' attention.

Aporia and Radical Empathy:
Frankenstein (Re)Trains the Reader

Syndy M. Conger

Mary Shelley's increasing conservatism in later life has frequently been used to suggest a foreshadowing conservatism in her youthful novel *Frankenstein* (see especially Scott; Sterrenburg). When I work with the novel in the classroom, however, I am repeatedly convinced that, whatever its overt themes, the book's covert demands on readers are radically subversive. Unlike other gothic tales of its day and ours whose rhythmic frights coerce readers to admire noble heroes and detest outlaw villains, *Frankenstein* creates what Friedrich Schiller called the "republican freedom of the readers" (8). Liberated from the tyranny of terror, readers can exercise their own judgment to evaluate the merits of the tale and its characters. This reader independence occurs subtly, through Shelley's use of a multiple point-of-view technique that first gradually discourages admiration for the tale's self-professed protagonist, Victor, and then encourages identification with the ostensible antagonist, the Creature. To tell the students this outright, however, is to deprive them of this freedom. As a consequence, I usually teach this book somewhat later in the course (Introduction to Prose Fiction) and invite maximum student participation through group-constructed study questions. I do not immediately cast them adrift with the text; instead I launch them into their study by locating the text both in its revolutionary period and in the early development of the gothic novel. After that I ask students to read the book in segments that correspond to the stories of the various narrators: Walton, Victor, the Creature, and then, again, Walton. The questions students formulate take many shapes but invariably center on the two major ones I discuss below.

The first day we discuss any book, I try to bring to the students' attention something special that they might not know but that could be interesting and useful to them. My aim on the first day on *Frankenstein* is to activate their expectations about Shelley's novel in particular and the gothic genre in general but without making them feel that I am necessarily challenging those expectations. Most recently, and most successfully, I have begun by talking about the central mystery surrounding the making of *Frankenstein*, which Mary Shelley herself best articulated in her introduction to the 1831 edition. How did the novel come about? Her multiple sources include parents, contemporaries, "waking dreams," and fantastic stories (vii). By far her most compelling explanation of its origin, however, because it matches a key scene in the novel itself, is her last one: she dreamed it (x–xi).

As I explain in a brief historical lecture, a clear, and very probably not accidental, connection exists between gothic novels and nightmares. Afterwards I ask the students to describe some of the key features of their dreams. They invariably discover (and I tell them so to increase their confidence and motivation) at least two of Freud's four characteristics of dreamwork: the conflation or condensation of images or human figures; the displacement of the important by the trivial; the pictorial dramatization of concepts; and elaboration, the voice-over narration of the dream that works to render its illogic logical (Freud, ch. 6). I share with them my conviction that dream literature engages its readers more completely on the emotive, imaginative, and cognitive levels than other literature. After reading to the students one or two particularly dreamlike passages from the novel, I ask them to look for similar passages as they read. Students soon realize that nearly all these passages have something to do with Victor's Creature. Indeed the Creature seems to engage them most completely, no doubt the result of Mary Shelley's expert management of a technique she almost certainly learned from her father, William Godwin (Clifford 604): the first-person retrospective point of view.

Question 1: Why does Victor, even when faced with the prospect of seeing others either injured or killed, remain silent? Students rarely show any spontaneous interest in Walton even though, as narrator and genuine outsider, he might be considered reliably objective and representative of the author's views. Occasionally they even mistake Walton for the editor of the edition we are reading and skip his section altogether to jump into chapter 1. If they do read Walton's letters, however, those letters seem at first to confirm their notion of what the story is about: a gripping tale of a mad scientist who, like God, tries to create life from death and who is ultimately destroyed by his own abortive creation.

Victor's initial narrative reinforces these preconceptions, allowing the students, in Wolfgang Iser's reader-response terminology, to continue the "consistency building" (or "illusion building") that is so "fundamental to the grasping of a text" (119). Victor's studies—and especially his willful study of books his father forbids him to read—seem appropriate for a young man destined to dream of creating life in a laboratory: Cornelius Agrippa, Paracelsus, Albertus Magnus, distillation, the air pump, electricity, and finally modern chemistry. Victor's obsessive work habits also correspond to the students' preconceived notions of the story: they are not surprised to read that Victor, in the course of pursuing his dream, loses all touch with time and season. Then, in the account of the momentous night in November when Victor finally instills the spark of life in his newly formed Creature, events begin to trigger in students the kind of surprise that Iser believes interrupts illusion building, disturbs involvement with character and story, and forces fruitful speculation (126–27, 187).

Students are generally unprepared by their encounters with *Franken-stein* films to implicate Victor in crimes other than the unnatural creation of life, but, beginning with that "dreary night of November," the text encourages them to do so. Some students are puzzled by Victor's sudden dreamlike transition from ecstasy to repugnance. Their questions often revolve around a passage that captures the abruptness of the shift: "Beautiful! Great God! . . . I had desired it [to create life] with an ardour that far exceeded moderation; but now that I had finished, the beauty of the dream vanished, and breathless horror and disgust filled my heart" (56). They are mystified by Victor's rush from the room and even more by his subsequent nightmare:

> I thought I saw Elizabeth, in the bloom of health, walking in the streets of Ingolstadt. Delighted and surprised, I embraced her, but as I imprinted the first kiss on her lips, they became livid with the hue of death; her features appeared to change, and I thought that I held the corpse of my dead mother in my arms; a shroud enveloped her form, and I saw the grave-worms crawling in the folds of the flannel. (57)

Victor wakes up a moment later to a sight like Mary Shelley's dream:

> [T]he miserable monster whom I had created . . . held up the curtain of the bed; and his eyes, if eyes they may be called, were fixed on me. His jaws opened, and he muttered some inarticulate sounds, while a grin wrinkled his cheeks. . . . [O]ne hand was stretched out, seemingly to detain me, but I escaped. . . .   (57)

Victor spends the rest of that night cowering in the courtyard, assigning names to his Creature that reflect his newly born horror: "demoniacal corpse," "mummy," "hideous . . . wretch," "a thing such as even Dante could not have conceived."

Victor's dream can be seen variously as an example of foreshadowing, as another instance of the gothic "dead bride" motif, or as a reflection of the desire to possess the mother (Hill 338–39) or of Shelley's ambivalent feelings about childbirth or motherhood (Moers, "Female Gothic" 81). Instead of encouraging students to assign a single interpretation to this dream, I challenge them to explore its emotive content. However it is read, the dream discloses appalling self-loathing and guilt, hints that Elizabeth's life may be in danger, and begins to raise doubts about Victor as protagonist. What hero would wish to escape so quickly from self-created responsibility? would dream that his mother and bride-to-be were one and the same?

would dream his bride-to-be into a shroud? And what hero, finally, would remain silent even when that silence threatened the lives of his family and closest friends? Students view Victor's persisting in silence with increasing impatience after the death of William, the trial of Justine, and the murder of Clerval. Even Victor's eloquent acknowledgment of guilt to Walton—"I had cast among mankind . . . my own vampire" (74)—does not deter them from insisting that Victor's supposed reasons for keeping the Creature a secret are flimsy excuses. To their growing list of questions, however, the students receive only Victor's answers. Their understanding of events is, at this point, limited to his perspective, a limitation they gradually begin to see as imprisonment. Victor's first-person narration is beginning to impede a carefree gothic reading of itself.

By the time the students begin reading chapter 9, their attitude toward Victor approaches *aporia*, an ideal state of mind described by the Greek skeptical philosophers as the perfect suspension of judgment that prevents either complete faith or doubt. Victor's version of his story represents him as protagonist and names him "victor," but his actions contradict his self-representation. They suggest he is a coward and a villain, indirectly responsible for two deaths and for the devastating unhappiness among the survivors. Students' initial admiration or sympathy for Victor now gives way to suspicion, and they wonder if they ought to believe the simple and soothing moral that Victor offers as his story's only message: "Learn from me, if not by my precepts, at least by my own example, how dangerous is the acquirement of knowledge" (52). Perhaps the story has another message, one that Victor's narration tries to displace?

Question 2: Why doesn't the Creature simply kill Victor and be done with it? This question, which invariably emerges when students read the Creature's narrative within Victor's tale, marks an important transitional moment in their reader-text dialogue. They have begun to recognize the complexity of the creator-creature relationship in this story: despite their rage against each other, Victor and his Creature are bound together, the Creature by his utter dependence on Victor, Victor by his obligations to the Creature. The students eventually see, too, the ways in which creature and creator duplicate and complement each other as if together they constitute a single, sadly divided personality.

The emergence of this second question signals the beginning of a shift in the students' allegiance from protagonist to antagonist. Despite Victor's tirades against the Creature as "monster," "fiend," "devil," and "vile insect" (95) and despite the Creature's undeniable crimes, students grow increasingly uncertain about hating the Creature once he has begun to tell his own story. Students may feel a bond with the Creature because they identify with him as unloved child, as misunderstood helper, as ugly duckling, or as unhappy student (Oates 545–47). Whatever facet of the Creature attracts them, however, their new hesitation in rejecting him depends to a great extent on the way in which Mary Shelley allows the reader to see through the Creature's eyes.

I believe this shift in perspective occurs in chapter 10, where the Creature, in a last desperate attempt to interest Victor in his tale, covers his eyes: " 'Thus I relieve thee, my creator,' he said, and placed his hated hands before my eyes, which I flung from me with violence; 'thus I take from thee a sight which you abhor. Still thou canst listen to me . . .' " (97). Victor, both literally and figuratively blinded, will no longer be the reader's "eyes"; the Creature he has rejected and execrated will now tell his side of the story. Shlomith Rimmon-Kenan succinctly explains the dramatic perceptual reversal this moment marks: the "focalized object" now becomes not only the "focalizer" of the novel but the "dominant focalizer," the point-of-view character whose ideology becomes the norm by which other characters and ideologies are evaluated (81). Just how does Shelley achieve this reversal?

We all know that the novel consists of a series of interlocking first-person narratives, each thematically mirroring the others. But very little attention has been paid to the differences between the Creature's manner of story-telling and Victor's. Both tales recount progress from innocence to experience, but only the Creature's tale reveals an innocence so absolute at the outset and so utterly devoid of preconceived notions or even differentiating categories that it quickly establishes him as a trustworthy, albeit naive, narrator. Limited in his ability to interpret what he sees, he nevertheless records his experiences faithfully:

> Soon a gentle light stole over the heavens and gave me a sensation of pleasure. . . . I gazed with a kind of wonder. . . . No distinct ideas occupied my mind; all was confused. I felt light, and hunger, and thirst, and darkness; innumerable sounds rang in my ears, and on all sides various scents saluted me. . . .   (99)

Several recent critics have maintained that, out of context, the Creature's voice is occasionally indistinguishable from Victor's (Cantor 107; Newman 146; Oates 546). What they fail to note, though, is that the Creature's narrative generally engages its reader on many more levels than Victor's usually does. His ignorance of the simplest objects makes his early narrative something of a puzzle that teases the reader's mind; his close record of sensory experience certainly appeals to the reader's imagination; and his emotional responses appeal to the reader's emotions. The narrative invites the reader to help complete the story that the Creature does not have all the words to tell (Schug 607); at the same time, the Creature's nonjudgmental stance gives the reader, especially the student reader, the confidence to accept that invitation.

Of the three levels of engagement, the most compelling for students is the emotional level (see R. J. Dunn 414; Oates 545); it is also the one that distinguishes the Creature's tale throughout. Victor, the precocious student of chemistry, shares his ideas and his deeds with the narratee but tends to forget as narrator what he forgot as character: feelings. In fact, he admits to Walton that his studies "interfere[d] with the tranquillity of his domestic affections" (54). The Creature's tale, in contrast, never strays far from his feelings; for him they are the precious residue that renders his experiences valuable:

> I found a fire . . . and was overcome with delight. . . . [H]uts . . . cottages, and stately houses engaged my admiration by turns. . . . [G]rievously bruised by stones . . . I escaped to the open country and fearfully took refuge in a low hovel. . . . [T]he aged cottager won my reverence . . . the girl enticed my love. . . . He raised her and smiled with such kindness and affection that I felt sensations of a peculiar and overpowering nature; they were a mixture of pain and pleasure . . . and I withdrew from the window, unable to bear these emotions. (99, 101, 103)

This is not to say that the Creature does not grow intellectually or talk about his growth. But what enhances his attractiveness is his record of the accompanying emotional growth from childlike wonder, delight, and dread to more mature (because more selfless) reverence, love, and empathy for others—the De Laceys, the drowning girl, even his own condemnatory creator—a capacity, its bears pointing out, that his creator does not share (Schopf 46–47). To many readers of Mary Shelley's day, the Creature's empathy would clearly identify him as his creator's moral superior; it also would align Mary Shelley with the British empirical philosophers of the preceding century (especially John Locke and David Hartley) who stressed the centrality of sympathy to moral behavior and of experience in the shaping of moral character and, for that matter, in the acquisition of all knowledge (Sidgwick 218–23; Lamprecht 115–17). This progressive philosophy, embraced in varying forms by radical thinkers from 1770 on, provided Shelley with a plausible apology for the Creature's eventual transformation to murderer (his repeated rejection experiences, which frustrate his desire for companionship, drive him to murder [Schopf 46–47]) and gave the author a rationale for her own markedly nondidactic stance toward her reader. The reader, too, must determine right and wrong from experiencing, albeit vicariously, the lives of creator and creature. Even today's students, whose knowledge of eighteenth-century ethics may be quite limited, are nevertheless inclined, like their predecessors, to empathize with the character who empathizes with others. This story within the story, this moving record of emotional and moral progress, seems to work the magic necessary to transform the Creature into the novel's dominant focalizer. It lets readers judge the Creature in terms of internal merit rather than external appearance, an alternative route they are even more apt to follow once they realize that Victor cannot and indeed does not contradict the Creature's tale after it is told. On the contrary, it convinces Victor—and readers along with him—that he has wronged his Creature and should make reparation for it.

The Creature, like Victor, has a nightmare; but his is the recurring waking nightmare of violent rejections, starting with that of his creator, including the rejections of Felix De Lacey and the friend of the drowning girl, and ending, at the beginning of his career of crime, with the rejection of Victor's little brother, William. The day after he has failed to gain the De Laceys as allies, the Creature recalls, "the fever of my blood did not allow me to be visited by peaceful dreams. The horrible scene of the preceding day was forever acting before my eyes; the females were flying and the enraged Felix tearing me from his father's feet" (131). Like Victor's nightmare, this vision conveys disapproval of self, but the dominant emotional chord struck by the dream is hurt, horror, and grief at losing, once again, a potential friend. The Creature's nightmare is that of the innocent victim, not the guilt-ridden perpetrator. Once students have heard the Creature's anguished cry, have read the record, in dreams and reality, of his repeated, unmitigated, and undeserved pain, they no longer seem able to subscribe solely to Victor's "elaborations" or rationalizations for his ambitions. Victor's story has been irrevocably written over, or at least glossed, his deeds have been revealed as crimes, and his distortions have been discovered. Before Victor destroys the Creature's promised mate, when he looks out the window to see the Creature looking in at him, the point of view is ostensibly Victor's: "I saw by the light of the moon the demon at the casement. A ghastly grin wrinkled his lips . . ." (159). In terms of sympathy, however, the students by now are standing—as they did during the entire De Lacey segment—next to the Creature on the outside of the window looking in. They have come to feel an empathy for Mary Shelley's social outcast—a radical empathy—that they cannot resist, one that induces them not only to reread Victor's story but invites them to read other stories differently thereafter.

Probing the Psychological Mystery of *Frankenstein*

Paula R. Feldman

Students in my English Romanticism class complain on first reading *Frankenstein* that this so-called horror story is not very frightening. I use the Socratic method to help them discover for themselves the interesting psychological dimensions that embrace the true horror of the story. We become literary detectives trying to solve a mystery, trying to make sense of things that don't seem, on the surface at least, to make much sense.

After spending some class time eliciting students' initial observations about the book and then discussing some of the more obvious topics, I point out that several puzzling circumstances in this novel bear further scrutiny. "Why," I ask, "does Victor Frankenstein, having worked for years to create a living being, abandon it just at the moment he accomplishes his dream?" Students initially respond that Victor flees because the Creature is hideously ugly, but I remind them that someone who has been working with dead body parts is not likely to be squeamish. I read aloud the opening paragraphs of chapter 5, asking them to listen for clues to an explanation that makes more sense. Soon they realize that what is frightening is not how the Creature looks but *that* he looks: not until his dull yellow eye opens does Victor seek to escape. Victor seems frightened by the autonomy of his Creature; he can no longer control it as he did when it lay lifeless on the table. Sometimes, a student will point out the similarity between Victor's feelings and those a parent might experience with a newborn child.

We leave this subject temporarily to concentrate on another curious occurrence. "How," I inquire, "does Victor know, after the death of young William, that the Creature is the child's murderer?" "Because," students volunteer, "he *sees* him." "Now wait a minute," I protest. "What kind of evidence is that? He *sees* him? Would you expect that statement to hold up in a court of law?" Acknowledging that they wouldn't, they point out that, all the same, Victor Frankenstein is correct—the Creature is, indeed, the murderer. "Still," I observe, "the last time he saw the Creature, he had just been created and had only just opened his eyes. How does he know anything about this creature's character, let alone that he is a murderer? By what process," I persist, "does he discover the truth?" Students admit that the process does not appear to be a rational one involving induction or deduction. I read aloud Victor's thoughts in chapter 7: "Could he be . . . the murderer of my brother? No sooner did that idea cross my imagination than I became convinced of its truth. . . . *He* was the murderer! I could not doubt it. The mere presence of the idea was an irresistible proof of the fact" (73–74). "What kind of a thought process is this?" I prod. Students recognize now that it is intuitive, as if Victor is looking inside himself for the answer. I point out here that while Victor Franken-stein's method of solving the murder would seem, on reflection, to be highly unusual, nevertheless, we, as readers, do not balk when we encoun-ter it in chapter 7. I hint that the author may have prepared us in some way to accept it.

Elizabeth's murder is the third strange circumstance I encourage my students to consider. "How is it," I ask, "that although the Creature clearly warns Victor that he will be with him on his wedding night, Victor goes right ahead and marries Elizabeth, showing no concern for the danger in which he will be placing his bride?" Students repeat Victor's protestations of obtuseness. They call to mind his egotism. "Come on," I say, "who could be that obtuse? Who could be that egotistical? Victor isn't stupid." They agree that Frankenstein's actions are puzzling. "Could it be," I propose, "that Victor marries Elizabeth precisely in order to murder her?" Students initially resist this suggestion. For further evidence we look to the dream Victor has just after bringing his Creature to life:

> I thought I saw Elizabeth, in the bloom of health, walking in the streets of Ingolstadt. Delighted and surprised, I embraced her, but as I im-printed the first kiss on her lips, they became livid with the hue of death; her features appeared to change, and I thought that I held the corpse of my dead mother in my arms; a shroud enveloped her form, and I saw the grave-worms crawling in the folds of the flannel.   (57)

Victor's kiss is the kiss of death, and this passage clearly prefigures Eliza-beth's fate as his bride. Students remain skeptical.

I call their attention to Victor's admission, just after deciding that the Creature is the murderer of young William: "I considered the being whom I had cast among mankind and endowed with the will and power to effect purposes of horror . . . nearly in the light of my own vampire, my own spirit let loose from the grave and forced to destroy all that was dear to me" (74). I read this passage aloud, slowly, and then hold up a picture of Boris Karloff portraying the Creature. "Who is this?" "Frankenstein," they gasp, recognizing the frightening implications of that response.

The stage is thus set for me to introduce the notion of the double. Stu-dents can now see how Victor Frankenstein's flight from his newborn cre-ation makes sense as a scene of unendurable self-confrontation. We talk about how Victor has achieved his self-imposed isolation in Ingolstadt by repressing something in himself that the Creature embodies; the Creature is forced to lead a life of his own, acting out what Victor is struggling to keep from consciousness. I call attention to the many times throughout the novel that Victor falls asleep or loses consciousness and how he explicitly acknowledges his own culpability when he first sees the corpse of each of the "monster's" victims. For instance, Justine's imminent death provokes him to acknowledge, "I [am] the true murderer" (84). He greets the lifeless form of Henry Clerval with the telling exclamation, "Have my murderous machinations deprived you also, my dearest Henry, of life? Two I have already destroyed; other victims await their destiny . . ." (169).

Next, I point out a passage in which the Creature reminds Frankenstein of their physical kinship ("my form is a filthy type of yours, more horrid even from the very resemblance" [125]) and challenge the class to look for deeper similarities. Students generally notice that both are isolated, intelligent, and originally innocent, but that Victor's and the Creature's innocence has been blasted along with their hopes. They recognize the two figures as Byronic: tortured by consciousness, longing for oblivion, unable to remove the curse that plagues them or (for most of the novel) to die. Both come eventually to mourn the loss of all those they love.

I call attention to the similarity of many of their utterances. For example, each in his own way cries to a mocking universe, "if ye really pity me, crush sensation and memory" (142), just as each describes himself repeatedly as a "miserable wretch." Each, motivated by blind revenge, destroys himself as he seeks the annihilation of the other. One is the slave of the other and at the same time master and executioner.

Next, I ask students to describe the characteristics that differentiate Frankenstein from his epipsyche. They notice that while Frankenstein is accepted by society but chooses isolation, his Creature is an outcast but yearns for companionship. They generally see Frankenstein as selfish and egocentric but his Creature as benevolent, sympathetic, and kind, transformed only by the cruelty and neglect of society. Students contrast the tumultuous early life of the Creature with the harmonious childhood of his creator. Someone usually volunteers that the Creature looks deformed on the outside but Frankenstein suffers from an internal deformity. They note the asexuality of Frankenstein and the implied sexuality of his Creature, as well as the added cruelty that Frankenstein has a bride while denying one to the Creature. Sometimes a student suggests parallels between the Creature and Freud's concept of the id and between Frankenstein and Freud's concept of the ego. While Frankenstein is ambitious to distinguish himself in the pursuit of knowledge, the Creature wants only to love and be loved. Students find it useful to see these polarities drawn on the board in the form of two opposing lists.

Such lists help clarify what the two characters embody, as do explicit statements in the novel. For example, Frankenstein himself observes that his crime is not the pursuit of knowledge in itself but the fact that such a pursuit "has a tendency to weaken your affections and to destroy your taste for those simple pleasures in which no alloy can possibly mix." As such, it is "not befitting the human mind" (54). Frankenstein allows his ambition to suppress his natural need for human love and sympathy. By denying its worth, he forces that essential part of his being to pursue a solitary, incomplete existence.

I follow up these insights with another question: "What does Walton have in common with these two?" As students list resemblances, I prompt them to see that Walton possesses characteristics of both Frankenstein and his Creature. Walton aspires to distinguish himself in the realm of knowledge, but his ambition is tempered by a love for his fellow beings. In hopes of accomplishing his mission, he chooses isolation from his family and home, yet he feels this separation strongly and yearns for companionship. The apparently tangential Walton turns out to be one of the most important characters in the book. He is Mary Shelley's model of the healthy, integrated personality—someone who can strive for distinction but who turns back when his actions might harm others.

Once I have established for students that it is legitimate and productive to probe the psychological dimensions of the novel, I do so at length. This novel, I argue, is truly a horror story, but not of the usual sort. Despite its imperfections, it has remained popular because it articulates the psychological horror of the author's own emotional landscape and, in so doing, subliminally touches responsive chords within us all.

Frankenstein is, in fact, autobiography told in the language of dreams. It expresses the unresolved contradictions of Mary Shelley's life. Until relatively recently, critics virtually ignored the psychological aspects of the novel and the import of its having been inspired by a nightmarish vision.[1] Yet *Frankenstein* not only has the character of an extended and elaborated dream; like a dream, it expresses in veiled terms the innermost wishes and fears of its author.

I begin our exploration of Mary Shelley's inner world with the most striking example of her dream life recorded in her journal. There, on 19 March 1815, shortly after the death of her first child, she writes, "Dream that my little baby came to life again—that it had only been cold and that we rubbed it before the fire & it lived" (*Journals* 1: 70). "Does this dream sound familiar?" I inquire. Students immediately recognize that this vision of a corpse miraculously imbued with life anticipates the famous reverie from whose terrors Mary Shelley would awaken slightly more than a year later to find herself with the germ for *Frankenstein*. "I saw," she recalls in her 1831 introduction, "the pale student of unhallowed arts kneeling beside the thing he had put together. I saw the hideous phantasm of a man stretched out, and then, on the working of some powerful engine, show signs of life and stir with an uneasy, half-vital motion" (x–xi). I suggest that the resemblance between these two visions is not merely coincidental; both derive from a deep, personal preoccupation that finds further expression in the novel and in her life.[2]

We take another look at this introduction, and I call attention to the passage in which Mary Shelley bids her "hideous progeny go forth and prosper" (xii). "She is referring here to ——— ?" (I pause to let students complete my sentence.) "Victor Frankenstein's monster!" they volunteer, blithely tumbling into my trap. "Not at all," I insist, and, to prove my point, read them the passage immediately following in the introduction: "I have an affection for it, for it was the offspring of happy days, when death and grief were but words which found no true echo in my heart. Its several pages speak of many a walk, many a drive, and many a conversation, when I was not alone . . ." (xii). Now students see clearly that this "hideous progeny," this "offspring," is Mary Shelley's own novel, her artistic creation. It is a novel about itself and about its author's relation to it. At its heart lies Mary Shelley's individual struggle with the act of creation, a struggle characterized by fear as much as by ambition. In a profound sense, the novel is Mary Shelley's monster let loose.

Students are now receptive to my argument that Mary Shelley's ambivalence regarding her artistic capabilities is central to the novel. I insist that when Victor Frankenstein promises to "unfold to the world the deepest mysteries of creation" (47), readers must take "creation" in its widest sense. He is not merely a scientist or inventor. To see him as such would mean ignoring the original vision of the "pale student of unhallowed *arts*" (my italics) who kneels beside the thing he had put together. Later in the same passage Mary Shelley remarks, "His success would terrify the artist" (x–xi). Casting Frankenstein in the form of a scientist seems to have been a matter of dramatic expediency at a time when the word *art* could still mean science as well as fine art. *Frankenstein*, then, is the story of an artist and the artist's progeny, just as Mary Shelley was herself the child of artists.

At this juncture, I introduce students to pertinent biographical information. From the day of her birth, I point out, Mary Shelley was regarded as "the only offspring of a union that will certainly be matchless in the present generation" (Taylor 1: 19). The daughter of Mary Wollstonecraft and William Godwin could be nothing less than exceptionally talented. However, in the summer of 1816, her promise was as yet unfulfilled. "My husband," she relates in the introduction, "was from the first very anxious that I should prove myself worthy of my parentage. . . . He was forever inciting me to obtain literary reputation, which even on my own part I cared for . . ." (viii). Years later, she remarks in her journal, "I was nursed and fed with a love of glory. To be something great and good was the precept given me by my father: Shelley reiterated it" (entry for 21 Oct. 1838,

Journals 2: 554). But despite others' expectations and despite her own will to achieve, she seems to have felt intimidated by the writers surrounding her. She says in her journal, "[I]ncapacity & timidity always prevented my mingling in the nightly conversations of Diodati—they were as it were entirely tête-a-tête between my Shelley & Albe [Byron]" (entry for 19 Oct. 1822, *Journals* 2: 439). And she describes Shelley as possessing a genius "far transcending" hers.

Now I suggest to students that if we view the ghost-story contest at Diodati against this background, the dream that inspired *Frankenstein* takes on increased significance. By her own confession, Mary Shelley felt mortified each time she had to admit that her "anxious invocations" had not yet yielded a story (x). But not just any story would do; it had to be worthy of its distinguished company and of her heritage. "In our family," her stepsister, Claire Clairmont, once remarked, "if you cannot write an epic poem or novel, that by its originality knocks all other novels on the head, you are a despicable creature, not worth acknowledging" (Nitchie 141). If we think of Mary Shelley's dream, at least in part, as a response to these anxieties, it seems symbolically to express inner fears about her creative capabilities. As an artist, Mary Shelley is horrified to see that what she creates is imperfect; its motion is "uneasy" and "half-vital" (xi). She runs to escape from it, then tries to put it out of her mind, but it returns, and she is forced to confront its odiousness. Despite its intrinsic merit, its countenance is ugly. It is frightful not only because it disappoints expectations by not perfectly embodying the inspiration that brought it into being but because it gives visible, public form to the artist's inadequacies.

Most students are, by this time, intrigued by what I have told them about Mary Shelley's life and its relation to the novel. They want to know more. I point out that the waking dream that inspired *Frankenstein* had nothing of murder in it. Even so, creation and destruction motifs are intimately linked both in the pages of Mary Shelley's book and in her own experience. Her imagination, I argue, expanded on her original vision by drawing on the psychological material associated with four profoundly disturbing deaths: those of her mother; her firstborn child; her half sister, Fanny Imlay (whose suicide occurred six weeks into the eight-month gestation period of the novel's composition); and Harriet, Shelley's first wife (whose suicide took place two and a half months after that).

I caution students that, if it seems curious to think of a nineteen-year-old asserting, "To examine the causes of life, we must first have recourse to death," they need only recall that Mary Shelley's birth nearly coincided with the death of her mother. It is not uncommon for children in such circumstances to hold themselves personally accountable for the mother's death—to feel an unconscious sense of guilt or to feel their birth to be murder, however inadvertent. Ironically, Mary Shelley's own first experience of giving birth was followed almost immediately by the death of her premature infant. Moreover, she had had warning of her lonely half sister's depression that summer at Diodati, and after Fanny's death she was, like Percy Shelley, filled with remorse and self-accusation for not having been more attentive. During her early life with Shelley, she must have had many occasions for wishing Harriet Shelley dead and out of the way. Harriet's suicide simplified Mary's life considerably. Yet, clearly Mary harbored intense feelings of guilt, which she articulated twenty-three years later in her journal entry of 12 February 1839: "Poor Harriet to whose sad fate I attribute so many of my own heavy sorrows as the atonement claimed by fate for her death" (*Journals* 2: 560). Students can see from this passage that Mary Shelley felt she had wronged Harriet and concluded that her crime had rebounded, heaping misery on her own life. (Sometimes a student volunteers that Mary Shelley's plight sounds much like Victor Frankenstein's.) At any rate, I argue that Mary Shelley appears to have felt some measure of responsibility and guilt for all four of these deaths, and her submerged response seems to have dictated much of the emotional landscape for the portrayal of murder in her novel. On some level, she must have felt that she, like her character, was a blight on others. Frankenstein, students recall, does not literally murder by his own hand but does nonetheless, bear responsibility. Death haunts him, I suggest, as it must have haunted Mary Shelley.

Near this juncture in our discussion, I can usually count on at least one skeptical student to raise an important objection: "Did Mary Shelley intend all these things you see in the novel, or are you just reading in what isn't there?" This question gives me the opportunity to tell students about the pitfalls of second-guessing authorial intention and about the varied ways in which readers can legitimately interpret a text, despite what the author may or may not have had consciously in mind. As I confess to the students, Mary Shelley probably did not consciously intend to embed in *Frankenstein* the autobiographical elements we have been noticing. Observing that the creative process is highly complex and that the author's subconscious often plays a crucial part, I ask students, "Have you ever had a dream that seemed to have little significance until a friend suggested an interpretation so obvious you wonder how it could ever have escaped you?" Fiction, I explain, can sometimes be like dreams in that way. An author may be consciously unaware of a work's subliminal sources or, for complicated psychological reasons, may fail to make the connection between her own and, say, a fictional character's situation. But that shouldn't stop readers from making whatever connections the evidence implies. Even so, I acknowledge to students, a psychological reading should not be undertaken without detailed knowledge of an author's inner life. For such knowledge of Mary Shelley, we must depend on her letters, journals, and other fictional works. Although those interpreting works by living authors may have more direct personal knowledge, all psychological interpretation requires not only extreme care but an acknowledgment that it is highly speculative. In *Frankenstein*, the dreamlike quality of the work seems to invite such an interpretation, as do some of Mary Shelley's own statements about writing.

For example, she writes to Maria Gisborne on 22 November 1822, "Perhaps it would be better not to write at all; but the weakness of human nature is to seek for sympathy" (*Letters* 1: 291). I try to persuade students that *Frankenstein* is as much about sympathy and rejection as it is about creation and destruction—that they are, in fact, two variations on a single theme. Mary Shelley's journals and letters suggest that although she felt guilty about the harm she had caused others, she felt at the same time injured and rejected. Thus, *Frankenstein* is a plea *for* sympathy and acceptance as much as it is *about* these human needs.

Drawing on the biographical evidence, I argue that Mary Shelley's familiarity with rejection probably came quite early. Many children in similar circumstances interpret their mothers' deaths as desertion. It is not improbable that Mary Shelley, like Frankenstein's Creature, felt abandoned by the one who gave her life. Godwin, a remote parent, hardly filled the void, and Mary's relationship with his second wife, Mary Jane Clairmont, was difficult at best. Students can see that, growing up, Mary must often have felt overlooked and alone, deprived of the sympathy that comforts most children.

When she eloped with Shelley, Mary must certainly have anticipated some moral indignation. Yet students can see from the evidence I present from her letters and journals that she was genuinely shocked by Godwin's outrage and disillusioned by this unexpected discrepancy between his actions and his ideals. Later she remarks, "Until I knew Shelley I may justly say that he [Godwin] was my God—& I remember many childish instances of the excess of attachment I bore for him" (*Letters* 1: 296). She felt profoundly injured by a rejection coming from the one person whose approval she most desired. She writes to Shelley, "I know not whether it is early habit or affection but the idea of his [Godwin's] silent quiet disapprobation makes me weep as it did in the days of my childhood" (*Letters* 1: 57). That she records having read or reread all the major works of both parents during 1814 and 1815 seems to indicate a desire to be "with" her parents in some meaningful way during those initial years with Shelley (see her reading lists, *Journals* 1: 85–97). Isabel Baxter, her closest girlhood friend, broke off the friendship at her parents' request. Students see that Mary must have felt increasingly rejected and isolated, like Frankenstein's Creature.

But, I argue, her creative work also helped distance her from others. Recalling our study of the last section of "Kubla Khan," I remind students that in the Romantic myth of the artist-hero, one of the most dangerous aspects of the imagination is its potential for isolating the individual. Proud defiance of conventional life and the insights of an artistic sensibility can be a curse. Blake once expressed the pathos of the artist's dilemma in his famous complaint:

> O why was I born with a different face?
> Why was I not born like the rest of my race?
> (*Complete Writings* 828)

Moreover, Mary Shelley felt torn between the demands of being a creator, where the act of composition is necessarily solitary, and the demands of being a procreator, a wife and mother, where being with others is essential.

I ask students to turn yet again to the novel's introduction, in which Mary Shelley, recalling her childhood, writes, "[M]y dreams were all my own; I accounted for them to nobody; they were my refuge when annoyed—my dearest pleasure when free" (vii). I tell them that in later life, ironically, these dreams often took the form of introspective brooding and deep depression, causing her to shut out of her life those very people whose affection she most needed. Frankenstein's declaration, "I shunned the face of man; all sound of joy or complacency was torture to me; solitude was my only consolation—deep, dark, deathlike solitude" (86), is of a piece with statements Mary Shelley confides in her letters and journals. She writes, for example:

> I am not given to tears; & though my most miserable fate has often turned my eyes to fountains—yet oftener I suffer agonies unassuaged by tears. . . . when to destroy every thing around me & to run in to that vast grave (the sea) until fatigued I sunk to rest would be a pleasure to me. (letter to Maria Gisborne, 17 Sept. 1822; *Letters* 1: 260–61)

Students can see the very images of this confession anticipated when Frankenstein muses, "[O]ften . . . I was tempted to plunge into the silent lake, that the waters might close over me and my calamities forever" (87).

To Maria Gisborne, Mary Shelley exclaims, "And instead of this [committing suicide] I write, & as I write I say Oh God! have pity on me!" (*Letters* 1: 261). Frankenstein's lamentations, I argue, are Mary's own, suppressed in the presence of those around her but poured out on the pages of her novel. Frankenstein revealingly remarks at one point:

> I checked . . . my impatient thirst for sympathy and was silent when I would have given the world to have confided the fatal secret. Yet, still, words like those I have recorded would burst uncontrollably from me. I could offer no explanation of them, but their truth in part relieved the burden of my mysterious woe.   (177)

These cathartic acts of Frankenstein are much like Mary Shelley's writing of her novel.

Next I show students evidence of the sharp disparity between the inner and outer world of both Victor Frankenstein and his creator, who describes herself as "one who entirely & despotically engrossed by their own feelings, leads as it were an *internal* life quite different from the outward & apparent one" (*Journals* 2: 438). This misleading appearance was a cruel contradiction in the character of a woman who maintains, "I cannot live without loving & being loved—without sympathy—if this is denied to me I must die" (*Journals* 2: 498). On 11 November 1822, she records in her journal her response to a charge often brought against her by those who knew her best: "[H]ave I [a] cold heart? God knows! but none need envy the icy region this heart encircles—And at least the tears are hot which the emotions of this cold heart forces me to shed" (*Journals* 2: 444). On the pages of *Frankenstein* she drew the two sides of her personality in the form of Victor Frankenstein, the artist who coldly chooses isolation, and his epipsyche, the rejected Creature who passionately craves human society and sympathy.

By the end of our study, most students agree that one of the great triumphs of *Frankenstein* is that it both includes and imaginatively transcends autobiography, speaking to the human condition or, as Mary Shelley herself puts it, "to the mysterious fears of our nature" (ix).

NOTES

[1]Psychological readings by Ellen Moers (*Literary Women*), Martin Tropp, and Marc A. Rubenstein were among the earliest.

[2]For example, see the scene in the novel where Walton initially discovers Victor Frankenstein exhausted and nearly frozen. Frankenstein faints but Walton explains, "We . . . restored him to animation by rubbing him with brandy and forcing him to swallow a small quantity. As soon as he showed signs of life we wrapped him up in blankets and placed him near the chimney of the kitchen stove. By slow degrees

he recovered . . ." (24). At other crucial points throughout the novel, Victor Frankenstein faints and is rejuvenated. This resurrection theme probably owes something to the discussions at Diodati concerning the reanimation of dead matter and to Adam's dream of God fashioning Eve in book 8 of *Paradise Lost*. But its personal derivation is also quite clear. For instance, on 5 March 1817, Mary Shelley writes to Leigh Hunt, "I had a dream tonight of the dead being alive which has affected my spirits" (*Letters* 1: 32).

Language and Style in *Frankenstein*

Stephen C. Behrendt

Frankenstein is not an easy read for most students. Diction, syntax, and stylistic features seem determined to interpose themselves between the reader and Mary Shelley's compelling tale. Students frequently remark that the reading is boring, although they often mean that they have been frustrated by the difficult and distancing prose style. Judicious classroom exploration of the nature, function, and context of the novel's language, however, generally helps to reduce—or at least account for—that difficulty for student readers. I recommend two principal routes: The first, more general one relates the novel's language and style to external circumstances; this approach is effective when the novel is being studied within the broad spectrum of the history of ideas, particularly in a course in British fiction. The second, more self-contained approach focuses on what the novel's language reveals about the attitudes and conditions of its characters and its author.

As the daughter of Mary Wollstonecraft and William Godwin, whose works she read repeatedly, Mary Shelley was well acquainted with the rhetorical complexity, detachment, and preponderance of the passive voice that characterized eighteenth- and early nineteenth-century intellectual discourse. Furthermore, because she belonged to a community of prolific writers, poets, and journalists (including Percy Shelley, Byron, Leigh Hunt, and William Hazlitt), she felt obligated and encouraged to write, as her 1831 introduction to *Frankenstein* indicates (vii–ix). In her reading (recorded in her journals), as in her writing, Mary Shelley aspired to encyclopedic expansiveness, invoking within single contexts complex writings that might be only marginally related. This tendency recalls Godwin's conviction (repeated often to both the Shelleys) that a reading program ought to consist of a tableful of open books, all of which are being read at once, in a rotation of browsing (J. Dunn 54). Such a program virtually ensures that intertextuality will occur in one's writing. The burden this writing imposes on the reader is evident in *Frankenstein*, where language and style indicate not just what is happening (i.e., they convey narrative information) but also how what is happening is organized, reported, and—ideally—perceived (i.e., they reveal the intellectual traditions utilized in the text that readers should recognize and respond to).

Many students—including English majors—are unprepared for a text that makes these particular demands of them: they both need and appreciate guidance and reassurance. It is helpful to establish intellectual and stylistic contexts for the novel. The language and style of *Frankenstein* reflect not only the gothic tradition, to which Mary Shelley's reading tastes and those of her husband and their friends had drawn her, but also discursive philosophical writings like Godwin's *Political Justice* and Wollstone-craft's *Vindication* and the "novel of ideas." To this latter category belong her father's *Caleb Williams* and *Mandeville*, her mother's *Maria*, and an apparently lost novel called *Hubert Cauvin* that Percy Shelley was writing at about the time he met Mary. Novels of ideas are typically cumbersome affairs whose closest relatives are philosophical, social, political, and economic writings. By reading aloud some passages from Godwin's or Wollstonecraft's works, students see the stylistic similarities and the complex and reserved authorial technique, in which the narrative "through line" is often interrupted or suppressed while the author drives home a philosophical or political point. I introduce such passages as background to clarify the relation between *Frankenstein*'s aesthetics and its didactic intentions. This is also a good place to mention the effects of Percy Shelley's editorial revisions: they frequently complicate and formalize the author's straightforward and idiomatic writing (Mellor, *Mary Shelley* 58–69), and they show that use of stylistic features based on an aspiration to encyclopedic expansiveness extends beyond Mary Shelley to her entire literary milieu.

Like the philosophical and sociopolitical writings to which it is related and indebted, the novel of ideas depends on rational consideration. Readers are expected to absorb, assess, and form considered judgments, rather than to let the story sweep them along by emotion as it does with the gothic or sentimental novel. I remind students that Walton and Frankenstein are both scientists and that even the Creature learns by what we loosely term the scientific method.

The instructor who is not teaching *Frankenstein* within the context of a period or genre survey may want to examine the novel's language in terms of what the characters reveal about themselves. The preoccupation with communication and its converse, the failure of communication, extends even to the novel's form. *Frankenstein* is, after all, an epistolary novel, although the initial epistolary format first metamorphoses into a journal format and subsequently all but disappears, reappearing only at the very end. In the process, the novel moves away from being a document formulated by a single author (Walton) for an audience of one (Margaret Saville) and becomes instead a polyphonic work in which meaning is relative, the product of a complex interaction among characters, speakers (some of whom are also writers), and readers (both within the narrative and outside it, in the classroom). Mary Favret's discussion in "The Letters of *Frankenstein*" is especially helpful here.

I like to have students read key passages from *Frankenstein* so that they may discover not only what the language reveals but also what it conceals. Walton's first letter, for instance, discloses facts about his academic background. Although he gave only a year to poetry, he devoted six years to physical conditioning and the study of mathematics and the sciences. Does his renunciation of poetry, in which he had "lived in a paradise of [his] own creation" (16), reflect a failure of imagination? Perhaps. Or has he decided that in a modern world that spurns poets and their creations only scientific endeavor offers the promise of "glory" (17)? Certainly his letter adopts a rather severely formal idiom that reflects his new province, the rationalistic language of empirical science. Yet the ending of this letter reveals sincere personal feeling—an unmistakable emotional side to his existence—that is echoed elsewhere.

After we look carefully at the first letter, I ask students to examine the second on their own. They typically recognize there the conflict between emotions and the rationalist mechanisms of language by which emotions are expressed (or not) to others. Having no friend, Walton must filter his experiences through language, "a poor medium for the communication of feeling" (18). The importance of language and its inadequacy in communication are stressed repeatedly by all the major characters. Both Walton and Frankenstein are students of language, though it is the romantic Clerval (who in the 1818 text is himself an accomplished poet [Rieger 39]) who takes up the study of the more exotic Oriental languages, in which Victor joins him (66–67). I like to point out in Walton's second letter, too, the emotional and sensory responses Mary Shelley added about the aurora borealis (in her autograph additions to the copy of the 1818 text that she presented to her friend Mrs. Thomas in 1823, included in the Rieger edition; Rieger 16) and about the love of mystery and the marvelous (1831 text; Rieger 231). Both additions further underscore Walton's uneasy position as a rationalist and scientist possessed of an imaginatively responsive and sympathetic humanism. This letter sounds a related theme that I encourage students to trace among the other characters: phrases such as "I cannot describe to you," "It is impossible to communicate," and "I do not understand" (20–21) echo in speeches throughout the novel, as when Victor reports that his remorse and guilt over having created the Creature plunged him into "a hell of intense tortures such as no language can describe" (86). The recurrence of such expressions shows students how the parallel experiences of the characters extend even to the linguistic level.

Once we have begun to discuss the language characters use to represent themselves both to themselves and to others, I suggest that we consider whether, like Coleridge's Ancient Mariner, Victor Frankenstein is essentially a man of words, not of actions, and that his whole existence is largely a semantic one. That is, for Margaret Saville (and ourselves as readers), Victor exists only as he is reported to her: as a tale. So, too, for Walton is the Creature only a tale (except for Walton's brief glimpses of him at the beginning and the end, which are meant to validate his physical existence).

Indeed, Victor's presence, like the Ancient Mariner's, is meaningful only in his words, only in what he seeks to communicate through the faulty medium of language. And yet the complex language in which he portrays himself and his history distances us from him (and him from us) even as it engages us.

For many students, the key to understanding Victor lies in regarding him not as a scientist but as a particular kind of scientist, and here, too, Victor's words provide that key. Unlike Walton, who maintains a lively interest in others and who communicates in a variety of forms, Victor is the mechanistic investigator who treats everything and everyone as a depersonalized case study—just as he treats the unfortunate Creature. I point out Victor's remark about Elizabeth in the 1818 edition: "I loved to tend on her, as I should on a favourite animal" (Rieger 30); he regards her like a "possession" (35). Victor portrays himself as a determined scientific quester, attempting at the same time to conceal his fundamental lack of humanity, a lack that only becomes apparent in "slips" like these. Hence the irony of the way Victor describes Clerval and Elizabeth, whose imaginative vitality rather puzzles and amuses him. Characterizing himself as ambitious and analytical, Victor condescendingly paints them as lively and communicative, and it is clear that if he draws this distinction at all ruefully, it is only now in retrospect, in his final hours.

Finally, we consider the Creature, whose entire existence is a pitiful record of the breakdown of communication, despite his poignant efforts to express himself. From the beginning he is shut out; Victor observes that when the Creature lifted his (Victor's) bed-curtains, "he muttered some inarticulate sounds." Victor continues, "He might have spoken, but I did not hear" (57). That line epitomizes both Victor's life and the Creature's predicament, encapsulating the point that Shelley makes everywhere: Victor neither communicates nor "hears" in any meaningful fashion. When the Creature confronts Victor on the Mer de Glace, he first says, "I entreat you to hear me"; when Victor says, "I will not hear you," the Creature takes away the option: "I demand this from you. Hear my tale" (95–97). The Creature's history comes full circle, for, when Victor destroys his mate, the Creature returns to his inarticulate state, uttering only "a howl of devilish despair and revenge" (159). The Creature has the last word, though, delivering his eloquent and moving final speech over the dead Frankenstein, who he says "cannot answer him" (208).

In one of the novel's finest ironies, only the Creature seems to appreciate the liberating and humanizing potential of language, a point worth exploring. In observing the "godlike science" of speech practiced among the family of cottagers, for instance, he remarks that "every conversation . . . now opened new wonders" to him (106, 114). This delight in the life and imaginative creation conveyed by language recalls Elizabeth and Clerval, the characters whose innate vitality is most like that of the Creature; when he murders them the act is a form of self-annihilation. In his earliest stages of consciousness the Creature seeks interaction with others; by contrast Victor increasingly withdraws to the secrecy of his laboratory. The Creature wishes to bring pleasure to others, while Victor wishes to bring fame and adulation to himself. One is generous, the other selfish. What knowledge Victor does acquire, he either misuses (privately, but ultimately publicly) or keeps hidden away. Consequently, his greatest discovery, the secret of life, is never revealed. Although his secretiveness keeps him in a position of power (Favret 9), the value of that power diminishes even as Victor's life does.

To clarify these essential differences in language use, I cite some passages from the novel to demonstrate Victor's fondness for passive-voice constructions, as opposed to the Creature's preference for the active voice—especially in his description of his earliest memories and in his final speech. I also suggest that the strong active voice we hear in the Creature's speech may be Mary Shelley's own voice breaking through the formal facade of depersonalized (and depersonalizing) rhetoric that characterized the novel's principal male speakers and writers (see Johnson; Mellor, *Mary Shelley*). Passive constructions defer and deflect responsibility from the agent and subtly hint that causal relations only partially involve the agent: "The window was broken by me" suggests a fragile window ready to self-destruct with only minor participation by "me," whereas "I broke the window" makes clear the agent's responsibility for the event. Victor repeatedly invokes the responsibility-shifting power of the passive voice to exonerate himself rhetorically from the catastrophic chain of events for which he is directly and unavoidably responsible. The Creature's final speech, in which the active voice predominates, is startling by comparison:

> I have murdered the lovely and the helpless; I have strangled the innocent . . . I have devoted my creator . . . to misery; I have pursued him even to that irremediable ruin. . . . I shall quit your vessel . . . I shall collect my funeral pile and consume to ashes this miserable frame.   (210)

When Victor does finally engage the Creature in an active-voice interchange, as on the Mer de Glace, it is to threaten and to condemn, not to establish community: "There can be no community between you and me; we are enemies" (96). Elsewhere, he relegates to dependent clauses his acts and activities whose consequences are the greatest and most terrible.

Other illustrations of Victor's preference for passive construction abound, particularly those linked with long and elaborate sentence structures. In tracing them, students come to appreciate how much this man of words isolates and insulates himself in a fabric of deception whose raw material is language itself.

This language-bound novel returns again and again to crucial events that depend on successful or, more commonly, failed or suppressed communication. As her father does in *Caleb Williams*, Mary Shelley explores in *Frankenstein* the consequences of repressing communication. Godwin's Caleb fears that the "truth" he knows about Falkland is too fabulous to be believed (and in both the endings Godwin composed Caleb suffers a mental collapse); similarly, Victor believes that what he knows about the murder of William, for which Justine pays the price, would be regarded as "the ravings of insanity." Consequently, he resolves "to remain silent" (74), even as he consistently refuses to tell Clerval or anyone else what he has been doing. The unnatural quality of such suppression is underscored by Victor's increasingly hysterical behavior and by the apparent disease (of a clearly psychological origin) to which he falls victim after the Creature escapes from the laboratory. Significantly, once his "illness" passes, he resumes his correspondence with Elizabeth.

Still, Victor Frankenstein "remain[s] silent" almost to the end. Only on board Walton's ice-bound vessel does he at last find the friend and confessor to whom he can pour out his tale, much as the Ancient Mariner's prayer springs forth when he recognizes the dignity of life and blesses the water snakes. Only at the end of his life, once he has presented his history as a monologue, does Victor engage at last in the apparently unprejudiced and noncompetitive conversation to which he had been a stranger since his youth. Walton's comment is important: "His eloquence is forcible and touching; nor can I hear him, when he relates a pathetic incident or endeavours to move the passions of pity or love, without tears" (200). At the terrible cost of his own life and those of family and friends, Victor finally learns to communicate. Yet even this effort is not entirely guileless egalitarian communication. Victor is still attempting, from his deathbed, to control events by means of words, exerting psychological pressure where physical force is no longer possible. His speech to Walton's unwilling sailors (203–04) offers clear evidence of his recalcitrance, as does his dying request that Walton "undertake [his] unfinished work" and destroy the Creature (206). Who can refuse a dying person's last request? Walton can, we discover, and his expression of that refusal (and the soul-searching it entails) to his sister—who represents the warmth, family, and community toward which he has now redirected his ship and his thoughts—is a gesture of courage and self-sufficiency.

Frankenstein is a difficult novel to read, no matter how practiced and sophisticated the reader. Nevertheless, when students begin to see that there are demonstrable reasons for the way it is written—that characters express themselves as they do for the internal audiences they are addressing—they invariably come to a greater appreciation of *Frankenstein*'s language and style, even if they never go so far as to like them. Moreover, students begin to see more clearly the function of language in generating—or denying—power within society as a whole. Victor's failure to take appropriate responsibility for his language mirrors his failure to take responsibility for his Creature, and his history constitutes both a parable and a warning about problems that remain very much a part of contemporary existence.

CONTEXTS OF STUDY

Frankenstein and the Uses of Biography
Betty T. Bennett

Mary Wollstonecraft Shelley created one myth; her critics, another. All her works, including *Frankenstein*, are generally interpreted as roman à clef, supposedly grounded in the biographical facts of her life. The fundamental problem with this approach is that there exists no accurate critical biography on which to base those interpretations. In fact, in almost every instance, critics writing about *Frankenstein* have not consulted even the primary material available. Most often, their basic—unspoken—premise is that women's writings must have a one-to-one correlation with their personal, emotional lives. Larger, intellectual issues and artistic ability are treated as accidental or unconscious. It is no surprise that such restricted interpretations fail to explicate *Frankenstein* fully or to explain its significance for Romantic and twentieth-century studies.

This is not to dismiss a biographical approach to *Frankenstein*. Rather, through creative use of available resources, teachers can develop a fuller, more accurate picture of the author and thereby establish a sound basis for biographical exploration of the novel. Such material will also be useful for reading *Frankenstein* in the light of other critical methodologies (e.g., feminist, mythic, psychological, structuralist).

My premise in this discussion is that the teacher has already introduced students to the major sociopolitical and aesthetic aspects of British Romanticism. I also take as a given that William Godwin (*Caleb Williams; An*

Enquiry concerning Political Justice), Mary Wollstonecraft (*A Vindication of the Rights of Woman*), and Percy Bysshe Shelley (himself strongly influenced by Godwin and Wollstonecraft) figure in such a discussion. The challenge, then, is to set Mary Shelley into this context.

To "resee" Mary Shelley, I suggest that teachers prepare their own minibiographies of the author. Class discussion of *Frankenstein* should begin with that overview of the author's life, followed by a series of questions that stem from the overview. The best sources for the minibiography are *The Letters of Mary Wollstonecraft Shelley* and *The Journals of Mary Shelley. Shelley and His Circle* (ed. Cameron and Reiman) provides solid, elucidating introductions to the Shelley circle, with the exception of the essay on Mary Shelley herself, which was written before the advent of the new scholarship.

The introductions to the three volumes of the *Letters* provide a contextual, narrative guide to Mary Shelley's life based on the letters. Her life as daughter, parent, wife, and writer is set in its social and cultural milieu. If students cannot read through the volumes, the letters cited in the introductions can serve as starting points for discussion of her perspectives and responses, her literary objectives, and her shared intellectual life with Shelley. The *Letters* should be supplemented with citations from the *Journals* that indicate the author's remarkable depth and breadth of reading (including Milton's *Paradise Lost*, Volney's *Ruins of Empires* and Goethe's *Werther*, influences that she calls special attention to in *Frankenstein*), record the progress of her writing, and reflect her personal, emotional life.

I recommend asking class members for their picture of Mary Shelley based on this material. Their answers generally include the following characteristics: independent, intellectual, daring, family-oriented, career-oriented, cultured, assertive, diffident, ambitious, ambivalent—a strongly antimonarchical political reformer and an advocate of love versus power. The idea is to allow the students to assemble their own picture of this complex person—a composite derived from biographical facts. Next, I briefly sketch the dominant social expectations for middle-class women—subservience and domesticity—and ask the class to compare Mary Shelley's characteristics to those standards. Students readily see that Mary Shelley was remarkably different from most women of her era. This difference becomes a major biographical theme in *Frankenstein*.

Before moving to the novel itself, I like to establish another way in which Mary Shelley biography is used and not used in her fiction. To do this, I select and compare the alpine passages in *Frankenstein*, the *Letters*, the *Journals*, and Mary Shelley's *History of a Six Weeks' Tour*. In this way, students directly experience how she transformed her observations into literature. (The same kind of comparison can be done with the travel passages.) She does not simply take life and record it; she transmutes it through imagination into art, using some parts, discarding others. By this time, Mary Shelley, writer, should be established, and teachers can proceed with an analysis of *Frankenstein*.

To guide this discussion, I pose two questions that the class, as a group, eventually answers. First, why did *Frankenstein* become an instant success? We consider the initial stage adaptation, *Presumption*, in 1823, and subsequent productions; the references to *Frankenstein* in Parliament and in newspapers. Second, why does *Frankenstein* increasingly haunt us today? I cite the references in newspapers and the increasing numbers of essays, stage depictions, and editions of the text, including those in foreign languages—Italian, Japanese. Next, just as we established "our" Mary Shelley based on biography, I ask the class to point out the fundamental issues raised by *Frankenstein*. From the novel's specific circumstances (Frankenstein breaks social and familial rules; the Creature's isolation) I guide the class in developing a list of the book's larger moral and ethical issues. For discussion purposes, I generally break these into the two categories that follow, but teachers can structure these issues according to their own choice and time constraints:

1. *Authority:* the question of obedience to established authority, God, monarch, or parent as part of political, social, technological, or industrial (vs. agrarian) change.
2. *Values:* nature; education (of Frankenstein, the Creature, Walton, Safie, or readers of the book); love (vs. power); responsibility (abandonment leading to questions of the creative process or of gothic horror).

Clearly *Frankenstein* raises the question of the role of authority. Walton's disobedience of his father's injunction against going to sea serves as a minor counterpoint to Frankenstein's disregard of filial obligation (his six-year self-exile) and Frankenstein's larger hubris in usurping godly power to create life. It might be argued, from the conclusion of *Frankenstein* narrowly viewed, that the message of the novel is that one should remain within one's proper role and that the concept of the great chain of being is fundamental to Mary Shelley's perspective. There is, however, another breakdown of authorial obedience in the novel that invalidates the argument for stratification. The Creature himself disregards the omnipotence of his maker in his insistence on a companion creature; in the murders of Frankenstein's brother, friend, and fiancée; and finally in his assumption of power over his creator in the hunt and chase that forms one of the several book narratives. Moreover, the novelist and most readers are sympathetic to the motivations for these acts of disobedience. We come, then, to a more complex vision of the role of authority as something the individual may question, disregard, or even defy.

To understand better Mary Shelley's view of authority, we return to our minibiography and examine her relationship to her parents, as she felt about them personally and as they exemplified the era of radical thought in Britain. Both Godwin and Wollstonecraft actively advocated fundamental change in social authority, and Mary Shelley often reread their works. Godwin argued for an egalitarian state, free of laws and government, to be organized in small communities in which everyone labored and studied daily and to be developed through a process of evolutionary, mass education. Wollstonecraft argued for republican ideals and gave particular voice to the concepts of female education and independence. Furthermore, the personal lives of Mary Shelley's parents in effect exemplified a breakdown of traditional standards. Some examples: Godwin opposed legalized marriage (Godwin and Wollstonecraft married five months before their offspring's birth to protect the child in an England that had not changed); he believed that the greater good of the populace came before personal family considerations; he lived by the precept that wealth should be distributed according to need. Wollstonecraft was extraordinary in having a writing career; her first child was born out of wedlock; she traveled unescorted to France and Scandinavia. Two points should be acknowledged here: first, Godwin and Wollstonecraft were active participants in, and leaders of, the larger antimonarchical radicalism of the 1790s; and, second, children do not necessarily follow their parents' ideals. But Mary Shelley did, though she tempered their views through her own imagination, intellect, and sensibilities. (*Frankenstein* is both dedicated to Godwin and indebted to Godwin's *Caleb Williams*, which argues that a social system with the wrong values will corrupt all. Frankenstein's quest for power symbolizes a parallel destructive value system.)

Mary Shelley learned sociopolitical as well as personal disobedience from both her parents. For example, she intended to pursue a writing career (still in the male domain) from a very early age, publishing her first work at eleven (*Monsieur Nongtongpaw*) and her *History of a Six Weeks' Tour through a Part of France, Switzerland, Germany, and Holland* and *Frankenstein* at twenty. She eloped with the married Shelley in defiance of society and—important to note—her father; Godwin refused to see the couple until their marriage two years later. In 1827 she arranged for illegal passports so that a female friend could pass as a man.

In recognizing Mary Shelley's own disobedience to the established order (rather than the passive role normally assigned her), teachers stimulate their classes to understand her societal sympathies. Discussion of the major sociopolitical upheavals should follow, so that students recognize how much her biography places her in the midstream of Romanticism. The points I cover in class are outgrowths of the breakdown of established authority at the end of the eighteenth century seen as part of great social change on many levels and in many sectors of the world. I remind students that the American Revolution and the French Revolution established a precedent for Continental revolutions in the name of self-government throughout the nineteenth century. The fight for expanded rights occurred as four hundred years of agrarian society gave way to the beginning of the era of industry and technology that continues today. With a new inventiveness, industrial experimentation, and a new interest in science came artificial lights, coach construction, furnaces, flying machines, electricity, and steam engines. Methodist societies taught the working class how to read the Bible, opening the way for them to read newspapers, penny sheets, and pamphlets as well. Fundamental to these changes was the occurrence of shifts in the means of acquiring wealth and power. Monarchs struggled but fell, and the eighteenth-century great chain of being gave way beneath them.

Mary Shelley's biography demonstrates that her inheritance included acting on her parents' ideals, even when Godwin no longer did. The change in Godwin might have come about, as it did for many who dreamed of reform, when the French Revolution for individual freedom became the Napoleonic wars of conquest. As a result, England entered an era of political repression and retrenchment. Mary Shelley reacted to that conservatism and defied it in eloping with Shelley, becoming, in a sense, the living personification of her parents' ideals. Mary Shelley's letters and journals illustrate her awareness of these social issues as well as her belief in the need for governmental reform. In *Frankenstein*, she voiced that same unwillingness to adhere to established systems that did not benefit humanity. Frankenstein fails as a scientist and as a person because he is driven by a quest for power. This quest, formerly the domain of royalty, became the sociopolitical standard for the technocrats and merchants of nineteenth-century England.

Teachers should point out that in Mary Shelley's view expanded participation in a social order based on power was not an improvement. Again, her biography gives more clues to our understanding of *Frankenstein*. In eloping with Shelley, she gained new happiness but also undreamed-of difficulties like hiding from debt collectors, Godwin's rejection, the death of her firstborn, and a peripatetic life. The fulfillment of her love brought with it a host of destabilizing factors. In the internal struggle of *Frankenstein*, she works out both her personal and her sociopolitical belief in love and humanistic values that stand in opposition to power. Frankenstein's egocentric quest for power results in the creation of a new order he is incapable of accepting—he flees from the Creature. And the Creature, constructed of ill-fitted parts from the old order, cannot exist as Rousseau's noble savage in a world that values conformity and authoritarian power. *Frankenstein* represents an ambivalent vision of this newly forming society, a society that will demand conscious and responsible choices or be condemned to its own self-destruction. The novel, in confronting an uncertain future in an atmosphere of increasing social and technological mobility and change, questions whether reliable values can exist in an era in which change is fundamental and respected. Mary Shelley argued that they could.

First, in true Romantic spirit, she believed in the reciprocity of humanity and nature. By citing her letters and journals, teachers can illustrate the sense of joy and inspiration that she felt in rural settings throughout her life. She emphasizes this theme in *Frankenstein* through the scientist's isolation from the physical world as he monomanically pursues his objective and through his later realization of the gulf between his work and nature. The Creature, by contrast, is meant to win the reader's sympathies through his deep appreciation of nature and his desire for companionship. In these respects, the Creature and Mary Shelley are in harmony.

So, too, can we demonstrate that they agree on the need for a well-rounded education: Teachers can begin by reviewing Godwin's and Wollstonecraft's precepts about education and then give examples of these ideas as expressed by Mary Shelley. A discussion of Percy Shelley's contributions to Mary Shelley's education should follow, pointing out that he expanded his companion's learning by introducing her to the knowledge he had acquired through privileged schooling and extensive study. Many examples from the *Letters* and *Journals* show the importance Mary Shelley placed on learning. These can be compared with her description of the education of the protagonists in *Frankenstein*. Students will readily see that she contrasts the Creature as a humane, sensitive product of history, philosophy, literature, and science (through his study of Frankenstein's experiment journal) with Frankenstein, who remains narrow and self-centered in his exclusive pursuit of science. The role of education in the novel is further underscored by the attention paid it in the personae of Walton and the cottagers. Finally, students should see that readers of *Frankenstein* are being guided from accepting an obvious equation (scientist = good; Creature = evil) to a deeper, more comprehensive understanding of human values.

Proper education, according to Mary Shelley, opens the mind to the realization that love—domestic and universal—not power, makes life valuable. She works out this belief on many levels but primarily through the interaction of Frankenstein and his Creature. In a reversal of the Promethean myth, this new Prometheus fails to take responsibility for his creation. Ironically, Frankenstein's failure to care for the Creature locks them inextricably together. Indeed, they are often studied as "self" and "other self," with personal boundaries broken as so many boundaries of the era were broken. The doppelgänger approach, in recognizing the possibility of evil in oneself, is both a realistic psychological phenomenon and a denial of the eighteenth-century idealized "man of good feeling." This blurring of lines has biographical relevance in its realization of the multiplicity of the individual and its suggestion of Mary Shelley's own complexities.

At this juncture, it is inviting to discuss with the class examples of the various "biographical" personifications that critics have applied to the creator and his creation: (1) Frankenstein represents Godwin, the Creature Mary Shelley; this view is based on the depiction of Godwin as a "single," cold parent who caused his lonely daughter to subconsciously seek vengeance; (2) Frankenstein represents Shelley, the Creature Mary Shelley; this view is based on the depiction of Shelley as cruel to his wife and her as subconsciously wanting vengeance; (3) Frankenstein represents Mary Wollstonecraft, the Creature Mary Shelley; this view is based on the child's feelings of abandonment at birth, compounded by her guilt at having caused her mother's death as well as her guilt at the death of her first child.

Problems exist for each of these characterizations if one tries to force them into a one-to-one biographical correlation. For example, while Mary Shelley was writing *Frankenstein*, all evidence indicates that Shelley was a loving and supportive figure rather than a source of grief to his wife. The argument that Frankenstein is Godwin is based on Godwin's supposed habitual coldness. However, evidence suggests that he was a caring father, though one certainly distracted by his ever-constant challenge to earn a living. As for his daily habits of writing and reading, Mary Shelley emulated that pattern—and no one has accused her of being an uncaring mother. Mary Shelley loved and admired her father. The one time she felt, and was, abandoned by him was not in early childhood but after she eloped with Shelley, creating a breach she was anxious to heal. Perhaps, subconsciously, she was seeking vengeance for this abandonment in the Creature's murder of her father's namesake, William. But if she subconsciously killed William, her father, she also killed William, her son. This act would be inconsistent with both her possible birth trauma and her acute, well-documented suffering at the deaths of her children, particularly William. Much more likely, William's death was for her the worst thing she could imagine. This idea is consistent in terms of *Frankenstein* because this worst death is in fact the climax of the book. Mary Shelley's lifetime sense of loneliness and abandonment may well have had its roots in her mother's death in giving birth to her. What the novel and her life substantiate is the close identification of Mary Shelley's feelings of loneliness (whatever the source) and the Creature's.

The one-to-one correlation leads to other difficulties of critical interpretation as well, the most important being the role of the creator. Frankenstein, the failed creator, is the work of Mary Shelley, the successful creator. *Frankenstein* can be viewed as a fulfillment of her aspirations and of the confidence placed in her by the two other creators she most admired and loved: Godwin and Shelley. It also represents a communication with her mother, whose presence (spiritual and literary) and absence were central to her daughter. Mary Shelley's basic creativity cannot be attributed to the subconscious or unconscious or accidental because her *Journal* and her *Letters* amply demonstrate how very self-aware an author she was and how she relied on, and nourished, her own imagination.

Class discussion should finally lead to the two important questions posed earlier: Why was *Frankenstein* an instant success? What accounts for our increasing interest? Mary Shelley's biography provides the answer. Through her family relations, ambitions, values, intelligence, and imagination, Mary Shelley mirrored the major questions of her era—and ours. She lived at the very beginning of an era of rapid social and technological change in which fixed values were largely replaced by relative ones and a stable order replaced by one in constant flux. Her Creature can be seen as a metaphor for the unprotected being who seeks its rights in a new, potentially hostile world. While she welcomed change, she was convinced of the need for a sound philosophy to deal with that change. For Mary Shelley, a world with no absolutes requires individuals and governments to make decisions on the basis of love and responsibility for the general good. In *Frankenstein*, she gives us her vision of the outcome should we fail. We are increasingly drawn to *Frankenstein* as we recognize in our society the shadow of Frankenstein and his Creature.

Frankenstein and Marx's Theories of Alienated Labor

Elsie B. Michie

Labour does not only produce commodities; it
produces itself and the labourer as a commodity and
that to the extent to which it produces commodities in
general.
What this fact expresses is merely this: the object
that labour produces, its product, confronts it as an
alien being, as a power independent of the producer.

Karl Marx

Marx's writings on alienated labor allow students to see in *Frankenstein* an
economic and political subtext that might otherwise remain invisible.
Given sections of the *Economic and Philosophical Manuscripts* (*Selected
Writings* 75–112), which contain Marx's early, noneconomic descriptions of
alienation, together with Shelley's novel, students invariably notice a series
of passages in Marx that sound as if they were virtual commentaries on
Frankenstein. Discussing the similarities between the two texts helps them
understand that Shelley's novel reflects or represents the same economic
moment Marx describes, the moment in which the dominant mode of production becomes the production of commodities. To come to this conclusion, however, students must begin to read *Frankenstein* as what Fredric
Jameson calls a socially symbolic act. Shelley's novel contains no explicit
depictions of workers, the marketplace, or the forces of production. With
the application of Marx's writings, details that appear literal in *Frankenstein*—descriptions of what Victor does while making the Creature, his subsequent interactions with it, the physical makeup of the Creature—take on
symbolic resonance and become visible as part of the novel's systematic
attempt to deal with the issue of material production and the problems
that arise from it.

Because such a symbolic reading is difficult, students approaching *Frankenstein* through Marx turn to the most obvious representation of alienation in Shelley's text, the Creature's relation to its creator and through
him to the entire world around it. They see immediately that the Creature
suffers the misery and vents the anger of the alienated laborer, and they
observe that the terms from Marx's analysis of alienated labor describe
precisely the situation of the Creature. The appearance and the actions of
the Creature confirm Marx's assertion that production renders the worker
both "deformed" and "barbaric" (79). (Franco Moretti's reading of the
Creature as a representation of the proletariat can be useful here.) The
Creature experiences the kind of exclusion that Marx describes the worker
as experiencing, particularly during its stay at the De Laceys'. There,

touched by Safie's beauty and the domestic felicity of the bourgeois family, it expects to be accepted into society once it has learned how to speak, but it discovers instead, as Marx says, that "labour produces palaces but only hovels for the worker; it produces beauty, but cripples the worker . . . it produces culture but only imbecility and cretinism for the worker" (79–80). (Teachers may explore the link between production and imperialism by using Spivak's analysis of the same scene at the De Laceys' in "Three Women's Texts and a Critique of Imperialism.") Taken as a whole, the novel can be understood to show the relation between creature and creator as a reflection of the relation between workers and those who control the forces of production. The paradoxes in *Frankenstein*—that the Creature is much larger and apparently more powerful than Victor yet is incapable of producing anything without him and that Victor is inextricably bound to it and it to him—accurately represent the bond between worker and capitalist as both become involved in the process of production.

When we consider Victor as another figure standing for the alienation of the worker, students begin to have difficulties. This new reading seems contradictory because the novel clearly represents Victor as coming from the upper, moneyed classes. The problem here is that we are moving from the easy one-to-one correspondence of a strictly allegorical reading, which sees Victor as entrepreneur and the Creature as worker, to a symbolic reading, which sees issues of production represented at various locations throughout the novel. To make such a shift, I ask students to look at the places where Marx represents the workers' experience of alienation. Passages like the following describe with uncanny accuracy the issue that critics find so problematic in *Frankenstein*, the relation between Victor and the thing he has made:

> The worker puts his life into the object and this means that it no longer belongs to him but to the object. . . . So the greater this product the less he is himself. The externalization of the worker in his product implies not only that his labour becomes an object, an exterior existence but also that it exists opposite him, that the life he has lent the object affronts him, hostile and alien. (79)

When students take a closer look at the details of Victor's story, they begin to see that it lays out, in narrative form, the series of stages that Marx's writings describe workers going through as they become alienated from the objects they produce. In class discussion, I point out that this reading of Shelley's novel gives us a fictional or "lived" instance of the themes Marx subsequently articulates in his theories of alienation in much the same way that Freud's case studies provide narrative or lived instances of his psychological theories.

Reading *Frankenstein* as a narrative about production solves a number of the problems that arise in discussion when students approach the novel as a story about a creator and his creation. For instance, students frequently ask why Shelley fails to describe the actual moment in which the Creature comes to life; teachers can answer that she depicts Victor caught up not in an act of creation but in a process of production. As a result, her descriptions concentrate not on the moment of creation but on the alienating effects of the process that leads up to that moment, thereby illustrating Marx's assertion that "alienation shows itself not only in the result, but also in the act of production, *inside productive activity itself*" (80; emphasis mine). The literal details Shelley uses to convey Victor's state of mind while he is making the Creature—his isolated apartment, his inability to contact his family or even notice the changing of the seasons—can be read to represent what Marx describes as the two most immediate consequences of the worker's alienation from the product of his (Marx's usage) labor: alienation from nature and from other men. The Creature's behavior once it has been made makes more sense to students when they read the novel as a story of production rather than creation. In Marx's terms, the Creature represents the externalization of Victor's alienation. The Creature, once produced, works to break any attachment Victor might form to the outside world. I note here that in the 1831 version Shelley added passages in which Victor articulates his alienation first from his family and then from the rest of society: "I felt . . . as if never more might I enjoy companionship with them" (142) and "I felt that I had no right to share their intercourse" (176). Victor becomes a mouthpiece, clearly expressing the isolation from the rest of his species that Marx asserts is the consequence of production under capitalism.

Once they read *Frankenstein* as an account of production, students can analyze what that account reveals about nineteenth-century attitudes toward production and alienation; in the process they use Shelley's narrative to comment on Marx. Asked where *Frankenstein* most clearly represents the process Marx describes as alienating the worker from "his own body . . . his intellectual being, and his human essence" (83), students cite the scenes in which Victor is involved in physically producing the Creature. I ask them to think of that section of Shelley's novel as a symbolic version of what Marx describes theoretically in his essay "Alienated Labour" (*Selected Writings* 77–87). We then read the process of making the Creature as a fictional representation of what Marx later describes as the experience in which the worker "does not confirm [but] denies himself, feels miserable instead of happy, displays no free physical and intellectual energy, *mortifies* his body and ruins his mind" (80; emphasis mine). From this perspective, the materials Victor uses to make the Creature, parts of dismembered corpses, are emblematic of the way production breaks down what Marx calls the "body" of the natural world into a series of "dead" component parts to be used in manufacturing. When asked what effect contact with such materials has on Victor, students explain that it makes the process of production disgusting and that, to keep working, Victor must avoid triggering such a sense of disgust by denying or repressing natural responses like taste and smell. I point out that this repression divides Victor from himself, so that one part of him is involved in the material process of production but the other part denies that involvement. We then compare the Creature's description of Victor's journal as containing "the minutest description of my odious and loathsome person . . . in language which painted [Victor's] own horrors" (124) with Victor's earlier description of his act of "creation." While Victor consciously insists he was intent only on creating ideal beauty and was horrified at the results when the Creature was completed, the journal entry reveals his awareness of what was happening during the process of production. Shelley's novel thus suggests that the ultimate nineteenth-century self-alienation arises not from production itself but from the denial of the materiality of that process.

If we analyze the figure of the Creature itself, students come to see it as a representation of materiality. I ask them to describe how the Creature is depicted in the various film versions of the novel. (Paul O'Flinn's article tracing the history of the popular "reproductions" of the Creature is useful here.) Students immediately point out that the classic visual images of the Creature stress its physical massiveness, the seams on its face, and often the bolts in its head. The significance of these details, we conclude, is that the Creature's size emphasizes its presence as a massive material object and that the seams on its face are the external or visible signs of its existence as a manufactured product. The Creature is ugly or horrifying because it does not present a smooth surface but is clearly fissured, showing the sutures that join it together as an assemblage of heterogeneous parts. The Creature is also monstrous because the machinery that makes it run is too close to the surface and therefore too easily seen: as Victor explains, the "yellow skin [that] scarcely covered the work of muscles and arteries beneath" (56). Looking again at the previous scene at the De Laceys', teachers can show students that when the Creature functions as worker rather than product, it is still acceptable only as long as it is invisible. The De Laceys are uninterested in the source of their benefactions when the worker who provides them remains unseen. But as soon as the Creature becomes visible, it is cast out completely. The Creature can thus be read, both as product and worker, as an embodiment of production, and its treatment suggests that material production is what nineteenth-century society, as depicted in the novel, desires to repress.

When students now stand back from the novel and look at it as a whole, they see that the central symbolic gesture it systematically makes is to replace stories of creation with accounts of production. This gesture of replacement is represented most clearly when the Creature discovers itself to be a product, when it turns from reading *Paradise Lost*, a fiction it takes for truth, to reading Victor's laboratory journal, which sets forth "the whole detail of that series of disgusting circumstances which produced" the Creature's "accursed origin" (124). This exchange, as Peter Brooks explains, "substitutes for myths of creation a literal account of the monster's manufacture" (210). We then turn to the "Author's Introduction" that Shelley added to the 1831 edition, in which she links the whole question of creation and production to her own position as an artist. The gesture Shelley makes in that preface, of telling the story of what led to her writing of the novel and insisting that she was not simply inspired, emphasizes that the novel was not created out of nothing but produced from "determinate conditions" (Macherey 68). As she says, in talking about myths of creation:

> Invention, it must be humbly admitted, does not consist in creating out of void but out of chaos; the materials must, in the first place be afforded: it can give form to dark, shapeless substances but cannot bring into being substance itself.   (x)

Considering the "Author's Introduction" together with their reading of *Frankenstein*, students see Shelley's novel not just as an account of production but also as a manifesto that insists, as Macherey puts it, that "art is not man's creation, it is a product (and the producer is not a subject centered in his creation, he is an element, in a situation or a system)" (67).

This reading of *Frankenstein* as an account of production can be connected to other approaches to the novel and used to comment on them. Thus, to analyze *Frankenstein* in the context of Romantic poetry, teachers can interpret Shelley's insistence on substituting accounts of production for myths of creation as a critique of Romantic theories of abstract creativity. In the most identifiably Romantic scenes in the novel, those set in the Alps, Shelley shows Victor calling on the spirits of nature but receiving in response not the abstract creations of his poetic fancy but the material and uncontrollably alienated product of his labours, the Creature itself. Or, to give a feminist reading of the novel and deal with Mary Shelley as a nineteenth-century woman author, teachers can point out that the "Author's Introduction" mixes terms associated with production with those associated with reproduction. Words like *mechanism, component part,* and *manufacture* stand beside words like *offspring, progeny,* and *cradle* (x–xii). In the first paragraph Shelley refers to the novel she has produced as a "hideous idea" and in the penultimate paragraph as a "hideous progeny." The shift from idea to progeny suggests that the introduction is documenting the novel's passage from abstract to concrete, from ideal to material, the moment of potential alienation, which Shelley treats in the language of childbirth.

Reading *Frankenstein* in terms of production does not preclude other interpretations of the novel by linking them to a single authoritative reading. Instead it opens up new possibilities by helping teachers to avoid replicating nineteenth-century ideology, as we do, for example, when we insist on talking about the "Creature" rather than the "monster" or on calling it, as Harold Bloom does, "the total form of Frankenstein's creative power" (215), thereby repressing or denying the presence of production in *Frankenstein*. When we read the novel as a critique or analysis of that ideology, we can use that reading to revise or rethink a whole series of other approaches that may also have become entangled in replicating the nineteenth-century ideologies.

Frankenstein and the Sublime

Anne K. Mellor

In my courses on Romanticism and on literature and the visual arts, the problem of the sublime looms large. I have found that *Frankenstein* is a surprisingly useful text in teaching the meaning of the sublime as it relates to the nineteenth century and the nuclear age. To get at this issue, I begin by asking my students the following questions:

1. Is the Creature in *Frankenstein* good or evil?
2. Is he innately so? Or does he become good or evil?
3. If he becomes so, what causes this change?

As the discussion develops, the class usually divides into those who believe the Creature is good and those who believe he is evil. The former cite the Creature's assertions: "I was benevolent and good; misery made me a fiend" or "My vices are the children of a forced solitude that I abhor; and my virtues will necessarily arise when I live in communion with an equal" (Rieger 95, 143; all subsequent page numbers refer to the Rieger edition). After pointing out that the Creature here invokes Rousseau's notion of the "natural man," born free and good but everywhere enchained by society, I turn to the rest of the students, who usually cite Victor Frankenstein's immediate perception of the Creature as evil: "Abhorred monster! Friend that thou art! The tortures of hell are too mild a vengeance for thy crimes. Wretched devil!" (94); they also cite the long list of the Creature's crimes (burning the De Lacey cottage, murdering William, Clerval, Elizabeth).

To clarify the question of whether the Creature is innately good or evil, a Romantic child of innocence or an Augustinian child of original sin, I ask the class to look at the central scene in which the Creature first sees himself:

> How was I terrified, when I viewed myself in a transparent pool! At first I started back, unable to believe that it was indeed I who was reflected in the mirror; and when I became fully convinced that I was in reality the monster that I am, I was filled with the bitterest sensations of despondence and mortification. (109)

This passage suggests that in *Frankenstein*, identity is a process not so much of knowing (re-cognition) as of seeing. Even though the Creature is unable to recognize himself in the mirror of the pool, "unable to believe it was indeed I," his eyes convince him: "I was in reality the monster that I am."

Since the Creature's internal sense of himself (his belief) differs from his external perception of himself, he becomes the emblem of the very questions we are pursuing: What is the thing in itself? How do we perceive it? Do we perceive what is really there? I ask the class how the characters in *Frankenstein* perceive the Creature. They quickly respond that all but one see him as evil, monstrous, frightening. Frankenstein interprets the Creature's affectionate embrace as an attempt "seemingly to detain" him and flees from "the demoniacal corpse to which [he] had so miserably given life" (53); the old man in his hut, perceiving the Creature, shrieks and runs away (100); the villagers pelt him with stones (101); the rustic whose drowning girlfriend the Creature saves shoots him (137); Felix, horrified by his appearance, throws him down with superhuman force in order to rescue Father De Lacey from his grasp (131); even the innocent William Frankenstein sees him as an "ogre" and a cannibal (139). I point out that all these characters are endorsing Johann Lavater's and Johann Spurzheim's contemporary theories of physiognomy and phrenology—the assumption that the external human form or the shape of the skull accurately manifests one's internal moral qualities.

The one character who does not immediately read the Creature as an evil monster is, of course, blind. Father De Lacey listens to the Creature's eloquent speech and hears truth in his assertion,

> I have good dispositions; my life has been hitherto harmless, and, in some degree, beneficial; but a fatal prejudice clouds their eyes, and where they ought to see a feeling and kind friend, they behold only a detestable monster.   (130)

Father De Lacey articulates the students' own response: "there is something in your words which persuades me that you are sincere" (130). As several students observe, the reader—as opposed to the filmgoer—has not seen the Creature but only heard descriptions of his appearance. At this point in the novel, the reader's sympathies have shifted away from the horrified Victor Frankenstein and toward the speaking Creature, whose eloquent language is at least as powerful as the words earlier spoken about him. But whether the blind Father De Lacey reads the Creature's innate character correctly, we as readers can never know, because he is ripped out of the novel by his prejudging son.

Walton is the other character who does not immediately reject the Creature on the basis of a first impression, primarily because he has heard—through Victor—the Creature's autobiography. Confronting the Creature for the first time at Victor's deathbed, Walton is initially repulsed: "Never did I behold a vision so horrible as his face, of such loathsome, yet appalling hideousness. I shut my eyes involuntarily" (216). But, because he is thus momentarily sightless, he is also attracted to the Creature: "I called on him to stay" (216). Walton's responses to the Creature continue to veer between hostility and sympathy. But Walton's final judgment on the Creature's moral nature is mute; after the Creature's *apologia pro vita sua* Walton says nothing, and in the final sentence of Mary Shelley's manuscript (which differs from the 1818 text; see "Choosing a Text" in this volume), he significantly loses "sight" of the Creature "in the darkness and distance."

This last sentence brings us back to the fundamental epistemological problem in the novel: How are we to see the nature of the Creature? Walton, who of all the characters in the novel knows him best, has "lost sight" of him. The Creature thus represents the confrontation of the human mind with an unknowable nature, with the experience that eighteenth-century philosophers such as Immanuel Kant and Edmund Burke called the sublime. The Creature inhabits the very landscapes that Burke explicitly identified as the locus of the sublime experience in his *A Philosophical Enquiry into the Origin of Our Ideas of the Sublime and the Beautiful*:

> whatever is fitted in any sort to excite the ideas of pain and danger; that is to say, whatever is in any sort terrible, or is conversant about terrible objects, or operates in a manner analogous to terror, is a source of the *sublime;* that is, it is productive of the strongest emotions which the mind is capable of feeling. (39)

I show the students several examples of sublime landscapes, landscapes that seem to threaten the viewer's life, culled from Salvator Rosa's depictions of towering mountains, huge dark caves, and marauding bandits; from John Martin's images of the biblical deluge; and from Caspar David Friedrich's depiction of a shipwreck in the frozen arctic seas. Confronted with these scenes, the students themselves experience the process Burke describes, a movement from terror or fear to astonishment (as the instinct of self-preservation is gradually relaxed) to admiration and perhaps reverence and respect, as they acknowledge the awesome revelation of a power (call it nature or God) capable of creating such overwhelming landscapes.

Returning to the novel, students quickly recognize that the Creature inhabits such sublime landscapes, whether in the Alps near Geneva over which violent storms rage, the desolate rocks of the Orkney Islands off the Scottish coast "whose high sides were continually beaten upon by waves" (161), or the "mountainous ices of the ocean" at the North Pole, where the

Creature is finally "lost in darkness and distance" (Rieger 221). Not only does the Creature bound through such sublime landscapes, but he also embodies the sublime. His gigantic stature, his enormous physical strength, and especially his origin in the transgression of the boundary between life and death—all render him both "obscure" and "vast," qualities that are the touchstones of the sublime. His very existence seems to constitute a threat to human life.

I suggest to the class that Mary Shelley's calculated association of the Creature with Burke's sublime is intended to do more than rouse a powerful aesthetic response in the reader. It also raises the question of what we know and how we know it. When the human mind encounters a sublime landscape, it tries to determine the meaning of the image before it. Burke and Kant suggested that the meaning of such an immense landscape is the infinite and incomprehensible power of God or nature (the thing in itself). In this reading, what is signified (divine omnipotence or the *ding an sich*) is greater than the signifier (the landscape and our verbal or visual descriptions of it). With Thomas Weiskel, we might call this mode the "negative" sublime, since the human mind is finally overwhelmed or negated by a greater, even a transcendent, power.

As contrast, I ask the students to read the Mount Snowdon episode of Wordworth's *Prelude* and Coleridge's "This Lime-Tree Bower My Prison." These two Romantic poems suggest that the meaning of a sublime landscape may lie, rather, in its capacity to inspire the poetic imagination to a conception of its own power as a "mighty mind" or "almighty spirit." In this reading, what is signified (the landscape) is less than the signifier (the poetic language produced by the creative imagination); hence this mode can be called the "positive" sublime, since the human mind finally confronts its own linguistic power. I then remind students that the aesthetic experience of the sublime they received from looking at the paintings by Rosa, Martin, and Friedrich was based not on nature but on art, on the power of a visual language created by human beings.

With this distinction in mind, I ask the students to determine whether Frankenstein's Creature represents the positive or the negative mode of the sublime. Again, the class usually divides. Some say the negative, observing that the Creature is a vast power beyond Frankenstein's linguistic control. As he threatens Frankenstein,

> Slave, I before reasoned with you, but you have proved yourself unworthy of my condescension. Remember that I have power; you believe yourself miserable, but I can make you so wretched that the light of day will be hateful to you. You are my creator, but I am your master; obey! (165)

In this reading, the Creature represents the power of universal human destruction, the unthinkable, unimaginable, unspeakable experience of a deluge or a nuclear holocaust. He is the thing in itself, the elemental force of nature that can annihilate all human life.

But insofar as the Creature is the unknowable thing in itself, I remind the students, he is always already interpreted or read by the characters in the novel and by themselves. In this sense, he also represents the positive sublime, the meanings or systems that human beings construct out of the elemental chaos of nature. Like Kant, Mary Shelley forces us to see that the human mind always imposes a phenomenological order on an unknowable noumenon and that these orderings or semiotic constructions are the social ideologies that we call reality.

I argue that Mary Shelley's purposes in the novel are finally ethical rather than epistemological. After showing students several of Diane Arbus's photographs of freaks, the Jewish giant, transvestites, and transexuals, I ask them how they have responded to these images of the unfamiliar, the abnormal, the unique. Invariably, they express unease, discomfort, anxiety, even repulsion and fear. I suggest that human beings typically interpret such images negatively. In other words, we use language to name the normal and the abnormal, the human and the nonhuman, and thus to fix the boundaries between them. As Michel Foucault has pointed out in *Madness and Civilization* and *Discipline and Punish*, we use language as an instrument of power, as a way to define the borderline between reason and madness, between the socially acceptable and the criminal, and thus to control the terrors of the unknown.

In Mary Shelley's novel, this linguistic process of naming the unknown, the Creature, becomes a discourse of power that leads directly to the creation of evil. By consistently seeing the Creature as evil, the characters in the novel force him to become evil. Whatever his moral nature might be, the Creature becomes a monster because he has been denied access to a human community, to female companionship, to parental care, to love. His violent rage and malicious murders are the direct result of a humanly engendered semiotic construction of the Creature as terrifying and horrible. Mary Shelley thus shows us that when we see nature as evil, we make it evil. What is now proved was once only imagined, as William Blake said in *The Marriage of Heaven and Hell*. Having conceived his Creature as a "devil" and his "enemy" (94, 199), Victor Frankenstein has made him so.

Moreover, since we can consciously know only the phenomenological or linguistic universes that we have ourselves constructed, if we read or imagine the Creature as evil, we write ourselves as the authors of evil. In Blake's pithy phrase, "we become what we behold." Frankenstein gradually becomes the monster he constructs: "I considered the being whom I had cast among mankind . . . nearly in the light of my own vampire, my own spirit let loose from the grave" (72). Many students notice that, by the end of the novel, Victor and his Creature have become indistinguishable—they embody one consciousness, one spirit of revenge, one despair. More literally, Frankenstein has become the monster he named: in the popular imagination informed by the cinematic and comic-book versions of Mary Shelley's novel, his name, Frankenstein, has become the monster's.

Mary Shelley's answer to the questions originally raised in class—is the Creature innately good or evil?—is thus one of radical skepticism. Since the human mind can never know the thing in itself, it can know only the constructions of its own imagination. Because the mind is more likely to respond to the sublime or the unknown with fear and hostility than with love and acceptance, the unfettered imagination celebrated by the Romantic poets is more likely to construct evil than good. Mary Shelley believed, I argue, that the Romantic imagination must be consciously controlled by love, specifically a love that sees all the products of nature—the old, the sick, the handicapped, the freaks—as sacred life-forms to be nurtured with care and compassion.

Finally, I point out that Mary Shelley's criticism of the unfettered Romantic imagination and its celebration of the sublime entails a different aesthetic commitment, an affirmation of the beautiful over the sublime. As Burke wrote, the sublime appeals to the instinct of self-preservation and rouses feelings of terror that result in a desire for power, domination, and continuing control. But the beautiful appeals to the instinct of self-procreation and rouses sensations of erotic and affectional love. I illustrate this distinction by showing the class several examples of beautiful landscapes by Claude Lorrain and Richard Wilson, emphasizing the sensuously undulating curves, balanced symmetries, controlled tonal harmonies, and careful framing of these compositions. The idealized figure of Clerval in the 1818 edition of Frankenstein explicitly prefers the brightly colored and gently undulating landscapes of the beautiful, the banks of the lower Rhine (153), for instance, to the "majestic and strange" mountains of the Swiss Alps (153). By celebrating the beautiful over the sublime, Mary Shelley through Clerval advocates a loving acceptance of all the productions of mother nature (significantly, in this novel even the Alps are gendered as female). Only by reading the sublime, the unknowable, as lovable can we prevent the creation of monsters, monsters both psychological and technological, monsters capable of destroying all human civilization.

Frankenstein in the Context
of English Romanticism

William Walling

Perhaps the safest prediction one can make about teaching *Frankenstein* is that many students will be both surprised and impressed by their experience of the novel. Expecting, if anything, to be diverted by crude melodrama, they find instead that they have been moved; and few students fail to notice that they have encountered a work of unmistakable seriousness. Yet substantial as Mary Shelley's achievement is in its own right, *Frankenstein* also provides an enormously useful entry point into some of the central preoccupations of English Romanticism, preoccupations that may be most fruitfully explored in the classroom through a shared reading of the novel.

One broad and critical issue, however, looms large even before reading begins: the question of the relation between the Romantic movement and the expansive rationalism of the Enlightenment. Here, of course, *Frankenstein* holds an unusually prominent place—perhaps, in popular awareness of the issue, the most prominent place of any work in the Romantic period. Thus some students will likely volunteer that the very name Frankenstein has passed into the common language as an admonition against the monstrous potential of science. (A more formal route to this realization would be a dictionary assignment on the various connotations conveyed by the title of Mary Shelley's novel.)

In popular apprehension, then, *Frankenstein* surely represents one of the more extreme counterstatements to the optimism of the Enlightenment. But students in a course on English Romanticism will have little difficulty in recognizing the striking similarity of another extreme counterstatement, in a poem from a collection often cited as the beginning of the English Romantic movement. "We murder to dissect," Wordsworth tells us in "The Tables Turned" (in the *Lyrical Ballads* of 1798), impelled by the corrosive power of our "meddling intellect." This resistance, discussion should show, becomes even more intense in the signification of Mary Shelley's title, for the name *Frankenstein* now suggests that our meddling intellect may be impelled beyond dissection into the creation of its own murderer.

In their stark simplicity, extremities like these make clear the contentious relation English Romanticism often bears to the dominant values of the Enlightenment. Because much of our teaching aims to demonstrate the genuine complexity in what could be taken for mere assertion, the outlines of this cultural conflict offer a useful context in which to begin the reading of the novel. Moreover, with this reading, richer significations become apparent, and students should be alerted to a sustained pattern of imagery whose particularities help to clarify both the relation of English Romanticism to the Enlightenment and the resonant place of *Frankenstein* in the Romantic movement itself. Since such claims demand a good deal of support to be persuasive, the instructor might want to work through the details in a class session.

The pattern of imagery I have in mind is, fittingly enough, concentrated around the ambiguity of light. On the novel's first page, as Walton describes to his sister the intense ambition that is driving him to journey farther and farther north, he muses on the beneficent wonders he will find when he finally reaches "a country of eternal light" (15). Of course, Walton never reaches that country, but his optimism about the nature of light functions as ironic prologue to the tale he will soon hear from Victor Frankenstein. For, at the age of "about fifteen," Frankenstein had been warned of the potential in light to "dissect" (in Wordsworthian terms) the organic unity of nature:

> As I stood at the door, on a sudden I beheld a stream of fire issue from an old and beautiful oak which stood about twenty yards from our house; and so soon as the dazzling light vanished, the oak had disappeared, and nothing remained but a blasted stump. When we visited it the next morning, we found the tree shattered in a singular manner. It was not splintered by the shock, but entirely reduced to thin ribbons of wood. I never beheld anything so utterly destroyed. (40)

The warning, as students discover, is "ineffectual" (41), and readers soon encounter the rich irony of Frankenstein articulating the conventional— and conventionally positive—imagery of intellectual discovery as he describes a crucial moment in his research: "I paused, examining and analysing all the minutiae of causation . . . until from the midst of this darkness a sudden light broke in upon me. . . ." So suffused is the narrative with ironic play on illumination, in fact, that Frankenstein promptly offers the certitude of natural light as a verification of the authenticity of his science: "The sun does not more certainly shine in the heavens than that which I now affirm is true" (51).

But this potentially destructive light is rather different from either the intellect's or the sun's, and it is surely more brilliant than "the dim and yellow light of the moon" that first gave him an inkling of his creation (57). For, more than a year later, the same kind of light that destroyed the beautiful oak makes pellucidly clear to Frankenstein the monstrosity of what his intellect has brought into being:

> A flash of lightning illuminated the object and discovered its shape plainly to me; its gigantic stature, and the deformity of its aspect,

more hideous than belongs to humanity, instantly informed me that it was the wretch, the filthy demon to whom I had given life. (73)

That this revelation comes in the form of an electrical discharge deserves stressing. Even as an adolescent, Frankenstein had mused on "the more obvious laws of electricity" in the wake of the oak's destruction (40). But the revelatory flash of lightning that occurs now, more than a year after he had infused "a spark of being" into a "lifeless thing" (56), suggests that even the best-informed scientific hopes of Mary Shelley's time, including those for the potential of electricity, must submit to the dramatic ironies of her fable.

It is thus especially appropriate when, after Frankenstein's death, the "wretch" who owes his very being to the conjunction of an electrical spark and a highly charged intellect now declares his intention to extinguish the "light" that remains to him in "torturing flames" (210–11). Many students should be able to identify this allusion, particularly if the course has already treated the English Romanticists' frequent use of the Promethean myth. The teacher can also point out the coherence of Mary Shelley's overall conception in the formal terms students usually find impressive, for the "torturing flames" (211) that are foreshadowed at the end of *Frankenstein* bring us full circle to the subtitle that begins it—*The Modern Prometheus.*

Students should readily recognize the pronounced affinity between the myth of Prometheus and the pattern of imagery they have been pursuing. Indeed, the "equivocal potentialities" of the light Prometheus brings to humankind (Bloom 213) are essential to all versions of the myth, whether the light is taken as fire, heightened human consciousness, or life itself. In this novel, the Promethean myth implicates itself richly into the crucial— and crucially ambiguous—pattern of imagery concerning light and the promise of electricity. All the equivocal potentialities sometimes coalesce incandescently under Mary Shelley's pen, as on the "dreary night in November" when Frankenstein begins "to infuse a spark of being into the lifeless thing that lay at [his] feet," while a dying "candle" gives off its "half-extinguished light" (56). Moreover, students should find much to discuss in the fact that this last passage, with its extraordinary resonances, is the one Mary Shelley claimed was the genesis of composition (xi).

As I have already suggested, however, the Promethean theme also brings *Frankenstein* into provocative relation to a number of major Romantic texts. Two use Prometheus in the title: Byron's short, bleakly splendid "Prometheus" (1816) and Percy Bysshe Shelley's formidable lyric drama of passionate hope and troubled skepticism, *Prometheus Unbound* (1818–19). Other Romantic texts, more typological in allusion, share with *Frankenstein* the articulation of a Promethean resonance. Most notable are those poems of Blake's that give prominence to a figure sometimes nameless (as in "the new born fire" of "A Song of Liberty," 1793), sometimes called Oothoon (asking for "Theotormons Eagles to prey upon her flesh," in plate 2 of *Visions of the Daughters of Albion*, 1793), sometimes called Fuzon (as in *The Book of Ahania*, 1795), but most often called Orc (as in *America*, 1793, and *The Book of Urizen*, 1794).

Still, Prometheus hardly exhausts Mary Shelley's conscious use of myth, and instructors might want to explore two other areas during class discussion. One is quite overt. Like Blake's *Marriage of Heaven and Hell* (1793) and Percy Shelley's preface to *Prometheus Unbound* (1819) and his remarks in *A Defence of Poetry* (1821), *Frankenstein* engages in the bold revaluation of another bearer of light, Milton's fallen Lucifer, Satan. Blake's and Percy Shelley's revaluation focuses primarily on Satan and Milton's conception of God. Mary Shelley's revaluation of Milton's mythology is more diffused—as her epigraph of the title page should suggest to the class, since it is drawn from a speech of Adam's in book 10 of *Paradise Lost*, well after any significant role for Satan. ("Did I request thee, Maker, from my clay / To mould me Man, did I solicit thee / From darkness to promote me?" [10. 743–45]). Indeed, an influential feminist interpretation of *Frankenstein* sees the novel as "a mock *Paradise Lost*," with its "striking omission of any obvious Eve-figure" covertly indicating "that for Mary Shelley the part of Eve *is* all the parts" (Gilbert and Gubar 230).

This challenging reading of *Frankenstein* makes the second area of possible exploration more accessible: the frequent Romantic confrontation not so much with Miltonic myth as with the Miltonic presence in literary tradition. Blake writes an epic called *Milton* (1804); Wordsworth suggests, by direct allusion to line 646 of book 12 of *Paradise Lost*, that his epic will begin where Milton's breaks off (1.15 in the 1805 text of *The Prelude*; 1.14 in the 1850 version); and Keats wrestles with the question of Milton's influence both in his letters (e.g., the letters to J. H. Reynolds, 3 May 1818 and 21 Sept. 1819) and in his two versions of *Hyperion* (1818–19).

Sooner or later, however, discussion should return to the more modest pattern of imagery in *Frankenstein* that centers on the problem of light. Here, too, Mary Shelley's novel shares in a significant and generalized practice of the period. Blake, for example, in his "Introduction" to the *Songs of Experience* (1794), vocalizes with indeterminate irony a postlapsarian longing for the renewal of "fallen, fallen light" (10); Wordsworth, in his "Ode: Intimations of Immortality" (1802–04), contrasts the memory of an earlier "celestial light" (4) to the drearily encroaching "light of common day" (76) that too often characterizes adulthood. Coleridge, in a poem written at least partly in response to Wordsworth's "Ode," creates one of the most profoundly ironic images in all of English Romanticism when he describes a *"green* light," utterly devoid of vivifying power ("Dejection" [1804], 44; emphasis mine).

But it is in the poetry written by the members of Mary Shelley's own generation that the imagery of light closely approximates the problematic issue *Frankenstein* raises of the relation between Romanticism and the Enlightenment. Most striking is Percy Shelley's last major poetic effort, *The Triumph of Life* (1822), where the play on images of light is truly astonishing, from the energetic description of a sunrise in the first twenty lines to an account of another kind of illumination, which the poet-narrator encounters when he turns his back on the natural light. This new light is "icy cold," yet so glaring that it "obscure[s] with blinding light / The sun" (77–79). A dazzling orchestration that follows includes the "kindling green" (310) of spring (as if to turn Coleridge's "green light" inside out) and the ambiguous "Shape all light" (352) of Rousseau's fictionalized history in the last third of the poem. Equally brilliant, if less coruscating, Keats's *Hyperion* and *Fall of Hyperion* rest on a premise so basic that few commentators mention it: that the very nature of light can change—or, more accurately, that there can be a change in the valorization humanity confers on different kinds of light.

As the class will already perceive, the significance of the place *Frankenstein* holds in this complex drama is ensured. At the level of popular judgment, a point to which some instructors may want to return now with increased emphasis, the novel stands foremost among Romantic works that warn of the danger in the light privileged by the concept of the Enlightenment—including, not least of all, the active light in lightning and the scientific promise of electricity. Students should be encouraged to find how much of the evidence in the text helps to explain the popular view. Even when reduced to shadowy implication, for example, the imagery of intense intellectual light versus a passive natural light seems to be pointing often in only one direction, as in the description Frankenstein gives Walton of the summer of his most committed scientific research:

> The summer months passed while I was thus engaged, heart and soul, in one pursuit. It was a most beautiful season; never did the fields bestow a more plentiful harvest or the vines yield a more luxuriant vintage, but my eyes were insensible to the charms of nature. (53)

But despite the attractive plausibility of this simple contest, the Creature's hope for his extinction in "torturing flames," a hope that seems very close to a longing for self-transcendence (211), should bring students back to the demands of a more rigorous reading.

Such a reading will show that, however precariously, *Frankenstein* shares in the ideology that perhaps best characterizes English Romanticism as a literary phenomenon: the belief in a mental light both stronger and more truly humane than anything embodied in the expansive rationalism of the Enlightenment. The poets, of course, called this stronger light "imagination," and students who have participated in a class in English Romanticism should be aware of the enormous significance that the ideal of imagination held for the poets—in particular, Blake, Wordsworth, and Coleridge.

It is here, however, that the same students might be encouraged to see that for the poets of Percy Shelley's generation, imagination is a far more troublesome concept. Byron is openly skeptical, if not entirely dismissive of the supposed value of imagination. Percy Shelley combines a passionate need to believe in imagination with an acute awareness of the probable illusiveness of all mental structures. And Keats's work reflects an ongoing debate with himself on the authenticity of imagination.

Students ought to recognize the family resemblance, then, in the disillusionment Frankenstein expresses after he has embodied his imaginative desire: "[N]ow that I had finished, the beauty of the dream vanished, and breathless horror and disgust filled my heart" (56). Indeed, if students are fresh from their reading of Keats, Frankenstein's disillusionment will seem uncannily like the sudden perception of a "foul dream" that informs the climax of *Lamia* (1819; 2.271). But the instructor should also point out that Mary Shelley's use of the Promethean theme, not to mention Walton's despondency at turning back and the dying Frankenstein's continued hope (204, 206), gives the novel a strong counterpoint to mere disillusion, along with a complexity denied it by popular interpretation. For although "the modern Prometheus" dies before the end of *Frankenstein*, leaving Walton to return to domestic ordinariness, the flames that animated Frankenstein's quest continue to burn, at least in the realm of his Creature's longing. Students who have just finished a reading of Keats need only be reminded of another possibility, no matter how remote, that the poet himself evokes: "The Imagination may be compared to Adam's dream—he awoke and found it truth" (to Benjamin Bailey, 22 Nov. 1817).

No consideration to *Frankenstein* ought to conclude without some recognition of its theme of profound isolation. If Enlightenment values have been discussed, the theme should be transparent enough to students. Thus Frankenstein's Creature, in the midst of his narrative, will state, "Increase of knowledge only discovered to me more clearly what a wretched outcast I was" (125). But the emotional force of this theme may be the most memorable aspect of the novel for many students. A defensible point worth making, then, is that in Frankenstein's "wretch" Mary Shelley has created the ultimate in solitaries for an age seemingly overwhelmed by contrary impulses about the question of "solitude."

Any number of analogous examples from Romantic poetry suggest themselves: Blake's Urizen striving to create a universe "[f]rom the depths of dark solitude" (*Book of Urizen*, ch. 2); Wordsworth's Solitary in *The Excursion* (1814); Byron's designation of human destiny as a "sad unallied existence" in "Prometheus" (52); the wandering poet of Percy Shelley's *Alastor* (1816), a poem whose subtitle is *The Spirit of Solitude*; and Keats's striking shift in tone to "a solitary sorrow" at the start of the third book of *Hyperion*. Mary Shelley, in her representation of a figure doomed to be forever friendless and alone, has created a truly terminal solitariness, made all the more poignant by the frequent pleas the "wretch" makes to Frankenstein for the creation of a mate.

With students sharing in such a recognition, the class may begin to discuss the poem most directly related to the novel—Coleridge's *Rime of the Ancient Mariner* (1798). Walton tells us of his fervent admiration for "that production of the most imaginative of modern poets" (20), and Mary Shelley either alludes to or quotes from the *Rime* at several other points in her novel. She may also have borrowed certain features from the poem— for example, Walton's voyage to a land of ice, a pattern of imagery centered on different kinds of light, and the fictional strategy of having a tale reshape the moral perspective of an internalized audience. But probably the most persuasive connection the instructor can make between novel and poem is to share with the class the lines in the *Rime* that Mary Shelley particularly admired:

> Alone, alone, all, all alone
> Alone on a wide wide sea!   (4.232–33)

The extremity of this vision of isolation is so vividly pathetic that among all the other works of English Romanticism perhaps only *Frankenstein*, with its unsettling power, and its solitary wretch at the center, approaches the starkness of Coleridge's vision.

SPECIFIC COURSE CONTEXTS

Teaching Frankenstein as Science Fiction

Terrence Holt

The function of science in *Frankenstein* to a great extent defines science fiction as a genre. More important, Shelley's use of science reveals that the critical tools necessary to understand science fiction are no different from those we use in reading any text. This principle, significant as it is for the instructor, often frustrates the expectations of students, who may enroll in a science fiction course hoping for something "nonliterary." Many students approach science fiction hoping to find a form of science, with all the comforting certainties that word suggests and none of the disturbing uncertainty of literature. The special challenge in teaching science fiction is to provide students a bridge from their expectations to an appreciation of the methods and goals of literary criticism.

Providing this bridge is difficult because the student in a science fiction course is typically a nonmajor, unfamiliar with and sometimes resistant to critical methods. My response to this situation has been to view the course as a missionary activity and to conceive of my mission as exposing students to as broad a range of critical approaches as possible. I concentrate on illuminating the ways in which science fiction uses a false front of scientific thinking as a disguise within which unscientific motives—essentially the same as one would find in any narrative—drive the plot. A discussion of the representation of science in *Frankenstein* provides a good beginning for the course and a paradigm for the genre as a whole.

The generic identity of science fiction has been heavily mystified. The most enduring view is that science fiction writers, working from sound scientific postulates, extrapolate the future of science and its impact on society or the individual. This argument appears naively in studies that are satisfied to track the prognosticatory success of various writers, but it also crops up in more sophisticated approaches that see science fiction as an experiment in the future of the historical process. In either form, the assumption is that science fiction is somehow fundamentally different, but this claim is troublesome. Emphasizing predictions that have come true requires that we ignore or, worse, rationalize the many examples of the genre that have not come true. This approach also glosses over a crucial question: Is there a relation between the writer's extrapolations and the actual process of scientific inquiry? Or, from another perspective, is there a difference between such extrapolation and the imaginative act by which any writer creates events that have no more reality than the inventions of science fiction? The answer to both questions is not really. Any claim that science fiction exists in a different relation to the empirical world than mainstream fiction does needs to find a better answer; to date, none has appeared.

This mystification of the status of science fiction probably reflects the mystique of science itself. Our customary relation to science is ignorance, a familiar relation, with familiar literary implications: the willed suspension of disbelief with which we purchase computers or read novels. Most of us do not understand, for instance, pharmacology. Someone in a white coat tells us that we need an injection, and we roll up our sleeves. An author tells us that the application of a spark to dead organic tissues will produce a living creature, and we read on. On neither occasion do we require a full explanation of the techniques involved, for—and this is crucial—we cannot distinguish a valid explanation from a fraudulent one. All we require is evidence of the practitioner's authority: the doctor's diploma or the writer's scientific-sounding rhetoric. In both instances, our willing acquiescence works to our advantage. Our belief in the efficacy of a drug is sufficient to create a placebo effect. When we read, the placebo effect is even stronger; indeed it is the only effect a text has to offer. Words on a page cannot create a living creature: they can only create our belief in one, and this is all a text requires. The function of science in science fiction, then, is best understood by reference not to what science does in such texts but to what it cannot do and which rhetorical devices perform in its stead.

The way science functions in *Frankenstein*, and in science fiction generally, is analogous to what engineers term a "black box." Rhetoric borrowed from science flows into it, and a viable plot flows out of it, but the exact nature of the process enacted within the box, under the rubric of science, remains obscure. In *Frankenstein*, the material flowing into the box consists of ideas and a location: Victor's early studies, a spark, and the laboratory. The result is the Creature, and through it the novel's plot. *Frankenstein* would not be possible without a black box at its center because of the one simple fact that the text goes to great lengths to evade: Mary Shelley did not know how to create an actual human being; she could only create the rhetorical semblance of one.

An important first step in considering *Frankenstein* in a science fiction course is to emphasize that Shelley's ignorance of techniques for creating artificial life does not reflect any ignorance of the state of scientific knowledge in the early nineteenth century. This proposition illuminates several critical aspects of the teaching of science fiction. First, the gender identification of science fiction (despite strenuous efforts by writers such as Ursula K. Le Guin and Joanna Russ) still tends to be male: it would be a serious mistake to start off such a course by allowing students to characterize a woman author as fundamentally ignorant about science. Second, since *Frankenstein* is properly the first text taught in such a course, a discussion of Shelley's knowledge of science provides an opportunity to bring home an important point: that what passes for scientific fact in a given text depends greatly on when the text was written.

Students should be aware of how the body of scientific knowledge has evolved historically for several reasons. They may have difficulty understanding why one classifies as science fiction early texts treating phenomena we no longer consider scientific (e.g., Poe's "Facts in the Case of the Late M. Valdemar"). If students overlook the role such theories as animal magnetism played in early nineteenth-century science, a great many of the founding figures of science fiction can seem irrelevant to the tradition. A more important reason, however, is that students who appreciate the historical contingency of science can understand how a principle once accepted as truth might now appear nonsensical. This understanding, in turn, can help them recognize the difference between logic and rhetoric: the difference, that is, between the scientific method and the pseudoscientific rhetoric science fiction substitutes for that method. To be viewed as fact, nonsense need be bolstered only by belief, and belief, in science or in fiction, is founded in ignorance. Scientific investigation proceeds by filling in ignorance, and thus old theories die. Science fiction succeeds by exploiting the reader's ignorance, and thus its fantasies flourish.

It is crucial to that exploitation that the writer know enough about science to construct a plausibly realistic facade of scientific learning around the text's central implausibility. Recent scholarship has demonstrated that Shelley's scientific knowledge was more than adequate to this task. In "*Frankenstein*: A Feminist Critique of Science," Anne K. Mellor identifies three sources behind the novel's scientific machinery that point in turn to at least two major paradigms of nineteenth-century science. Erasmus Darwin's taxonomical work, which helped lay the groundwork for the theory of evolution by natural selection, is important to the novel's implicit critique of Victor's Promethean ambitions. The inventor's hope of accelerating evolution and the ironic devolution of both creature and creator not only reflect the central strain in nineteenth-century biological theory but also introduce two enduring themes (these themes are central, for instance, to the work of H. G. Wells) of modern science fiction: evolution and its discontents. The hubris of Humphry Davy, who confidently predicted the triumph, through chemistry, of the human intellect over the material circumstances of existence, appears, ironically, in Frankenstein's education and in the Creature itself. Finally, Luigi Galvani's experiments, which investigated how electricity functions in the muscular and nervous systems of animals and human beings, provide the "spark of life" essential for the Creature's animation. (For detailed a discussion of the influence of these theories on the novel, see Mellor's "Feminist Critique.")

The first step in discussing *Frankenstein* as science fiction, then, should be to identify the novel's scientific background, stressing that what may seem improbable or antiquated to twentieth-century readers represented the state of the art at the time of the novel's composition. Such knowledge makes even more striking the paucity of scientific (or any other) information given us concerning the construction of the Creature itself. If Shelley's refusal to give these details does not indicate ignorance, what does it reflect? The answer, of course, is that *Frankenstein*, in portraying the creation of a human being, goes far beyond anything a contemporary scientist could have done. Shelley's difficulty stems from her story's central dependence on a departure from empirical knowledge. What lies beyond the empirical is the imagination, a realm governed by principles more familiar to the literary critic than to the biologist.

Shelley's means of overcoming this difficulty give the science fiction novel both its origin and its fundamental nature. The essential technique is a sleight of hand. The author uses a few scientific-sounding terms to distract her audience while the actual work of the literary imagination goes on unobserved. The technique requires only a few such gestures. The reader's conviction is so powerful that when Victor disappears into his laboratory, the novel need not follow him there. Descriptions of process or method involve no science whatever; what goes on inside the black box is no different from what gives form to any fiction.

This nonfunction of science within science fiction makes the genre's scientific conceits an unusually useful tool for teaching the fundamentals of literary criticism. Once a class has discovered how little science is involved, it is ready to notice the ways in which these devices lay bare other forces motivating the plot. Historical, psychological, and linguistic influences that shape the literary imagination find easily recognizable metaphors in the imaginary postulates and invented machines of science fiction. The form's stress on invention, in fact, gives the writer's imagination freer rein than it might otherwise have: seemingly cast off from social convention and free as well to invent its way around inconvenient facts, the writer expresses in relatively undisplaced forms material that, in more realistic texts, might take a more obscure disguise.

A classroom approach to this material might include the following steps. Once the actual scientific material is identified, students trace in detail the process by which Frankenstein makes his Creature. The instructor stresses the importance of cause and effect in the scientific method. In chapter 3, for instance, as Victor tells of the steps leading to his discovery, he confesses that his account of his life's work has been given in "rather a too philosophical and connected a strain" (45–46). The instructor, reminding the class of the meaning of *philosophy* in this context, invites students to point out disconnections in the novel's logic, its failures to explain, its many non sequiturs. As students identify these gaps the instructor reformulates them as questions: If there's no scientific reason for this, what other reasons might someone have for proceeding this way? What wishes or fears might cause such a leap of reasoning?

As students come to recognize the absence of scientific process (and to recognize what lies behind the appearance of that process), they should focus on Victor's interest in the subject of life. It is introduced as a mere appurtenance to a poorly defined "incident" that "happened" (50); students challenged to identify this incident will move the discussion in provocative directions, turning up either a circularity or another non sequitur. The terms in which Frankenstein explains his interest stress not natural philosophy but the supernatural: the quest starts, after all, with alchemy, and he tells us that even after he has supposedly abandoned these "exploded systems" he was "animated by an almost supernatural enthusiasm" (50). "Animated" is, in context, a charged term: yoked here with "supernatural," the two suggest that other forms of animation may be equally inexplicable by rational means.

Victor introduces the charnel-house elements of the process in another non sequitur, a bald claim that "[t]o examine the causes of life, we must first have recourse to death" (50). The imperative behind that "must," explained nowhere, raises another leading question: If there is no scientific principle at stake, what other forces might make the bodies of the dead a necessary precondition to this miraculous creation? Here, of course, students might be asked to consider who has recently died in the Frankenstein family and what that figure might have to do with the creation of life. Although this passage purports to recount Victor's fascination with the "minutiae of causation" (51), cause and effect is entirely absent from the logic of the account itself: first principles and unsupported assertions are thrown out seemingly at random "until from the midst of this darkness a sudden light" breaks in, "a light so brilliant and wondrous, yet so simple" that Victor becomes "dizzy with the immensity of the prospect which it illustrated" (51).

Victor's dizziness is part of a general coyness that overcomes his narrative at this point. He tells us that "the stages of the discovery were distinct and probable" (51), but of the stages themselves we have only an indistinct impression, rendered probable chiefly by narrative expressions of astonishment. Students should absorb two important points here. The first is that the text tells us to believe in the causes of its events but fails to provide the actual causes. This is a paradigm for the course as a whole, for the same technique appears repeatedly throughout the genre. Seeing this inconsistency is a skill that students hoping to understand literary criticism must master—the ability to see that a text may contradict itself. Second, students should consciously track the elements of Victor's explanation that seem designed to engage their credulity. A valuable introduction to close reading, this exercise can help them to recognize their own responses as effects produced by rhetorical techniques rather than as empirical perceptions.

The novel gives the instructor useful support by emphasizing both these points when Victor reports, "this discovery was so great and overwhelming that all the steps by which I had been progressively led to it were obliterated, and I beheld only the result" (51). Victor addresses his audience directly, in effect slamming down the lid on the novel's black box:

> I see by your eagerness and the wonder and hope which your eyes express, my friend, that you expect to be informed of the secret with which I am acquainted; that cannot be; listen patiently until the end of my story, and you will easily perceive why I am reserved upon that subject. (51)

This is the closest we get to science in *Frankenstein*. Far from specifying its techniques, Victor's narrative explicitly refuses to explain.

Having established that *Frankenstein* does not offer any scientific explanation of the process by which Victor makes his Creature, the class can turn to the crucial question: If the novel isn't about someone who made a human being in a laboratory, what is it about? Clues are available in the passages of chapter 4 in which Victor describes his mental state during the construction of the Creature (and it is worth noting that these passages are longer than those describing the process that evoked the state of mind). He describes that state as a "trance," suggesting once more something dreamlike rather than real. We also get a distinct impression of the quality of that trance:

> It was indeed but a passing trance, that only made me feel with renewed acuteness so soon as, the unnatural stimulus ceasing to operate, I had returned to my old habits. I collected bones from charnel-houses and disturbed, with profane fingers, the tremendous secrets of the human frame.   (53)

This passage, along with the reference to Victor's fear that his father might ascribe his isolation "to vice" (54) and especially the chapter's closing paragraph, demonstrates that the black box of this novel conceals something shameful. The language also suggests that, as with most shame and particularly that associated with the production of human beings, this shame is sexual. (Students inclined to hoot at the idea that sex existed in the nineteenth century can be convinced if shown an excerpt from almost any nineteenth-century medical manual's entry under "masturbation," especially when read alongside the symptoms of slow fever and nervous prostration Victor reports in the final paragraph of chapter 4 and the "exercise and amusement" he proposes as their cure.) Chapter 4 makes painfully evident that the novel's science conceals anxiety about reproduction; the false front of science, by cloaking this anxiety, allows the novel to dramatize it. From this point, the class should be ready to approach the novel in the terms of standard critical treatments.

Despite the neglect of scientific method in *Frankenstein*, a science fiction class need not retreat entirely from the novel's treatment of science. The novel also lends itself to discussion of a literary issue that does characterize science fiction: the use of scientific technologies as metaphors for literary technique. Having recognized the essential fictionality of Frankenstein's "spark of life," the class can discuss the imagery of light in which Victor figures this conceptual breakthrough. The trail leads eventually to the 1831 "Author's Introduction," which gives the inspiration for the novel itself in strikingly similar terms:

> Swift as light and as cheering was the idea that broke in upon me. "I have found it! What terrified me will terrify others; and I need only describe the spectre which had haunted my midnight pillow." On the morrow I announced that I had *thought of a story*. I began that day with the words "It was on a dreary night of November," making only a transcript of the grim terrors of my waking dream.   (xi)

"I have found it!" is, of course, a translation of the conventional "Eureka!," further associating Shelley's investigations with scientific inquiry (an association the author makes explicit in the closing paragraphs of the 1831 introduction). Perceptive students should notice not only that the novel, like the Creature, comes to its author in a burst of light but also that Shelley, as significant details in the passage suggest, finds creation as much a problem as Frankenstein does.

Students should consider the tone of the passage: Is "only a transcript" self-deprecating? To what extent might such a tone stem from the difference between her emphasized claim to have "thought of a story" and the seemingly unwilled mechanism by which (in her account) the story actually comes to her? How might the relation between the Creature and its creator mirror the relation between Shelley and her novel? Shelley's 1831 introduction also offers suggestions for such a line of investigation, as in her observation, "Invention . . . does not consist in creating out of void, but out of chaos; the materials must, in the first place, be afforded: it can give form to dark, shapeless substances but cannot bring into being the substance itself" (x). What does this passage have to say about the materials from which Shelley herself drew? What source is likely to have afforded her materials? What issues of origin might have remained "dark" and "shapeless" in her own life? Such questions lead readily into discussions of reproduction as metaphor for literary production.

The inventor or scientist as a figure for the author is a persistent motif in science fiction, one Shelley introduced to the genre at its inception. Shelley repeatedly calls Victor an artist: he is a "pale student of unhallowed arts" (x–xi), his discovery one that "would terrify the artist" (xi). Frankenstein himself tells Walton of his work, "I appeared rather like one doomed by slavery to toil in the mines, or any other unwholesome trade than an artist occupied by his favourite employment" (54–55). Discussing these parallels allows a discussion of intentionality (frequently a vexing question for nonmajors). The Creature's resistance to the conscious intentions of its author plays off consistently against the novel's suggestions that the Creature is Victor's doppelgänger; this contradiction opens up the possibility that Victor's own intentions may be mixed and, by extension, that the novel may mean more than it intends, that intentions themselves may be ultimately inscrutable.

Like the construction of the Creature out of dead, disarticulated parts, *Frankenstein* also figures its own construction out of discarded bits of prior literary forms—epistolary and journal and especially the gothic romance. Students, when asked to consider how the novel is like the Creature, may have trouble seeing this relation because it depends on an awareness of literary history. But, given the general idea, they can be surprisingly proficient at finding examples—which is itself a valuable exercise, helping them recognize form as something constructed and contingent, not a given or a radical invention.

This self-reflexive tendency, too, is characteristic of science fiction as a genre and is implicit in the central use of technology as a metaphor for literary technique. *Frankenstein* provides students with an opportunity to prepare for later considerations of this issue as well, in a variety of science-using narratives both outside and within science fiction. In the chess-game played out between author and reader, Poe's ludic use of simple machines like the concealed window catch in "The Murders in the Rue Morgue," his pseudoscientific use of mesmerism in "M. Valdemar," or the irrelevant (and inaccurate) discourse on hydrodynamics in "Descent into the Maelstrom" repeats the paradigm established in *Frankenstein*. Verne's machineries of transport have everything to do with the quality of narrative that Aristotelians term "profluence." Orwell's *1984* also uses imaginary technologies to describe the relation between writer and audience, offering springboards for Foucauldean or Freudian readings.

The great advantage of using *Frankenstein* to construct a course on science fiction is that it offers a pointedly opaque, superficial explanation of itself at precisely the moment when students expect the text to become most explicit. This lapse is so central to science fiction, in fact, that an entire course can focus on this one aspect of the genre, stressing the form's dependence on nonscientific modes of thinking. A course so constructed can expose nonmajors to a range of techniques of literary criticism and root classroom discussion in the issues that make this novel—and much of the science fiction canon—more than mere genre writing.

The Woman Writer as Frankenstein

Marcia Aldrich and Richard Isomaki

Students who study *Frankenstein* in women's literature courses often relate the woman writer's attitude toward her act of creating literature to cultural presumptions about conventional maternal and domestic roles. The two alternatives—to mother silently within the domestic sphere or to write as an outsider—have generally appeared mutually exclusive. No woman in the nineteenth century entirely reconciled this exclusivity in shaping her allegiances to social ties, familial inheritances, and literary ambitions. Because of Mary Shelley's experiences as the daughter of a woman writer and because the novel examines creation without a mother, *Frankenstein* offers a particularly good opportunity to explore the dilemma.

We provide a loosely psychoanalytic frame of study for our students, focusing on the mother-daughter relation and the daughter's struggle for identity in a masculine culture. The search for a satisfactory model of parenting in *Frankenstein* is not unlike a search for a satisfactory model of female authorship. We ask whether particular texts by women extend maternal ties by relying on this similarity of models or reject feminine inheritance by building on the annihilation of the mother. Connections can be made between *Frankenstein* and works written long after the Victorian "angel in the house" had apparently ceased to dominate as the image of woman. Sylvia Plath's *Ariel*, for example, evinces an irreconcilable conflict between literary creation and the maternal role.

We begin with Shelley's novel by pointing out that the popular transfer of the name Frankenstein from the monster's creator to the monster himself is true to the logic of the novel because the two characters are aspects of one being. (We call him "monster," not "Creature," since we want to emphasize his hideousness, not his humanity.) But Frankenstein is also the name of the book, and the logic of transference allows a comparison between Victor Frankenstein and his monster, on the one hand, and Mary Shelley and her novel as "hideous progeny" (xii) on the other, a parallel that Barbara Johnson discusses extensively. Shelley's 1831 introduction suggests that the two seemingly dissimilar processes of creation develop along similar lines. The history of the novel's composition as Shelley recounts it reflects a pattern of random chances like those involved in Frankenstein's search for the hidden secrets of nature. Both Shelley and Frankenstein, for example, begin their pursuits because they curtail outdoor activities in bad weather.

Once engaged in their respective projects, novelist and natural scientist obey the same law of creation, the need for raw materials. Recounting her struggle to come up with a ghost story for the famous competition, Shelley theorizes about the blank failure of her first attempts: "Invention . . . does not consist in creating out of void, but out of chaos; the materials must, in the first place, be afforded: it can give form to dark, shapeless substances but cannot bring into being the substance itself" (x). The same theory explains Frankenstein's need to recycle substances taken from the grave. The first reader to notice this parallel was Percy Shelley, whose preface indicates that the novel has preserved the "elementary principles of human nature" (its preexistent components) but has not "scrupled to innovate upon their combinations" (xiii).

The parallel continues after monster and book have been completed. Both Shelley and Frankenstein view their creations ambivalently because each has encroached on prerogatives reserved to others: Shelley's unfeminine presumption in writing a novel is like Frankenstein's usurpation of the mother's role in reproduction. Both distance themselves from their false creations, and yet the monster nevertheless acts as Frankenstein's agent, the book as Shelley's. Just as the monster revenges himself on those who have excluded him, the monsterbook covertly does Shelley's bidding, acting on the wrathful impulses that conventional feminine decorum could not sanction.

With the parallel established, we turn to biography, asking students what it means that the author of *Frankenstein*'s vexed view of creation was Mary Shelley. Like Walton, she harbored desires to make her mark on the world. To be something great was a duty to her parentage and to her marriage, and her introduction casts her novel as an inevitable product of her position in these institutional relations. Not to write would constitute a perverse turn away from the family voices directing her own. Yet, we suggest, Shelley's introduction undercuts her literary ambitions, justifying her fiction in other terms. It presents an older, seemingly reluctant author explaining how she came to write *Frankenstein* in the first place and distancing herself from her original production and her earlier ambitions. To deny the self-assertive act of creation, the introduction emphasizes her passivity: "My imagination, unbidden, possessed and guided me" (x).

If Shelley wrote in response to family voices, why this evident ambivalence? Why did she see her novel as a hideous thing? Students can frame answers to these questions by considering the complicated relations among these discordant familial and cultural voices and pressures. For instance, one context for Shelley's attitude toward her work is offered by the experience of Mary Wollstonecraft, whose domestic arrangements became notorious and who was attacked as a "philosophical wanton" (Gilbert and Gubar 222). Was Shelley subtly pressured into identifying her mother's artistry as monstrous, a deformation of literary and philosophical conventions, and her own birth (which killed her mother) as retribution? Certainly her awakening sexuality, her discovery of her mother's texts, her own preparations for a literary career, and Percy's courtship of her at the site of her mother's grave suggest important considerations that help account for the ambivalent birth myths in *Frankenstein.*

Shelley's difficulties with composition were the result not of personal trauma alone, of course, but also of overtly cultural forces. The drive to create something significant was hardly the norm for feminine behavior. Convention instead stressed self-effacement, substituting for literary fame an anonymous domesticity, the proper context for women's ambition. Her introduction suggests that Shelley was often asked how she came to "dilate upon so very hideous an idea" (vii), a question that nicely illustrates prevailing assumptions about women's proper demeanor and the appropriate channels for their creativity. Shelley's acquaintances frequently remarked on the contrast between her gruesome novel and her feminine manner. Lord Dillon puzzled in 1829: "I should have thought of you—if I had only read you—that you were a sort of my Sybil, outpouringly enthusiastic, rather indiscreet, and even extravagant; but you are cool, quiet, and feminine to the last degree . . ." (qtd. in Poovey 143).

We bring these personal and cultural forces together in the classroom to suggest the complex and ambivalent charge Shelley attached to the act of literary creation. This charge is effectively represented by Shelley's emphasis on her entry into the ghost-story contest ("I busied myself *to think of a story*" [ix]), the emphasis of the italics being repeated on her success in doing so ("I had *thought of a story*" [xi]). This repetition and typographical effect occurs in the body of the novel only with the monster's threat to Frankenstein ("*I will be with you on your wedding-night*" [161, 179; cf. 180, 181; Johnson 7–8]). What is the connection? Frankenstein's blindness to the meaning of this threat is palpable. So also is his lack of interest in the sexual, procreative act normally associated with that night, although his betrothal to Elizabeth has been arranged under the aegis of this procreation, as Victor's father makes evident (181). The aim is to breed a number of new little Frankensteins. To *think of a story*, apparently, is to *be with Frankenstein on his wedding-night*, a wedding night in which the possibility of domestic creation is killed.

We have now set up clearly the choice between literary creation and the domestic sphere, an issue with which the novel begins. The opening letters abound with suggestions of a parallel between large literary efforts and the Promethean explorations carried out by Frankenstein and Walton: Walton once hoped to inscribe his name in the eternal pantheon with Homer and Shakespeare (16); now a failed poet, he attributes his mysterious urge for the ocean to *The Rime of the Ancient Mariner* (20). Walton's letters to his sister also portray the voyage north and the possibility of a reunion with his sister as mutually exclusive alternatives, a replication of the woman author's choice between writing and motherhood.

Students are interested in domestic relations in the novel, which seem notably feminine even though the masculine views of Walton and Frankenstein are included. In a world where apparently only two possibilities exist, the conventional domestic life of self-sacrifice or the outlawed, selfish life of ambition, Shelley seems at first to advocate the former, exposing the fatal consequences of actions taken for self-aggrandizing reasons. Ambition needs tempering: Walton and Frankenstein, its representatives, are inflated and self-justifying men in whom personal ambition masquerades as selfless dedication to benefiting humankind—a rationale Shelley effectively punctures. Frankenstein and Walton pursue their explorations at the cost of fully human, social lives, powerless to curb the cycles of destruction they unleash.

One is tempted, therefore, to talk about Shelley's treatment of Frankenstein and Walton as a female critique of male ambition: they undervalue domestic ties, manifesting an insensitivity that leads to suffering. Yet, that insensitivity exists also in domestic relations between men and women, parents and children. Students are quick to note the power fathers wield and its ill effects: Frankenstein's and Walton's quests, for instance, are initiated against their fathers' prohibitions and can be construed as attempts to extract revenge. Caroline suffers poverty, isolation, and humiliation because of her father's blinding pride and egotism, while Safie's father uses her as a pawn for his freedom. Female characters perish for their loyalties or, like Agatha and Walton's sister, silently nurture affection for brothers who undervalue them.

Parenting, then, far from being the idyll Frankenstein portrays in his story of his childhood, reflects gender relations in disequilibrium. Dorothy Dinnerstein draws a connection between modes of parenting and monstrousness: the unequal allocation of duties to men and women creates a "semi-human, monstrous" state (5; qtd. in Johnson 2). Less than a year apart in age, Elizabeth and Victor differ significantly in their upbringing: Victor is "more deeply smitten with the thirst for knowledge"; to him "the world [is] a secret" to divine (36). Elizabeth, meanwhile, shines "like a shrine-dedicated lamp" in the Frankenstein home (37), content with the mere appearance of things. The flaws in domesticity are implicated in the violent disruptions Victor represents; not all yearnings, needs, and ambitions can be tolerated or nurtured within the domestic sphere. Creativity and domesticity are unreconciled within social bounds.

One question the novel raises, therefore, is whether Frankenstein's initial curiosity is inherently disastrous or simply becomes so because, being intolerable in the domestic realm, it is deformed through suppression. If the home is the place of victimized feminine virtue in a male-dominated culture in which ambition determines the shape of lives, Shelley seems to be attempting to integrate disparate roles that define curiosity and creativity as masculine and valued, domesticity as feminine and devalued. She questions this valorization by presenting extreme examples of masculine egotism, on the one hand, and of idealized domesticity, on the other. Caroline and Elizabeth may well represent those parts of herself, projected in idealized form, that represent the conventionally good mother, uncontaminated and split off from the more troubling aspects of behavior. Like Frankenstein and the monster, these characters represent aspects of warring selves. Walton's sister, Justine, Caroline, Agatha, and the saintly Elizabeth represent the angelic pole of feminine identity, insufficiently humanized. In fact, it is difficult to find figures in the novel that appear integrated and whole, but one might read those that are portrayed as Shelley's attempt to do more than simply mirror her own ambivalence through opposed characters of victimized women and indifferent men. Shelley aims to create a new order in which creativity and domestic sympathy not only coexist but check the tendency to exclusivity by tempering masculine ambition and empowering female sympathy.

We try to help our students unravel one more twist in the knot of complications in Shelley's attitudes toward her literary effort. One aspect of human bonding is the exchange of words: narration is a social act, cognate with the social and familial ties of responsibility that Frankenstein abrogates when he rushes from the scene of his creation. The threat to affectionate domestic relations entailed in Frankenstein's investigations is implied by his father's prediction: that when Victor ceases to think of his family with affection, he will stop writing letters (54). The monster's unavailing preparations for assimilation into the De Lacey circle include listening to the "wonderful narrations" of Volney's *Ruins of Empires* (114). Frankenstein himself does not want his story to come out a "mutilated narration" (199), hideous as his other creation, although this very narration is enclosed within the letters Walton writes to his sister. Both Walton's sister and Frankenstein's family feel justifiable foreboding over the men's ambitions, even if the relatives' understanding of the men is imperfect. Thus the continuation of Walton's and Frankenstein's quests is posed directly against the well-being of those whom they supposedly love. Significantly, Frankenstein's decision to tell Walton his story turns his monomaniacal pursuit of the monster back toward social bounds, and it seems that Frankenstein is himself transformed by the telling. Regaining the friend he lost on Clerval's death, Frankenstein certainly appears to change in Walton's eyes from one who, though amiable and attractive enough, must once have been noble (25) to one who is noble, even godlike

(200). Walton, meanwhile, learns from Frankenstein's story the lesson of sociability and returns for the sake of his crew.

Creation or narration per se does not result in monsters. Shelley paints a flawed, destructive version of creativity, deforming because it does not shape in combination with feeling: "Victor's worst sin is not the creation of the monster but his refusal to take responsibility for it" (Levine, "Ambiguous Heritage" 10). That is the real reason Frankenstein relates his story: not to dissuade Walton from his Promethean pursuit but to show him how to behave whether he succeeds or fails (28), a subtlety that students often miss.

While the approach to the novel we describe here is aimed at courses in women's literature, it might apply elsewhere as well. The comparison between two types of creation, of monsters and of books, could be widened to include other works, as for instance in a course on Romantic subjectivity. Our approach might also have its place in a study of the transformation of Romantic Prometheanism into the optimism of the Victorian assumption of progress, a transformation from transcendental to quasi-material aims. Dickens's *Great Expectations*, which alludes to Shelley's work, offers a useful contrast to the monster's dilemma in that Pip, full of Frankenstein-like expectations, tries to create himself anew, free of the supposedly degrading domestic ties to the blacksmith Joe. He learns that these affections and obligations are in fact unshakable, or ought to be, but not before he has destroyed his own hopes, much as Victor Frankenstein destroyed his.

Teaching *Frankenstein* from the Creature's Perspective

Paul A. Cantor and Michael Valdez Moses

Frankenstein has worked well for us in a wide variety of courses: in a basic undergraduate survey course in British literature, where it helped to chart the transition between Romantic poetry and Victorian fiction; in both undergraduate and graduate survey courses on Romanticism; in a course on tragedy as a genre, as an example of how tragic action can be transposed into a novel; and in a course on myths of creation as a genre.

Whatever the context, we often encounter difficulties at first because of the story's prominent place in popular culture and the consequent temptation for students to think that they are familiar with the contents of the book without having read it. Many telltale signs alert teachers that they are dealing with a student of James Whale (director of the 1931 film version of the novel) rather than of Mary Shelley. A comment in class on the poignancy of the Creature's inability to speak is a sure clue, and we know we are in trouble when we pick up a paper entitled "The Role of the Hunchback in *Frankenstein*." Having once made it clear to students that they must leave Boris Karloff and Colin Clive behind and read Mary Shelley's text, though, teachers can make the popularity of the Frankenstein story work to their advantage. The story could never have enjoyed the success it has had in the form of horror films if it did not somehow tap into a variety of adolescent fears and fantasies. Bearing in mind that Mary Shelley was the same age as many college students when she wrote the book, teachers ought to be able to make it speak with particular force to them. We have found that *Frankenstein* comes alive for students when we ask them about the ways in which they can sympathize and even identify with the Creature.

What Mary Shelley wrote is, after all, a grotesque variant of the bildungsroman. Literally at the center of *Frankenstein* is an account of the Creature's education, and the Creature's fundamental problem is the one with which many heroes and heroines of nineteenth-century novels grapple: how to find a respectable place in society. While the Creature's situation is certainly extraordinary, its troubles mirror basic human concerns and anxieties. The questions that torment the Creature have a familiar ring to the ears of college students: Why do I appear to be different from everyone else (even though I seem to share the same feelings inside)? How do I fit into society? Why have I been rejected by someone who should have taken care of me? How do I find a mate? Is there anyone to share my misery? By getting students to approach the Creature's experience in terms of such questions, a teacher can quickly break down their initial tendency to see the Creature's story as fantastic and remote from their own interests and concerns.

But the point of this pedagogical exercise is not to reduce the Creature's story to the level of undergraduate angst; rather, once students begin to view the Creature sympathetically as an outcast, they can begin to explore Mary Shelley's specifically Romantic concerns in the novel. The Creature takes its place in a long line of Cain figures in English Romanticism, beginning with Coleridge's Ancient Mariner (to whom Walton refers in his second letter). Like its creator, Frankenstein, the Creature has much in common with the self-image of Romantic artists. Isolated from ordinary humanity, the Creature is simultaneously cursed and blessed: cursed with an inability to participate in the normal joys of humanity but blessed with special insights into the human condition precisely as a result of its isolation. Teachers can talk about the Creature's feeling for nature, in particular its affinity for sublime landscapes. In a Romantic or a general survey course teachers can ask students to compare the Creature's sensibility with that of particular Romantic poets, such as Wordsworth, Byron, and Percy Shelley.

We have found it especially helpful to discuss *Frankenstein* in terms of Rousseau's philosophy (in her journal Mary Shelley indicates that she was reading Rousseau's *Reveries of the Solitary Walker* while working on *Frankenstein*). In particular, we assign Rousseau's *Second Discourse* or at least explain the central ideas of the work. In many ways, Mary Shelley's Creature corresponds to Rousseau's "natural man," having roughly the same combination of virtues and defects. In some ways the Creature—even in its own eyes—seems uncivilized and hence inferior to the citizens of society. Like Rousseau's "natural man," the Creature at first lacks the ability to speak and reason. But by the same token, in some ways the Creature seems superior to so-called civilized people. Again like Rousseau's "natural man," the Creature is stronger and more vigorous than the citizens of modern society. It can survive in circumstances that would kill the pampered products of civilization. The Creature possesses the virtues Rousseau attributes to "natural man"—in particular, independence and a natural sense of pity. In telling the story of the Creature's turn to crime, Mary Shelley re-creates Rousseau's chronicle of the fall of "natural man" into civil society, with all the attendant psychic strains and distortions.

Using Rousseau as background for teaching *Frankenstein* helps students to think about the novel in broader, philosophic terms. His revolutionary reconception of human nature can suggest ways for students to break out of their conventional responses to the Creature and to understand that its monstrousness is in part a social construction. In a sense Mary Shelley is portraying the distorted world of society, in which Rousseau's "natural man" appears as monstrous—a creature with all the natural impulses of humanity—indeed a being in whom the creatureliness of humanity is heightened to a new extreme—is rejected by society as inhuman for its failure to fit into its conventional molds. Viewed in these terms, the Creature's story becomes a case study in alienation, in precisely the sense of the term that Hegel and Marx inherited from Rousseau. The Creature's tragedy is that, forced to see itself through the eyes of others, it ultimately accepts their view of it as monstrous. Because of this development, the Creature gets locked into a life-and-death struggle with Victor Frankenstein, in which it can succeed in rivaling its creator only by matching his destructive power.

Once we have our students thinking about the Creature as a pole of sympathy in *Frankenstein*, we ask them to press further and consider whether there are ways in which Mary Shelley might have identified with her "hideous progeny" or, alternatively phrased, ways in which *Frankenstein* might reflect the concerns of a nineteenth-century woman. At first, these questions may puzzle students. How can the story of a decidedly male Creature—it is, after all, questing for a female throughout much of the book—embody a woman's concerns? But when we remind students of the centrality of education as a theme in *Frankenstein*, a light begins to dawn. Denied access to any normal means of education, the Creature is forced to educate itself. Moreover, the Creature must do so on the sly, learning to speak and read by eavesdropping on the education the De Lacey family gives to the Turkish girl, Safie. The Creature thus appropriates for itself an education that was meant for another. Many a woman in the nineteenth century, barred from the educational opportunities available to men and forced to improvise an education for herself, faced similar circumstances.

From a formal perspective, this reading of *Frankenstein* has the advantage of justifying the long De Lacey episode at the center of the novel or at least of explaining its role in Mary Shelley's overarching plan. These chapters, which deal with the De Lacey family and the Creature's education, may strike students as tame by comparison with those describing Frankenstein's creative labors and the Creature's revenge on its creator. It may be that Mary Shelley was seeking in the De Lacey episode a plot device to explain how her Creature became so articulate. Significantly, the film versions of *Frankenstein* always drastically reduce this segment of the story or omit it altogether, their producers and directors well aware that audiences are looking for something more sensational than an elementary lesson in French.

Looking at the De Lacey episode in the light of Mary Shelley's concerns as a nineteenth-century woman may not make the story any more gripping at this point, but it does give students a sense of how the book coheres thematically. At the center of her novel, Mary Shelley places a story of the education of a woman, a woman who is also a foreigner, an alien. Her status as an alien links her with the Creature, and indeed the way its education runs parallel with hers establishes a firm association between the two characters. That Safie comes from Turkey highlights the issue of the status of women. The Turks were of course proverbial for their low evaluation and mistreatment of women, and Mary Shelley uses the occasion of Safie's education to draw a contrast between proper and improper conceptions of the place of women in the world:

> [Safie aspired] to higher powers of intellect and an independence of spirit forbidden to the female followers of Muhammad. . . . [She] sickened at the prospect of again returning to Asia and being immured within the walls of a harem, allowed only to occupy herself with infantile amusements, ill-suited to the temper of her soul, now accustomed to grand ideas and a noble emulation of virtue. The prospect of marrying a Christian and remaining in a country where women were allowed to take a rank in society was enchanting to her.   (119)

In her fear that society will not accommodate her aspirations to virtue and nobility, Safie reveals her similarity to the Creature. And Mary Shelley does seem to be holding up Safie's case as an ideal of equality in education. That Felix instructs her in a scientific and historical book like Volney's *Ruins of Empires* suggests that he is trying to give her the same education he would give a man.

When one of us was teaching *Frankenstein* in a graduate course at the University of Virginia, a graduate student named Rosemary Graham wrote a paper that gives a remarkable new perspective on the issue of women and education in the novel. Graham argued that *Frankenstein* should be read in the light of Mary Wollstonecraft's *Vindication of the Rights of Woman* (1792), which Mary Shelley was rereading while working on *Frankenstein*. This work passionately advocates equality of education for women; much of its argument is directed against Rousseau's view of women and his idea that they should be educated differently from men (a view that Wollstonecraft associates with the followers of Muhammad). Rousseau developed his ideas on education in *Emile*, where the woman who is raised to be Emile's companion is named Sophie. As Graham pointed out, it is a brief step from *Sophie* to *Safie*. Thus by portraying Safie's education as radically different from that of Rousseau's Sophie and especially by having Safie educated in conjunction with the "male child" in her work, Mary Shelley may be continuing her mother's polemic against the French philosopher.

Having established the link between the Creature and Safie, we go on to explore the larger issues of gender raised in *Frankenstein*. In particular, we use the novel to raise the question of the extent to which gender is socially constituted. To be sure, the Creature is created as a male, and on one level of interpretation it might even be said to embody—and eventually to act out—the masculine aggressiveness of its creator. But from another point of view, throughout the novel the Creature may be said to be genderless or at least searching to establish a gender for itself. That desire of course is the point of the Creature's urging Frankenstein to create a suitable mate. It realizes that it can be truly male only in binary opposition to a female of its own kind.

In the absence of a mate, the Creature is forced to lead an existence that in terms of gender is profoundly indeterminate. As masculine as it may appear to be, at many points it is cast in a role that in the nineteenth century would have been viewed as feminine. The Creature, after all, in a curious way ends up speaking for the value of domestic life in opposition to Frankenstein, who, in his heroic quest as a creator, rejects the ties that would bind him to a conventional family. The Creature longs for precisely the warmth of hearth and home that its creator fails to appreciate. For all its strength, the Creature finds itself fixed in an essentially passive, reactive role, in which it is crucially dependent on the powers of its masculine creator to make it happy. The more one considers this aspect of the novel, the more one recognizes Mary Shelley's wisdom in associating the Creature with a poor, abandoned, persecuted female (the archetypal role assigned to the heroine in gothic fiction).

Discussion of Rousseau and Mary Wollstonecraft and of the issues of education and gender may seem at first to lead us away from the central concerns of *Frankenstein*. But as we have shown, the marginal becomes central in chapters 12–14 of *Frankenstein*. Mary Shelley brings together a strange group of liminal characters: the De Lacey family, exiled from their homeland for trying to help a foreigner; Safie, an Oriental in Europe, who is the daughter of "a Christian Arab, seized and made a slave by the Turks" (118); and finally of course the Creature, whose existence cuts across many boundaries and calls them into question. Is the Creature human or inhuman, animate or inanimate? In view of its hideousness conjoined with great power, is it a beast or a god? In view of the way it eventually turns the tables on Frankenstein, is it creature or creator? When students realize how persistently the Creature's existence works to subvert many of the conventional distinctions on which society rests, they can appreciate why in the deepest sense it appears monstrous to ordinary humanity. Thus the issue of marginalization is ultimately what ties together the diverse group of characters Mary Shelley juxtaposes in the middle of her novel and, more important, provides the most profound basis on which Mary Shelley, as a woman in the nineteenth century, could identify with her "hideous progeny," the Creature. In the end, by approaching *Frankenstein* from the Creature's perspective, teachers and students can connect the book with the most significant social and political issues of Mary Shelley's time, as well as raise some of the most pressing theoretical concerns of our own.

Teaching *Frankenstein*
in a General-Studies Literature Class:
A Structural Approach

Mary K. Thornburg

The first time I assigned *Frankenstein* to a class, I decided to give each student a brief chapter outline, which would help us keep the novel's events and characters straight during our discussion. I had no special teaching approach planned, but the book's length, number of characters, relative complexity of plot and setting, and especially its deviation from chronological order in the narrative recounting of events seemed to warrant a practical approach. When I looked at the outline I had prepared, however, I made a surprising observation. I could see patterns of movement, of balance among characters and events, in the architectonic design of the novel that not only clarified my previous understanding of relations, ideas, and key concepts but also suggested new ways of exploring the novel's significance.[1] I recommend this approach (or some modification of it) to anyone preparing to use this book in the classroom.

Although I drew up the structural outline myself the first time, I later realized that an outline is much more valuable to students if they prepare it and discover its patterns themselves. Individuals (or small groups, depending on class size) can be assigned one or more chapters for summary. The summary of each chapter should be very brief and should be worded so as to mention every separate significant event, including the specific participants. (Example: "Chapter 1—Victor tells of his parents' history and their marriage; he describes the adoption of Elizabeth." My own outline is appended to this essay. Although every class's outline will be slightly different in wording and perhaps even in the significant events it includes, these differences should not affect the usefulness of the outline, so long as discussion continues to refer closely to the book so that judgments of what is significant can remain flexible.) When the summaries are finished, the class as a group can examine and discuss them, modify them as desired (probably by paring extraneous words), and finally combine them in a finished version, which should be arranged so that the symmetry of the novel's five sections (Walton's opening and closing narratives and Victor's two-part narrative surrounding the Creature's story) is clear. The structural outline can be duplicated for student use (copies are especially helpful if students will write or make oral reports on the book) as well as projected on a screen or written on a chalkboard. The outline's effect is at least partly visual, so it is better to have it all on one page if possible.

Once the structural outline of *Frankenstein* is revealed, patterns will become apparent, and the class can begin to plot them graphically. (They can be marked in different colors on transparencies or on a chalkboard. Students seem to benefit from discovering and tracing these patterns individually, perhaps in felt-tipped highlighter pens, on their own copies of the outline; more than one copy might be made available to each student.) Among the patterns students will discover are those of plot synchronicity, of physical movement (the characters' travels), and of structural balance (since the outline will follow the novel's architectonic design, which is related but not identical to the plot structure).[2]

My classes mark plot structure first, assigning numbers to six time periods covered by the three narrators: (1) "historical" (the De Laceys' history, Walton's and Victor's family histories and early lives up to the death of Victor's mother); (2) Victor's studies in Ingolstadt before the Creature's completion; (3) the period between the Creature's completion and Justine's arrest; (4) the period from Justine's arrest to Victor's excursion to the British Isles; (5) the period from the British excursion to Victor and Elizabeth's marriage; and (6) the period from the wedding night to the end of the novel. These numbers, written beside the outline, make it clear what each narrator is doing during the periods of all three narratives. They also point out interesting parallels between incidents, such as the Creature's residence near the De Laceys and Victor's illness and confusion in Ingolstadt, and help to show the relations between the physical movements of the narrators.

After plot synchronicities have been established, physical movements can be shown for each narrator (and for other characters, if desired). At the top of the outline, my classes mark ten settings from west to east—the Orkneys, England, Italy, Geneva, Mont Blanc, the De Lacey cottage, Ingolstadt, Archangel (site of Walton's departure), the Arctic, and "darkness and distance" (the unknown region toward which the Creature moves at the end of the novel). Different colored lines plotting the movements of each narrator reveal patterns of clear thematic significance. For example, the novel's changes of physical setting, beginning and ending with movement toward and away from the Arctic regions, center—geographically and structurally—at the De Laceys' cottage in some unspecified rural area of western Europe. Characters cross and recross other points, and certain likenesses and contrasts among these places become visually apparent (for example, Mont Blanc, where Victor and the Creature meet and talk, and the De Lacey cottage are both central locations seeming to offer possibilities of reconciliation that are dashed by conflicts driving the characters apart). These lines also show important parallels between Victor's movements and those of the Creature, parallels that underscore the close relationship (and perhaps the unacknowledged parallels of purpose) between the two. When the narrators' physical movements are shown graphically over the structural outline, the balance of one setting against another becomes significant; moreover, when the movements of other characters (such as Clerval and Elizabeth) are introduced, contrasts involving amount of travel and reasons for travel become strikingly apparent. (Safie's journey to and from her home in North Africa, recounted in the De Laceys' story, presents an interesting contrast to the movements of the other female characters.)

Other sorts of movement—for example, what might be called the didactic movement (who learns what from whom; who teaches or attempts to teach someone else)—and other thematic movements can be plotted as well, perhaps on separate copies of the outline so that these patterns do not become confusing. At the same time, actually as part of this process, other patterns—patterns of balance among characters and incidents—will emerge. For example, Victor's account of Elizabeth's adoption falls almost exactly opposite his account of her death; the description of Victor and Elizabeth's visit to Justine in prison is balanced by the account of Victor's creation and destruction of the female creature; the death of Victor's mother and Victor's marriage to Elizabeth are also symmetrically balanced. Students may indicate these patterns of balance by circling or highlighting names or phrases on either side of the architectonic center of the novel—the Creature's recounting of the De Lacey family history—and by drawing light connecting lines from one to the other, in the margin or over the outline itself. The connections suggest relations that are sometimes obvious, sometimes surprising, and provide possible subjects for later discussion and study.

Students should now be ready to consider the relations and key concepts that these patterns suggest, either in class discussions or in individual and group reports, impromptu dramatizations, or written assignments.

Relations involving geographical setting may be explored with maps and pictures or verbal descriptions; for example, students may be helped to visualize contrasts and similarities between settings like the well-ordered commercial city of Geneva and the ancient university town of Ingolstadt, the picturesque majesty of the Alps and the raw Arctic wilderness. Individual characters and characters in combination (e.g., Elizabeth and Justine, Safie and Agatha, Victor and William, Clerval and the Creature) can confront each other dramatically as their positions within the structural outline suggest; these conjunctions are especially interesting when characters who do not actually encounter each other in the novel's plot are "brought together" and allowed to "discuss" topics of concern, through the medium of student dramatization. For example, what might Victor's father and M. Krempe or M. Waldman have to say to each other regarding the purpose of an education? What would emerge from a discussion of family relationships and feminine roles among Elizabeth, Justine, Agatha, and

Safie? Certain kinds of behavior (e.g., travel, courtship and marriage, study, letter writing) are engaged in by various characters throughout the book, and these behaviors, as suggested by the outline, may be explored in discussion or writing through comparison or contrast. All these activities bring out key concepts—home; relationships among parents, children, friends, and lovers; "ideal" masculine and feminine behavior; violence; creativity; and so on—which may be discussed as various characters or as the students themselves might define them.

An approach to *Frankenstein* based on the book's architectonic design can work by itself or, in modified form, with some other teaching strategy. Such an approach encourages the perception of the novel as a unified whole; presents plot, theme, characters, and setting visually and graphically as integral parts of the novel's structure; and provides students with a record of all the steps in the study process and of how those steps relate to one another and to the novel itself. Such a record may suggest reading and study strategies that students can bring to books they read in the future. The greatest value of this approach, it seems to me, is that it reveals *Frankenstein* as a living work of literature, one in whose meaning and significance each new reader and group of readers can continue to participate.

NOTES

[1] My understanding of *Frankenstein* is detailed in *The Monster in the Mirror*. In brief, it is that the Creature represents a combination of Victor's emotions and traits that he must reject as part of his conscious self-identity to conform to his culture's masculine ideal; in creating the Creature he is also "creating" himself as he must be in order to be worthy of the love and respect of society, his family, and especially Elizabeth. Since the self that Victor must adopt is a culturally formulated and essentially artificial construct, the other characters are actually collaborators in its formation and thus in the formation of the Creature, who is a figure of combined sensitivity, physical and emotional passion, strength, violence, and vengefulness. In my development of this idea, I am indebted to many writers, especially Kate Ellis, Masao Miyoshi, and Philip Stevick.

[2] Several writers have suggested that the architectonic design or structure of the gothic novel is a valuable aid to discovery of that novel's themes. In particular, I am grateful to Thomas Thornburg and Richard Jennings.

Appendix: A Sample Outline of *Frankenstein*'s Architectonic Design

Walton's Narrative	Letter 1	Walton looks for a ship, recalls his life's events
	Letter 2	He describes his crew
	Letter 3	His voyage of discovery begins
	Letter 4	He sights the Creature, meets and talks with Victor
Victor's Narrative	Chapter 1	Victor's parents' history; Elizabeth is adopted
	Chapter 2	Victor's happy childhood; his interest in science
	Chapter 3	His mother's death; to Ingolstadt; Krempe and Waldman
	Chapter 4	Work on the Creature; he neglects his family
	Chapter 5	The Creature awakens; Victor's illness and recovery
	Chapter 6	Elizabeth's first letter; Victor's decision to return to Geneva
	Chapter 7	His father's letter (William's death); his return home
	Chapter 8	Justine's trial; prison visit; Justine's death
	Chapter 9	Mourning and guilt; Victor's journey in the Alps
	Chapter 10	Victor meets the Creature on Mont Blanc
The Creature's Narrative	Chapter 11	The Creature's journey away from Ingolstadt
	Chapter 12	The Creature discovers the De Lacey family
	Chapter 13	Safie arrives; the Creature learns language
	Chapter 14	The De Laceys' family history
	Chapter 15	The Creature's books; he throws himself on the mercy of M. De Lacey: he is driven away by Felix
	Chapter 16	The Creature's revenge, flight, and suffering; his killing of William; his revenge on Justine
Victor's Narrative	Chapter 17	Victor's argument with the Creature; his promise to create a female creature
	Chapter 18	Procrastination; his father's worries; to England with Clerval
	Chapter 19	To Orkneys; work on female creature
	Chapter 20	Misgivings and destruction of the female; the Creature's rage; Victor is arrested
	Chapter 21	Imprisoned for Clerval's murder; saved by his father
	Chapter 22	Elizabeth's second letter; their marriage
	Chapter 23	The wedding night
	Chapter 24	Confused search for the Creature; his father's death and Victor's visit to magistrate; journey to Arctic
Walton's Narrative	Letter 4 (cont.)	Walton's ship in peril; his decision to turn back; Victor's death; the Creature's final appearance

Frankenstein in a Humanities Course

Donovan Johnson and Linda Georgianna

We have found that for a number of reasons *Frankenstein* works particularly well in an interdisciplinary course at a large public university. Our course is a three-quarter sequence that satisfies both the lower-division humanities breadth requirement and the freshman writing requirement. About thirty percent of our freshmen take the course, including a considerable number of biological science majors who are competing to enter medical school. In essence, the course is designed to give students a range of experience in reading and writing in the humanities. Our course objectives are to expose students to a wide variety of texts and issues and to give them practice responding to texts through a diversity of approaches. These objectives make the course substantially different from typical survey courses or courses that trace the history of Western civilization.

Each quarter is loosely organized by a theme, such as "violence in the modern world" or "the middle class in the nineteenth century." Emphasizing a particular theme enables us to give some consistent focus to the task of interpreting the various readings. Each quarter's instruction consists of two major elements: large lectures by faculty members on literature, history, and philosophy followed by small discussion and writing sections conducted by lecturers and advanced graduate students. Students attend two hours of lecture and two hours of section meetings each week. As a lecturer in the course and as the administrator responsible for its writing component, we work together to make sure that the integrated course objectives are met in each unit of the course.

Frankenstein is the focus of a unit in the fall quarter, during which term the theme is "knowledge and choice." This unit consists of two lectures, two discussion meetings, and an essay assignment. Including the novel in a unit on the development of the concepts of knowledge and choice in Western culture helps to highlight the text, particularly when it is read in juxtaposition to Dante's *Inferno*, which immediately precedes it in our course. Other texts treated in the fall term include Augustine's *Confessions*, Descartes's *Meditations*, and various contemporary texts dealing with questions of knowledge and choice in wartime. As with each of the readings assigned, students are given a set of study questions the week before they begin this unit to alert them to relevant passages and issues and to help them prepare for discussion. (See the list of study questions appended to this article.)

Three weeks of work on Augustine and Dante at the beginning of the quarter help students to develop one major set of terms and issues in relation to the theme of knowledge and choice. Then we introduce *Frankenstein* as a more recent reworking of some of these earlier conceptions. One of our aims is to demonstrate to students the complexity of the reading process itself. To that end, the lectures sketch out two plausible but rather contradictory readings of the novel. The lecturer works to make each reading as strong and plausible as possible in order to force students to develop readings that are truly their own. The first of these readings builds on the material of the first weeks of the course by asking students to read the novel through the eyes of Dante. The possibility of this reading is made concrete for students when we remind them of explicit and implicit references in the novel to *The Inferno* (57), to *Paradise Lost* (124), and to a number of Christian stories and beliefs.

The second reading, which we call the "monstrous" view both because it is largely articulated by the Creature and because many of Shelley's contemporaries considered it "foul" and blasphemous, suggests that humanity, like the Creature, was created by a vengeful or a perverse or at least a disinterested god. Human beings are "unfashioned creatures, but half made up" (27), and all their attempts at communion with others are thwarted by their own contradictory desires. In this view, knowledge brings not (as in Dante's view) salvation but envy, desire, and an increased consciousness of human alienation and suffering, relieved only by death, the extinction of all thought.

The first lecture, a reading of *Frankenstein* through the eyes of Dante, emphasizes the events leading up to the moment when Victor gives life to the Creature. By recalling one of the medieval genres introduced in the lectures on Dante, the exemplum, the lecture uses Victor's words to Walton to show how the frame story works to establish Frankenstein's narrative as an exemplum:

> When I reflect that you are pursuing the same course, exposing yourself to the same dangers which have rendered me what I am, I imagine that you may deduce an apt moral from my tale, one that may direct you if you succeed in your undertaking and console you in case of failure. (28)

This Dantean reading focuses on Victor's "moral failure": his choice to follow overreaching ambition ("What glory would attend the discovery if I could . . . render man invulnerable to any but a violent death!" [40]), his "fervent longing to penetrate the secrets of nature" (39), and his determination to "explore unknown powers, and unfold to the world the deepest mysteries of creation" (47). Inasmuch as Victor's unrestrained storm of enthusiasm to penetrate the secret of life isolates him, his *contrapasso* is the isolation imposed by the secret of the Creature's existence and the loss of life that dogs Victor wherever he goes. By contrast, the Creature's love of the De Lacey family and his desire for human ties highlight the perversity of Victor's isolating pride and ambition. Like the inhabitants of the inferno, Victor is a figure who both deludes himself to the end and actively promotes that delusion in others, as his speech to Walton's men reveals (203–04).

Following this lecture, discussion leaders begin by turning their meetings into workshops. Using the blackboard to model the process of developing writing from reading, they work out the exposition of a representative passage of the novel with the students. Then, by working with student-selected passages in small groups, they have students repeat this process. Some discussion leaders also help students to develop a close reading of a section of the novel, such as chapter 4, where the novel's major contradictions are established. Students are encouraged to look for evidence of Frankenstein's conflicting desires (such as to benefit humankind and to benefit himself) and the consequences of his choices (such as his increasing isolation and his preoccupation with death). Since many of the students taking the course are biological science majors, discussions become particularly lively when students are asked what Shelley finds worrisome about scientific pursuits.

The second lecture works primarily to construct the opposing, "monstrous" reading of the novel. This reading focuses on the Creature's Romanticist use of themes from *Paradise Lost* and from Christian tradition to interpret himself, his suffering, and the world. Identifying with both Adam and Satan in Christian tradition (124), the Creature reverses the traditional doctrine of original sin, reproaches his creator, and implores Frankenstein to bring him happiness:

> I ought to be thy Adam, but I am rather the fallen angel, whom thou drivest from joy for no misdeed. Everywhere I see bliss, from which I alone am irrevocably excluded. I was benevolent and good; misery made me a fiend. Make me happy, and I shall again be virtuous. (95–96)

Once the Creature's perspective is articulated, the second lecture concludes by listing and developing the contrasts between the Dantean and the monstrous views of knowledge and choice. In Dante's view, the Creator is all-knowing, all-good, and all-powerful. From the Creature's perspective, his creator is severely limited in what he knows and what he can accomplish, as well as flawed in what he intends toward his Creature. According to Dante, evil is the result of humanity's free choice, while the Creature considers it the result of deprivation. Finally, Dante believes that knowledge (of Christ, who is Love) can redeem, while the Creature's experience teaches him that knowledge brings increased consciousness of deprivation and that it leads ultimately to destruction for both creature and creator.

For the second discussion hour, discussion leaders guide students in extending the monstrous reading of the novel. Taking the lecture's exposition of the Creature's perspectives as a model and focusing on Walton's letters at the end of the novel, they ask students to flesh out the viewpoints of Frankenstein and Walton as well and then to compare the three viewpoints. Given their initial sense of the differences among these characters, students are often surprised to discover the striking ways in which each of the three also resembles the others, particularly in their ambivalence, in their metaphysical outlooks, and in their self-imposed struggles. Discussion leaders conclude the discussion by raising the question of our fascination with horror and asking students to relate their responses to the novel—which they generally express enthusiastically—and to Mary Shelley's explicit intention to "speak to the mysterious fears of our natures" (ix), the self-destructive capacity that lies close to the essence of self-knowledge in each of us.

In addition to the study questions that we distribute in advance, we hand out essay assignments. For this unit, students are to write the second in the series of three essays of three to five pages that constitutes their written work for the quarter. They choose between two assignments. The first allows them to define the parameters of their papers, while the second provides substantial focus and structure.

For the first option, we ask students to discuss in what ways and to what degree *Frankenstein* presents a reversal of certain beliefs basic to the traditional Christianity of Augustine and Dante. They are to select a particular concept or set of beliefs and to focus on a few major or representative passages to develop and support the contrast that they are attempting to describe. This topic invites students to build on what they have learned in the first three weeks of the course. It also motivates them to pay special attention to the contents of the lectures and to discern how those ideas relate to their own reading of the text. Using the lecture materials as prototypes, students learn to explore and articulate their particular interests and insights as they look at the cultural shift represented in the comparison of Dante and Shelley. We do not introduce the Romantic movement as such in this course. Nor do we explicitly stress what Northrop Frye characterizes as the great cultural and historical divide marked by Romanticism (3), although freshman students are for the most part fascinated by the tension between the two moments in Western tradition that this unit presents.

For the second, more structured paper option, students are asked to compare Ulysses's speech about exploring the ends of the earth in canto 26 of *The Inferno* (56–131) with the dying Frankenstein's speech to Walton's men (203–04). Students are to characterize what the two speeches reveal about Shelley's and Dante's contrasting attitudes toward knowledge. We remind them to consider these speeches carefully in relation to the contexts within which they appear. We suggest that they might make comparisons between what motivates Ulysses's desire for knowledge and what motivates Frankenstein's. We also suggest that they contrast the concepts of secret or forbidden knowledge that each work entails.

This second paper invites students to compare speeches that are often remarkably similar but that represent two different moments in the development of ideas of knowledge and choice. Because the passages are relatively brief, students must look closely at the boundaries of legitimate knowledge in each work as well as at the differences between Ulysses's desire for knowledge in *The Inferno* (and the role of that desire in his life and destiny) and the comparable desire and consequences in *Frankenstein*. In asking students to focus on speeches uttered in narrative works, we are asking them to pay attention to the rhetorical dimension and to the ideological and narrative dimensions. In this way we help students realize the complexity of these texts and of the reading process, both in their work as readers and in their work as writers.

Appendix: Study Questions

1. What are Walton's motives in traveling to the North? What are Frankenstein's motives in telling Walton his story? What does Frankenstein say that he and Walton have in common? How do the opening letters affect our expectations concerning the story itself? (letters)

2. What does Frankenstein say were his earliest interests and goals? How and why does he contrast his interests with those of his friend Henry Clerval? (ch. 2)

3. What are Frankenstein's motives in pursuing his scientific studies and discoveries? (chs. 2–4)

4. What "became a thing such as even Dante could not have conceived" (57)? In what sense could that thing be called Frankenstein's *contrapasso*? In what way does it differ? (ch. 5)

5. How does Frankenstein know that the Creature killed William? (ch. 7)

6. Describe the setting in which Frankenstein encounters the Creature in France. What is Frankenstein's reaction to the setting before he meets the Creature? (chs. 9–10)

7. Characterize the tone and style of the Creature's first words to Frankenstein, contrasting them with Frankenstein's speech to the Creature. Which of the two speeches sounds more moderate, learned, and reasonable? (ch. 10)

8. What is the demand the Creature speaks of on page 95, and why does he wait so long before specifying it?

9. In chapter 13, what view of human beings does the Creature infer from hearing *Ruins of Empires* read aloud? What definition of knowledge does he arrive at that makes him wish he had never "known [or] felt beyond the sensations of hunger, thirst, and heat" (115)? Who else in the novel voices this same wish and where does it occur in the book?

10. With what figures in *Paradise Lost* does the Creature compare himself when he begins his reading course in chapter 15? Why does he make these comparisons? Who in the Creature's own life has become "an omnipotent God warring with his creatures" (124)? Contrast the Creature's view of his creator with Dante's view of his.

11. Analyze the monster's argument that "the love of another will destroy the cause of my crimes" (140). What is his evidence and how does his story support his conclusion?

12. Examine Frankenstein's considerations and reasons for choosing not to create a mate for the Creature (158–59) and compare them with his reasons for creating the Creature in the first place. Has Frankenstein learned his lesson? If so, then how do you account for the disasters that follow? If not, explain what moral feelings he exhibits here.

13. Explain the sources of the interdependence between Frankenstein and the Creature during the chase in the final chapters. Why, for example, does the Creature leave clues and perhaps even food behind for his enemy?

14. What is the significance of the landscape that dominates the final scenes of the novel? Compare the setting and its significance with that of Coccytus in *The Inferno*.

15. Consider Walton's final assessment of Frankenstein as a "glorious creature . . . noble and godlike in ruin" (200).

16. Compare Frankenstein's remarks on the pursuit of glory on pages 203–04 with his earlier warnings to Walton on pages 25–26. With which set of remarks would Dante agree?

Bridging the Gulf:
Teaching *Frankenstein* across the Curriculum

Sylvia Bowerbank

I first taught *Frankenstein* to reluctant engineering students in a literature course instituted to bridge the "gulf of mutual incomprehension" between scientists and nonscientists—what C. P. Snow calls the "two cultures" (4). With a few exceptions, the students were initially antagonistic to the course. In response to a questionnaire on the first day, they generally dismissed the study of literature as a nonproductive, parasitic pursuit. Moreover, they were bewildered by literary criticism; one student complained that English teachers always "read too much into simple words." The course might be useful, they thought, if it taught them how to write lab reports. They chose to study engineering because it could lead not only to personal security and status but, potentially, to practical benefits for present and future generations. A literature course could, at best, wrote another student, "waste our time pleasantly." Their responses boiled down to a challenge: Why bother to study literature? The two cultures were face-to-face in the classroom.

What I learned from this teaching experience is that the compartmentalization of learning can be transformed into an asset in a literature course if it is addressed as an explicit theme. The course becomes an ongoing dialogue on the question, What kinds of knowledge are worth pursuing? To cultivate such a dialogue, I select interrelated readings, drawn from different historical periods, that deepen and challenge the students' present assumptions about knowledge. A typical reading list might include the following: Milton's *Paradise Lost* (at least books 4 and 9), Pope's *Essay on Man*, Blake's *Marriage of Heaven and Hell*, Ibsen's *Enemy of the People*, Doris Lessing's *Briefing for a Descent into Hell*, Marge Piercy's *Woman out of Time*, and Robert Pirsig's *Zen and the Art of Motorcycle Maintenance*. I also assign for comparison shorter works such as Wordsworth's "World Is Too Much with Us," Margaret Atwood's "Speeches for Dr. Frankenstein," and Howard Nemerov's "Cosmic Comics." Other useful readings can be found in *Poems of Science*, edited by John Heath-Stubbs and Phillips Salman. But, of all these works, *Frankenstein* most effectively engages the students' interest in the question of appropriate knowledge.

Frankenstein works well in the classroom for two reasons. First, the novel is an extensive, polarized exploration of two conflicting modes of knowing: the scientific mode and the sympathetic mode. The class may read the opening chapters of Victor Frankenstein's narrative as an account of a young man's choice between science and the arts, between a conquest over the unknown and a pursuit of harmony in his psyche and society. (Walton's less detailed framing story follows a similar pattern.) The teacher can quickly illustrate this pattern by showing how the minor characters work as polarized alternatives for Victor Frankenstein. At the one extreme is Professor Waldman, the representative for modern Prometheanism, who encourages Victor's scientific ambition to acquire "new and almost unlimited powers" over nature (47). At the other extreme is Elizabeth who, as "the living spirit of love," nurtures sympathy and social harmony (37). It is she who influences Clerval to study literature and to seek moral wisdom rather than power. Likewise, the Creature, because of his experience and education, undertakes a doomed search for sympathy. The novel's dire consequences stem from Victor's failure to value these two modes appropriately. But what is the appropriate value? This question excites students if teachers encourage them to connect Victor's dilemma to their own educational choices and to the personal and social consequences of those choices.

The second reason for *Frankenstein*'s success in the classroom lies in its lack of certainty. Because inconsistent characters narrate the novel from contradictory points of view, the reader cannot resolve the novel's dilemma by appealing to an authoritative position. The weakest lecture I ever gave on *Frankenstein* floundered because I repeated my published "solution" to the textual problems. All I left the students to do was to get it down in their notes. Fortunately, the novel's gaps, inconsistencies, and flaws work against the expert in the classroom and foster interpretative initiative. Readers are left to discuss and reconcile the polarities at the heart of the novel and of our culture.

My experience is based on teaching *Frankenstein* to large classes (100 or so students) that meet three times weekly, for two hours of lectures and one hour of tutorial discussion. I use the lectures to explore not only what *Frankenstein* says about the tension between the scientific and sympathetic modes of knowing but also how its gothic style works to complicate and deepen the understanding of that tension. Good lecturers, I believe, try to reveal their own processes of assessing materials and constructing an interpretation while nurturing the same process, but not necessarily the same interpretation, in students. One reliable strategy I use is to begin each lecture session by writing on the board the question the students will discuss in the next tutorial. With *Frankenstein*, a basic question works well at the start: Is Mary Shelley's novel as a whole in favor of or opposed to scientific knowledge? The question on the board as I lecture reminds the students that the process of knowing involves their engagement and assessment of the materials being presented.

My lecture offers two perspectives: an authoritative and a personalizing one. On the one hand, I provide the basic scholarly information a reader should know about *Frankenstein*—historical context, conventions of genre, biographical background, and key critical approaches taken in the past. On the other hand, I ask students to consider how this material is useful to their interpretations of the novel and to their resolutions of the issues the novel explores. I invite them to scrutinize the critical methods and theoretical assumptions I bring to my interpretations, and I both advance and undercut my views and those of other experts sufficiently to empower the students to venture fresh interpretations.

Thus, the students begin to understand that they have a personal stake in the choices available to Victor Frankenstein. I ask them to reflect on their own educational choices: Why are they pursuing arts or sciences? If they have further specialized, why did they choose commerce, history, geography, biology, or engineering? What personal and social reasons led them to reject other disciplines? These questions lead us back to the central problem: What kinds of knowledge should we pursue and why?

To encourage students to take a position, I have them discuss a one-page excerpt from Robert Pirsig's *Zen and the Art of Motorcycle Maintenance*, which contrasts the two modes of modern thinking (73–75). I ask the students to explain in writing why they identify with one mode or the other of the two modes. Although Pirsig's use of *classic* and *romantic* risks introducing a confusion of terms, the students easily recognize the familiar battle lines between the sciences and the humanities and are eager to debate. Here's part of his contrast:

> The romantic mode is primarily inspirational, imaginative, creative, intuitive. Feelings rather than facts predominate. "Art" when it is opposed to "Science" is often romantic. It does not proceed by reason or by laws. It proceeds by feeling, intuition and esthetic conscience. . . .
>
> The classic mode, by contrast, proceeds by reason and by laws— which are themselves underlying forms of thought and behaviour. . . . The classic style is straightforward, unadorned, unemotional, economical and carefully proportioned. Its purpose is not to inspire emotionally, but to bring order out of chaos and make the unknown known. (73–74)

Even a brief debate reveals that the classroom is a microcosm of the cultural split Pirsig describes. I suggest that the students respond to the whole passage because Pirsig goes on to examine how each mode simplifies, misunderstands, and underestimates the other mode. It is a short step from Pirsig's distinctions to Mary Shelley's contrast between the scientist Victor Frankenstein's pursuit of knowledge and that of the poet Henry Clerval (37, 66–67). Both *Frankenstein* and *Zen and the Art of Mo-*

torcycle Maintenance confront readers with the need to reconcile the split in modern intellectual life. I encourage the students to keep their written responses and, after we study *Frankenstein*, to check whether the novel has confirmed or changed their viewpoints and why. In the light of their own experiences, they assess the literary critic's claim that literature can foster a more holistic way of knowing.

As they read the novel, students readily see its pattern of dichotomized thinking. I use the lectures to enrich their reading by locating this pattern in its historical context. I draw their attention to the basic duality implied in the subtitle, *The Modern Prometheus*. The mythic Prometheus who brings fire from the gods to human beings also brings knowledge that allows human beings to control and transform their environment. In the ancient world Prometheus is bound, but in the modern world Prometheus becomes, in Marx's words, "the loftiest saint" of materialistic progress. The subtitle signals that the novel is about not just an individual but a cultural type; the "modern Prometheus" includes the scientist Victor Frankenstein and also Walton, the would-be discoverer of the North Pole, and all other contributors to human ascendancy.

To re-create ancient attitudes toward knowledge, I draw on three well-known sources: Hesiod's writings, Aeschylus's *Prometheus Bound*, and Genesis, chapter 3. The remnants of the Greek myth, as represented in Hesiod's "Works of Days" and "Theogony," describe Prometheus as a proud and deceitful thief, champion of the human species who steals fire and teaches us to aspire above our place in the natural order. But since the rightful, if regrettable, order of Zeus cannot be escaped, Prometheus is chained to a rock and his immortal liver is eaten again and again by an eagle. In *Prometheus Bound*, Aeschylus allows for a tragic ambivalence in the eternal conflict between Prometheus and Zeus, rebel and ruler. The acquisition of knowledge leads to an improvement in the material conditions of existence; yet human beings must suffer the consequences of Promethean pride. Prometheus symbolizes human ingenuity and progress, but he remains rightfully bound. Even the lost third part of Aeschylus's trilogy, *Prometheus Delivered*, would have reconciled Prometheus to Zeus's order, an outcome Percy Shelley calls a "catastrophe" in his preface to *Prometheus Unbound*. The ancients, in general, advocated restraining Promethean spirit. The biblical attitude toward knowledge, as expressed in Genesis 3, is similarly restrictive: aspiring to forbidden knowledge produces Adam and Eve's banishment from paradise.

To contrast the ancient attitude with the modern, I move briefly to the seventeenth-century battle of the ancients and moderns. On the one hand, Milton's *Paradise Lost*, for example, favors the ancient view that values moral perspective over acquisition of knowledge. When Adam accepts the true instructions given by Raphael, he learns appropriate knowledge. When Eve and Adam eat of the tree, they fall into the limited reasoning of humanity. To acquire knowledge is to understand how the material world works; to seek wisdom is to rehabilitate human reason in order to resee the world from a higher—a divine—perspective. On the other hand, the seventeenth-century writings of Francis Bacon promote the modern emphasis on useful learning; modern philosophers sought the advancement of learning to improve the material condition of human life.

My choices of Bacon and Milton are not arbitrary. Echoes of their writings help create the tension between moral and scientific knowledge in *Frankenstein*. In the early chapters, Baconian language abounds. Moreover, Mary Shelley selected the passages in which Bacon particularly advocates dominance over nature. I give the students a passage or two from Bacon's writing to show what I mean; for example, in *New Organon*, Bacon advises new philosophers to "penetrate" nature to "find a way at length into her inner chambers" (329). (Students can pursue this theme in Merchant, ch. 7.) In *Frankenstein*, the modern Prometheans are identifiably Baconian. Waldman defends the modern philosophers because they "penetrate into the recesses of nature and show how she works in her hiding-places" for "the solid advantage of mankind" (47, 48). Walton aspires to "tread a land never before imprinted by the foot of man"; he will confer an "inestimable benefit" on humanity; he will acquire "dominion" over "elemental foes" (15, 16, 26). The young Victor Frankenstein longs to unveil and "penetrate the secrets of nature"; he seeks to "pioneer a new way"; he pursues "nature to her hiding-places" (39, 47, 53). Mary Shelley's modern Prometheus achieves the highest of human aspirations to divinity: "A new species would bless me as its creator . . ." (52). But when the consequences of human progress are guilt, horror, and destruction, Victor falls back on the ancient attitude; for instance, he warns that intellectual success is "a serpent to sting you" (28), reflecting the belief that the original sin is acquiring knowledge.

To clarify *Frankenstein*'s cultural meaning, I find it particularly useful to contrast Mary Shelley's treatment of triumphant Prometheanism with those of her famous relatives, William Godwin, Mary Wollstonecraft, and Percy Shelley. A few passages from Godwin's *Enquiry concerning Political Justice* show that he shared the Baconian faith that the human estate could be restored through science and technology. Particularly relevant is the chapter "Of Health, and the Prolongation of Human Life," in which Godwin speculates that the human mind might overcome the death of the body and thus create a race of cultivated, virtuous adults impervious to the natural processes of childbearing and dying. Likewise, Percy Shelley's

Prometheus Unbound prophesies the triumph of Prometheus and our species's intellectual conquest of earth:

> The lightning is his slave, heaven's utmost deep
> Gives up her stars, and like a flock of sheep
> They pass before his eye, are numbered, and roll on.
> The tempest is his steed, he strides the air;
> And the abyss shouts from her depth laid bare,
> Heaven, has thou secrets? Man unveils me; I have
>   none.   (4.1.420–25)

To ensure that the students do not simplistically reduce *Frankenstein*'s
message to its overt didactic one, I confront them with the problem of
Victor Frankenstein's internal confusion. Victor tells his story to teach Walton to seek the values of conservative harmonism: "how much happier that
man is who believes his native town to be the world, than he who aspires
to become greater than his nature will allow" (52). Yet, in the end, he
exhorts Walton's crew not to return to their safe firesides but to continue
to the North Pole: "You were hereafter to be hailed as the benefactors of
your species. . . . Oh! Be men, or be more than men" (203–04). His last
words sum up his contradictory perspective: "Seek happiness in tranquillity and avoid ambition, even if it be only the apparently innocent one of
distinguishing yourself in science and discoveries. Yet why do I say this? I
have myself been blasted in these hopes, yet another may succeed" (206).
Once encouraged, the students will find many similar examples in which
Victor vacillates between advocating the values of staying home, cultivating
sympathy and harmony, and the values of enterprise, cultivating science
and progress.

Does *Frankenstein* favor or oppose scientific progress? Or, in other
words, is Mary Shelley a radical or a conservative? During the first discussion hour, I ask the students to take a position on the question and to give
significant reasons and textual evidence in support of their position. I
stress that the students should use the ensuing debate to refine (or rein-
force or even refute) their initial positions. This is a complex process, but
one illustration may indicate in general how it works. One usually reticent
engineering student came to class feeling that *Frankenstein* was an attack
not on science but on a bad scientist. During discussion he ferreted out
more and more textual details, mostly from chapters 3–5, to convict Victor
Frankenstein of violating the scientific code: (1) Victor is motivated by self-
glory rather than the public good. (2) For that reason, he rushes the
project, thus creating a gigantic monster. (3) He works in isolation and in

secret when he should work with colleagues who might restrain and evaluate his work. (4) He is too emotionally unstable for discovery; otherwise, why does he collapse in horror? A good scientist would see creating a monster as part of the trial-and-error process, as an experiment and not as a disaster. (5) He is ethically unsound in letting his experiment out of the lab without considering the consequences. The other students were not necessarily convinced that this was the ideal interpretation of *Frankenstein*, but they respected the engineer's skillful reconciliation of his personal values with an authoritative reading of the text. Discussion elicits a stimulating diversity of readings, and together students come to tolerate ambiguity and complexity.

The question for the second discussion hour is, What is the nature of Victor Frankenstein's guilt? It helps the students to get at the complexities of this question if they discuss it in three stages: How would each of the following characters answer the question: Walton, the Creature, Elizabeth, Clerval, Justine, Alphonse, Victor? How would Margaret Saville, the designated reader, answer the question after reading all of Walton's letters? How do the students answer the question? This third question is crucial in healing another manifestation of the compartmentalization of knowledge, namely, the widespread student habit of distinguishing between "what I really feel and think" and "what I say and write for courses." Many students consider this distinction necessary for academic survival, the tragic result being that they rarely see the classroom as a place to assess, develop, and integrate their intellectual, social, and personal pursuits. I repeatedly urge them to use the course as a place to discover what they want to argue about a topic. I ask the students to express their feelings on a topic, and then I help them gradually take responsibility for their views and assess the intellectual and social implications of holding such views.

If the discussion on guilt goes well, the students will progress from treating Victor as an individual to recognizing that he is a cultural type and from talking about the imaginary events in the novel to naming current Promethean successes. They easily supply examples of great inventions—everything from DDT to thalidomide--that went awry when released from the lab into society. For example, as I was teaching *Frankenstein* in January 1986, the space shuttle Challenger exploded. In an interview broadcast across Canada on the CBC, one NASA engineer described his anguish: he had spent years in careful research to benefit humankind; the step-by-step conquest of space had made him feel "godlike"; but tonight, he said, "I feel like a squashed Prometheus." Recent attempts to "play" the Creator—cloning, artificial intelligence, test-tube babies—are also relevant. Like Victor Frankenstein's successful "maternity" in the lab, these discoveries provoke the difficult ancient question about whether there should be limits to the pursuit of knowledge. Should science concern itself only with technical expertise—how it can be done—and neglect the moral question of whether it should be done? What I hope will come out of the discussion is an awareness of our profound ambivalence toward science. Discoveries may improve the human lot, but their consequences are often unforeseen and horrifying. Despite our technological successes, our modern culture shares the novel's tension between intellectual and moral knowledge. Is it the triumphant Prometheus that symbolizes humanity for us or the self-doubting, failed Frankenstein?

At the end of my first term of teaching engineering students, I asked them a final question: Which work studied in the course most challenges and transforms the contemporary reader's understanding and why? Most of them answered *Frankenstein*, which is perhaps not surprising given the personal relevance of the novel's theme. "*Frankenstein*," wrote one student, "questions the basic code I live by." Many students identified with Victor Frankenstein's tragic dilemma: "As an engineer," one student reported, "I believe science must be pursued to create a better world; yet, as the novel warns, the pursuit is unnatural and ultimately destructive." Even more remarkable, these students came to appreciate the novel as a "mosaic of unreliable viewpoints." The conflicting sympathies required of the reader of *Frankenstein* allowed them "to see the problem of the scientist's responsibility from various angles." From their struggle with *Frankenstein* and other works, they came to recognize why literature deliberately refuses to simplify an issue. One student even conceded that engineers needed to know "more about people and culture, which can best be learned through literature." Not all but most of the students appreciated the way literature could sensitize a reader to a more complex and holistic perspective on science. As one student discovered, "It is very necessary for engineers to understand that rational thinking and technology are only one aspect of our human experience." Clearly, the bridging of the "two cultures" can start in classroom conversations about the meaning of *Frankenstein*.

Reading *Frankenstein:*
Writing and the Classroom Community
Art Young

I teach *Frankenstein* in a junior-level course entitled The Romantic Age, a ten-week study of British Romantic poetry and prose that fulfills a humanities requirement. Most of my students are engineering or science majors who have no previous experience with college-level literature courses. In recent years, I have incorporated writing-across-the-curriculum techniques to provide opportunities for students to write their way to an understanding of literary texts.

Proponents of writing across the curriculum encourage teachers in every discipline to integrate writing into content courses so that students will have extensive opportunities to use writing both to develop knowledge (writing to learn) and to express that knowledge to others (writing to communicate). In addition to helping students gain proficiency with the written word, such programs encourage students to become active learners, capable of making meaningful contributions in a variety of contexts. Although my course includes several different writing assignments—critical essays, essay tests, poems, journals—in teaching *Frankenstein* I use a less traditional "writing-to-learn" assignment: a personal letter written to classmates that describes the writer's response to the novel. This assignment suggests a purpose and an audience different from those of the self-sponsored journal entries and critical essays that students submit for formal evaluation. Students think critically about the novel, share their reading experiences with classmates, and together develop knowledge about the novel. The letter assignment is designed to enhance the experience of reading literature for students who are skeptical of literary study and will probably not take another literature class.

Many of my students are not confident readers of literature. Some have confessed that they have difficulty finding the "deep meaning" in poems and fiction or that they never get out of a particular reading what the teacher got out of it. These students have a real need to feel empowered to read and talk about literature independent of the teacher's "deep meanings." The letter assignment puts into practice the pedagogical stance of Louise M. Rosenblatt: "Instead of a contrast or break between the ordinary reader and the knowledgeable critic, we need to stress the basic affinity of all readers of literary works of art. The general reader needs to honor his own relationship with the text" (140). My goal is to help students feel confident and competent as readers. They write to make discoveries about the novel and to provide a basis for collaborative activities with their classmates.

Students with technical backgrounds often feel as alienated from writing about literature as they do from reading literature. In conference, they confide that they "hate writing," that they have always done much better in math than in English. The personal-letter assignment engages these reluctant readers and writers. First, the form is familiar; most students have written and read letters previously, they read selected letters of the Romantics in my course, and they recognize the epistolary form of Mary Shelley's novel. The salutation and the acknowledgment of the reader with which most letters open enable students to begin writing with the sureness of recognition. Conversational in tone and style, the personal letter often mediates students' initial experiences with academic discourse. Writers can express emotions such as surprise or confusion because they imagine a friendly audience, one with whom they have shared experiences. They expect the teacher to read these letters as a trusted mentor who is willing to overlook mistakes in order to encourage risk taking. They know that the personal letter, like other writing-to-learn assignments, is not formally evaluated or graded. And finally, the rhetorical and expressive functions of the letter form allow student writers to focus their attention on their experience of *Frankenstein*. They can escape the anxiety and divided attention that frequently attend a less accessible and more demanding form such as the critical essay.

Before beginning our week-long study of *Frankenstein*, I distribute a list of over forty questions to preview the novel for the students, most of whom will have time to read it only once. Typical questions might ask students to determine whether Frankenstein is responsible for his actions or to assess the effects of hearing the story from the point of view of both Frankenstein and the Creature. The questions provide students with a sense of the possibilities *Frankenstein* presents to them as ordinary readers. During the same class period, I describe the letter-writing assignment, which is due the next class period. The letter should be brief—around three hundred words in length or about a half hour of composition. It should include a salutation and read like a personal letter to classmates. I tell the students that I will write a letter as well and that everyone will read everyone else's letters. Our goal is to share ideas and impressions about the novel with one another and perhaps see the novel anew as we learn together.

In preparing to teach *Frankenstein* in my course during the fall quarter of 1986, I wrote the following letter to my students:

Dear Classmates,

I enjoy reading and teaching *Frankenstein*. The novel, full of interesting speculations, was written by nineteen-year-old Mary when she and Percy Shelley were living in Switzerland with Lord Byron as a neighbor. The novel reveals many of the issues these young radicals were thinking about in the early 1800s. . . .

Mary Shelley's book is about human potential and human limitations, about the danger of pursuing science for its own sake—independent of moral values. Frankenstein, as you may remember, said he was only interested in science, and he left poetry to Elizabeth and moral reasoning to Clerval. I believe this was his flaw, along with his immense pride. He wanted to build a race that would worship him as a god—as their creator—and this pride blinded him to the poetry of creation and the moral consequences of his action.

When we consider what would have happened if Frankenstein had had better-developed moral and poetic sensibilities, interesting questions arise: Would he have created the Creature at all? Would he have created a being that was handsome and thus capable of entering society? Does modern science still pursue Frankenstein's dream?

Art

This letter was my attempt to enter the conversation as an ordinary reader in the context of a class devoted to reading Romantic literature. I wanted the letter to capture my enthusiasm for the novel yet focus on my experience of reading the novel. I gave each student a copy of the letter only after class discussion so that my participation in the assignment would not silence the conversation.

In the next class period, after a short lecture on Mary Shelley's life, the students broke into groups of four or five. Group members read their letters aloud and then asked questions, suggested clarifications, and compared ideas. During these discussions I divided my time among the groups, and then the entire class spent the remaining class time talking together. We discovered the areas that seemed to interest us most (Frankenstein's character and the question of his responsibility for his actions, the connections to modern science, the similarities to the Genesis story), analyzed the reasons for our interest, and considered other issues raised by our readings. The discussion was enhanced by our personal writing and our developing status as a community of learners.

Later, while reviewing the students' letters, I saw glimpses of the individual reading experiences that shaped our discussion of the parallel with the Genesis story. Here, in part, is what two students wrote:

Fellow Classmates,

I have just finished reading Frankenstein. After our readings and class discussions on the role of women during the 1700s and 1800s, it greatly surprises me to find the author of this imaginative novel to be a woman. Mary Shelley was indeed a woman of gifted talents.

One question that arose in my reading was what relationship does *Frankenstein* have to the Biblical Genesis story? The creature often refers to himself as the "Old Adam." Just as the Biblical account of God creating Adam; so had Victor Frankenstein created this creature. Yet, once Victor had seen what he had created and it showed signs of life, he fled. God, being both omnipotent and omniscient, never left Adam nor has he ever left us. Just as the creature learned to take care of his physical needs; so had Adam. The creature also sought from his creator a helpmate; so had Adam. Victor Frankenstein would not make a female companion for the creature. He realizes his creature had been the cause of the deaths of two innocent people, William and Justine. I understand the parallel of the creature & Adam, but the parallels of Victor Frankenstein & God stop after the creatures are created. Victor lacked a master plan for his creature. . . .

Maggie

. . . I noticed how similar the creature's predicament is to how ours is or at least seems to be at times. Adam and Eve were created perfect in the eyes of the creator, then they ate the apple and were kicked out of the Garden of Eden and in God's eye were probably much the same as the creature is to Frankenstein. Generally speaking God ignored Adam and Eve as Frankenstein tried to ignore the creature. Now as supposed descendants of Adam and Eve we try to get God's attention and try to get him to listen to us and help us as the monster tried to get Frankenstein to listen to him. The creature wants someone to share things with and someone to talk to who won't run away or be scared, someone to know him as a friend and maybe more. We all want that to different extents. The creature is asking Frankenstein for this other part of himself as many people ask it of God. . . .

Carol

In working out the implications of the parallels between *Frankenstein* and the Genesis story, Maggie and Carol related both stories to perceptions of human and divine purpose and to questions of responsibility and right action. At the beginning of her letter (not reproduced here), Maggie referred to previous class discussions of Mary Wollstonecraft, Dorothy Wordsworth, and the role of women in society. Many other students began or ended their letters with similar references to establish rapport with their readers. This rhetorical strategy also fulfilled an important reading strategy—to relate new experiences to old ones and to read each writer in the context of other writers and our community's previous experience. Maggie had made certain predictions about women writers of the early 1800s based on her limited reading experience and on some generalities generated by class discussion. When Mary Shelley did not fulfill those predictions, Maggie's surprise instigated reevaluation. She discovered that texts by women writers of the Romantic period could delight and inform— could lead her to pose questions worth asking and to develop knowledge worth having. Maggie compared and contrasted *Frankenstein* with her understanding of the Genesis story, but she was firm in stating that parallels between Frankenstein and God were not warranted after each had made his creation. Frankenstein tried to play God without a master plan, a plan he could not have developed, being neither omnipotent nor omniscient. Maggie assumed that her readers, her classmates, shared with her a common understanding and interpretation of the Genesis story.

Carol imagined a God quite unlike Maggie's, one whose attitude toward his fallen creature is similar to Frankenstein's attitude toward his awakened Creature. Both creators loathe and try to ignore what they have created. Victor's Creature asks his creator to give meaning to his life, just as we, the "supposed descendants" of Adam and Eve, ask God to give meaning to ours. Carol, too, assumed that her readers were familiar with the biblical story, but she did not assume that they shared a common interpretation of that story, as her use of the qualifier *supposed* indicates.

Both students were able to contribute to the class's understanding of *Frankenstein* through their written reflections in the letters. Carol wrote as if she were searching for further possibilities to explore, while Maggie's search appeared to stop with her assertion that the parallels "stop." In group and class discussion of these issues, both students were invited to consider further the ability of this text and our readings of it to enhance our understanding of personal experience and the experience of others.

In their letters, some students also speculated about the characters of Victor Frankenstein and his Creature, about why they acted as they did, about how they changed in the course of the novel:

> Dear Classmates,
>
> Wow! What a difference between the book and the movie! This is so much better. This book made me feel a sadness inside, that a novel never before has. There was sadness in nearly every circumstance in this book. What happened to Victor, the "creature," William, Justine, and so forth. All were sad.
>
> After hearing Victor's creation's tale, I was intrigued by the public's response to the creature. When Victor spoke of the creature's

abhorrent appearance, it didn't affect me at all. However, when the creature spoke of the public's response to his appearance, I felt sadness and compassion for him. I guess I feel that the creature was "guiltless" until he was judged so harshly by the rest of the world. To me, the monster was a newborn child, in a sense. He was not responsible for his creation, yet he had to suffer for it. This is somewhat like the child who's crippled at birth, and made fun of only based on his handicap.

I feel that people (and creatures, too) are born into this world as "good," and society and environment in turn mold them as evil. This goes back to the concept of childly innocence. I believe that the child is closer to God, naturally, than the experienced adult (like Wordsworth) who has been corrupted by society. . . .

Mark

. . . Frankenstein is guiltless as far as I am concerned. Yes, he created the creature, but I do not think there is any problem here. . . . Frankenstein is not capable of being responsible. I find it hard to make someone responsible for something they are not capable of. . . .

Carl

. . . Victor Frankenstein really hasn't grown through his experiences. At the end of the book, he tried to convince the sailors not to turn back from their quest for glory, no matter what the cost may be. That is the very type of thinking that started the whole story. . . .

Dee

Mark's letter had a familiar, conversational tone. He alluded to a common cultural experience, the movie version of the Frankenstein story. He used language colloquially, including patterns of expression (exclamations, fragments) that are closer to speech than to formal written discourse. The rhetorical strategies both assume and create a sympathetic audience to which he could comfortably express his feelings about the novel, about the "sadness inside." Mark reported that Victor's story about the Creature "didn't affect [him] at all" but that the story in the Creature's own words gave him a sense of "sadness and compassion." To explore the surprising empathy he felt for the Creature and to relate that feeling to a familiar personal experience, he developed the analogy of the "child who's crippled at birth." He analyzed his reading experience in terms of his perception of evil and his prior reading of Wordsworth's "Ode: Intimations of Immortality." Mark, a reticent student, used the invitation accorded by the form of the personal letter to communicate his experience and understanding of the novel to his classmates. Ordinarily he declined such invitations in class-room conversation. Nor did he attempt to express the emotional base of his reading experience in the formal critical essays assigned in the course.

In the brief selections I have quoted, Carl and Dee referred to episodes in the novel to support a judgment on Frankenstein's actions throughout the novel. Carl insisted that Frankenstein was ignorant about what he was doing and therefore could not be held responsible for his actions. That this was a minority viewpoint within our community surprised Carl, but he continued to develop this position in class discussion and subsequent journal entries. Dee expressed an interpretation of Frankenstein's character that was representative of the majority opinion, but she had the opportunity to hear from readers like Carl who disagreed with her.

After reading the letters, I put them on reserve in the library for the students to read. I asked them to synthesize the differing impressions with their own sense of the novel and to write journal entries that developed their perspectives in the light of this collaborative experience. Some examples of what they wrote follow:

> . . . I too think Frankenstein and Walton are much alike. After Tuesday's discussion I went back to the book and when Walton is telling Frankenstein's tale the creation is a "monster" but when Walton is telling about his conversation, the monster becomes a "demon." Walton is the adventurer so ready and willing to believe this fantastic tale. . . .
>
> Judy

> . . . Science is still like this today to some extent. They try to be moralistic but sometimes society itself demands that we advance so fast that not all the precautions are taken or something unforeseen happens. This was proven quite recently by the space shuttle explosion. The people responsible took turns laying the blame at each other's door but basically the pressure to advance quickly hurried things too much, pressure from society, government and the scientists themselves. . . .
>
> Marie

> . . .The comments on moral judgment are also interesting. I see many students here who have as little concern for arts and philosophy as did Frankenstein. Thus, the novel raises questions even today, as our class discussion showed. . . .
>
> Bernie

Reviewing classmates' letters led Judy and other students to reread portions of the text to clarify past readings or to correct misreadings. Some students joined Marie in relating *Frankenstein* to global events such as the shuttle explosion; others echoed Bernie in relating the novel to their immediate experiences, recognizing similarities between Frankenstein's attitudes toward science and the attitudes of students on campus.

Personal letters generate lively exchanges about the novel, orally and in writing, within the classroom community. Students learn to value their experience as ordinary readers and writers, and they understand how writing can lead to discoveries about literature for themselves and for others. They come to appreciate the value, pleasure, and usefulness of reading literature as the ordinary reader does: that they may engage in a conversation with authors, texts, and readers about issues of importance, and mutual interest, an engagement that can lead to self-knowledge and social empowerment.[1]

NOTE

[1] I want to thank my students for permission to quote from their writing. Their names have been changed to protect their privacy.

FRANKENSTEIN AND FILM

Lost Baggage: Or, The Hollywood Sidetrack

Harriet E. Margolis

As someone trained in comparative literature, I straddle various fences; for this essay I write in the guise of a "film person" teaching *Frankenstein* within the context of a film and literature class. While I can imagine a film class (probably a genre class focusing on horror films) that would include *Frankenstein* films without requiring a reading of Shelley's original, I cannot imagine a literature class including the novel without confronting the Hollywood versions of Mary Shelley's vision. Hollywood's influence over contemporary consumptions of the *Frankenstein* text is the topic that I wish to address here.

First, though, a word on sources. While films of *Frankenstein* have proliferated over the years, the *locus classicus* is the 1931 version adapted from Peggy Webling's play and directed by James Whale—the film that established Boris Karloff as a star, however typecast thereafter he may have been. *The Bride of Frankenstein* followed in 1935, with the same director and with Colin Clive and Boris Karloff again as "Henry" Frankenstein and "The Monster," respectively. The 1931 version drifts far from the shores of Shelley's original; the 1935 version makes efforts to right the course. Surprising as it may seem, given Mel Brooks's image, *Young Frankenstein* (1974; written by Gene Wilder, who plays the title character, and Mel Brooks, who directs) most lovingly hugs the contours of Shelley's landscape—and of the 1931 *Frankenstein* and of *The Bride of Frankenstein*. An obviously careful parody, *Young Frankenstein* is also a pastiche, deriving much of its humor from its egregious revisions of familiar images from such films as *King Kong* and *Dr. Strangelove* as well as from its more direct sources. In many ways, *Young Frankenstein* sticks closest to the concerns of Shelley's original; it may even be read as a serious and reassuring response to those concerns, a discovery students soon make when they discuss the specific similarities and differences in setting, characters, dialogue, and episodes among the novel, the 1931 and 1935 Hollywood versions, and Brooks's parody.

What, though, of the nonfilmic sources? How aware are contemporary students of Shelley's original concerns? The controversial scene on the lakeshore in which the Creature and the little girl play together with flowers—a scene whose unhappy conclusion usually gets censored—originated in theatrical versions (Tropp 87); quite unlike Shelley's novel, this scene and its variant in *Young Frankenstein* suggest that children, at least, find the Creature acceptable rather than horrific. Admitting the fallibility of marketing research, we must nevertheless allow the suggestion since, among other products targeted at children, Frankenberry cereal has met with some commercial success (its television advertisements have included precisely the lakeshore scene between Maria and the Creature excerpted from *Frankenstein* [1931]). From the 1930s on, children have accepted the Creature with fascination and delight; Shelley's original Creature would no doubt be thrilled except that his modern incarnation bears little kinship to the embittered and vengeful yet noble and enlightened savage who speaks for himself in the novel.

Significantly, it is "The Monster's Story," in which the Creature does speak for himself, that gets excerpted in the second volume of the Macmillan anthology *Literature of the Western World* (ed. Wilkie and Hurt), a basic text for introductory literature courses at many colleges and universities. For example, in my experience teaching *Frankenstein*, it was for various reasons impossible to expect the whole class to have read the entire novel. However, since the students had all completed a required class that used the Macmillan anthology as textbook, I could ask them to read the excerpt. Purists may object to a study of *Frankenstein* based on a fragment, but pragmatists will acknowledge the working possibility of the compromise. Although I think the Macmillan excerpt would be more useful if it also included the opening letters from Robert Walton to his sister, "The Monster's Story" nevertheless persuades students that Shelley's novel differs greatly from what most of us grew up with as the Frankenstein myth.

Generally, at least one student asserts that the original text has certain rights and that films of novels (or other originals) should stick to their base texts without modifications. I respond that cinema and literature are two different art forms, working with different limitations and opportunities, although often sharing a well-established narrative tradition. Each art form must be considered in its own right while individual exemplars must be considered on their own merits. I also point out that, although the 1931 *Frankenstein* appeared only about thirty years into the cinema's existence as an art form, Shelley's *Frankenstein* appeared only a little more than a century after the art form of the novel came into being—each work, that is, belongs to an evolving art form. I might digress further by observing that no art forms exist without predecessors and that most art forms have experienced vagaries in their public function and appreciation. In other words, I use the occasion to talk about art forms in their social context.

Virtually all novels adapted for the screen get simplified in the process; the more complex the novel, the greater the simplification is apt to be. Shelley's *Frankenstein* is no exception. Yet films like the 1931 *Frankenstein*, *The Bride of Frankenstein*, and *Young Frankenstein* exhibit complexities of their own. In teaching Shelley's *Frankenstein* to undergraduates who probably know the monster primarily through the movies, the trick is to help them negotiate the confusing terrain of source, variation, and, eventually, parody. Such exploration may lead to discussions of authorship (Shelley, after all, had her sources) and perhaps (depending on time and the caliber of one's students) to discussions of distinctions between high and low culture and the role of myth in popular culture. The film versions should not be seen as less interesting than Shelley's original just because they have been simplified for cinematic purposes; on the contrary, the cinematic omissions, deletions, and alterations may help students to understand Shelley's work more fully.

For example, the filmic versions eliminate Shelley's various narrative frames, entailing the loss, most significantly, of the figure of Robert Walton and the several formal shifts in point of view. Their settings are changed so that Victor Frankenstein's progressive removal from society no longer contributes to a theme of loneliness and isolation. Filmic versions also add assorted characters, such as the deformed assistant derived first from nineteenth-century melodramatic versions of the novel and ultimately from traditional stock theatrical characters. In addition, the films generally emphasize visually provocative and imaginative aspects of the technological processes involved in the novel—at the expense of discussing the moral consequences of these processes. However, these films have not so much rejected the historical and artistic context of Shelley's time as they have responded to the demands of their own epochs. Although the undergraduate may not recognize Shelley's explicit allusions to a literary tradition that includes Milton's *Paradise Lost* and the Prometheus poems by Percy Shelley and Byron, the principle behind allusions remains functional:

these films make their own allusions to several well-known films in the cinematic tradition.

Whether students read the entire novel or just "The Monster's Story," they must immediately consider formal differences between the literary and filmic versions. A simple yet heavily discussed characteristic of the cinema is that the camera cannot long maintain a first-person point of view. Robert Montgomery's *Lady in the Lake* (1946) is often cited as a failed attempt to sustain throughout an entire film a first-person narrative as we know the device from literature. Even with segments of a film, though, the camera typically—conventionally—adopts a third-person point of view (a convention, film theory argues, related to the distinction drawn between *histoire* and *discours* in linguistics and in linguistically influenced critical theory). The filmic conversion of the De Laceys and their education of Safie into the Creature's encounter with the hermit invites a digression on this distinction when time and course concerns permit. The real issue is that the formal significance of Shelley's shifts in narrative point of view gets lost in the filmic versions.

The most important loss is probably that of the epistolary frame, which ties the novel to two narrative genres: the frame story and the epistolary novel. Yet, in the opening sequence of *The Bride of Frankenstein*, Mary Shelley (played by Elsa Lanchester, who of course also plays the bride) explains how she came to write the story. In the 1931 *Frankenstein*, the presence of a token opening frame (in all senses) might also be argued, since the movie begins with Edward Van Sloan (who plays Dr. Waldman once the film proper starts) appearing from between the curtains on a traditional stage to announce that the producer, Carl Laemmle, has asked him to issue a "friendly warning." Van Sloan's speech describes Frankenstein as "a man of science, who sought to create a man after his own image without reckoning upon God" and his story as a strange tale dealing "with the two great mysteries of creation: life and death." The function of this introductory warning is roughly analogous to that of Walton's opening letters describing Frankenstein.

In other words, Van Sloan's warning simultaneously follows Shelley's original intentions and deviates from them, for it clearly serves not as a serious moral injunction to would-be explorers and Promethean challengers but as a theatrical come-on, suggesting the emotional pleasures of shock and horror to follow. Thus both the 1931 *Frankenstein* and *The Bride of Frankenstein* are identified with the concept of genre per se (if not exactly the genre of the epistolary novel), even if Karloff objected to the term *horror film*, preferring instead *terror film* (Glut, *Frankenstein Legend* 146).

The extent to which individual courses address the process of filmic adaptation may determine how much time is spent considering specific variations of setting, characters, dialogue, and episodes. One difference is that Shelley's novel has a relatively lonely quality, while the filmic versions seem cluttered with people. The relation between people and nature in novel and film, of course, differs radically, necessitating some class discussion about the Romantic concept of nature, on the one hand, and the history of cinematic mise-en-scène, on the other. The 1931 *Frankenstein* shows the influence both of the expressionistic sets for *The Cabinet of Dr. Caligari* (1919) and of the sets and the visualization of the eponymous character of *The Golem* (1920), the legendary tale of a robot created by a seventeenth-century rabbi. With *The Golem* the notion of influence in both film and novel dovetails, since Mary Shelley is said to have known of the Jewish legend, and Robert Florey, originally scheduled to direct the 1931 *Frankenstein* and involved in the project long enough to settle some of its characteristics, was definitely aware of Paul Wegener's performance as the Golem (Tropp 87–88). The few crowd scenes mentioned in passing in the novel become significant visual elements of the first two films: most of these scenes were filmed on a set (imitated in *Young Frankenstein*) of a European village from the 1930 antiwar film *All Quiet on the Western Front* (Glut, *Frankenstein Legend* 145). (For more detailed discussions of various connections between these two films and contemporary events, see Tropp 88–89, 97, 99–105; Tropp's most significant point is that the 1931 film responds to the sense of chaos after World War I, whereas the 1935 *Bride* acknowledges the growing unpleasantness of Hitler's social policy, specifically his emphasis on eugenics.) Another difference between the novel and the films is that true friendship between sympathetic souls plays a major role in the novel; the 1931 *Frankenstein* perverts the idea by converting the sensitive Henry Clerval into Victor Moritz, who, stiffly played by the matinee idol John Boles, makes unwelcome advances toward Elizabeth. Both *Bride* and *Young Frankenstein* have the Creature welcomed by a blind hermit who is grateful for the company; in each version, the Creature's nobility and undeserved mistreatment are emphasized, first by the attack of the hunters in the original film and then by the hermit's clumsiness in the parody.

The theme of friendship leads necessarily to discussion of the Creature's character. Whale's mise-en-scène strongly emphasizes religious imagery throughout the 1931 *Frankenstein* and in significant sequences in *Bride*. Whereas the novel emphasizes the comparisons between the Creature and Adam, on the one hand, and Lucifer, on the other, Whale's imagery explicitly sets up the Creature as a Christlike figure. What is the nature of the beast, and does he deserve the treatment he receives? That the Creature is a sympathetic character who has always gotten less than his due becomes comically blatant in *Young Frankenstein*, when young Frederick Frankenstein reduces the Creature (brilliantly played by Peter Boyle) to tears simply by telling him, "You are good"; Frederick continues his soothing behavior, saying, "This is a nice boy. This is a good boy. This is a mother's angel and I want the world to know, once and for all, and without any shame, that we love you."

Young Frankenstein shows that scientist and creation are complementary; the medical exchange in which young Frankenstein risks his life to correct the Creature's cerebral imbalance conclusively demonstrates that it takes both body and brain to make up a complete man, especially one who can satisfy a woman. Yes, *Young Frankenstein* "sinks" to burlesque, opting in the process for a variation on Hollywood's traditionally simple solution that love will conquer all, but the film does not neglect the more serious questions raised by the notion of artificially created life. The parody shows that Frederick the scientist is also Frederick the very fallible man who would like to surmount death in godlike fashion but who also knows his limitations and can feel remorse for the potential havoc he has wrought.

These questions, as well as those about the distinctions between human life and machine "life," periodically surface in Hollywood films. Students will probably comment on some of the contemporary films that discuss these issues: *Creator* (1985), in which Peter O'Toole plays a genially mad scientist (unlike his evil counterpart, Dr. Pretorious, in *Bride*) who wishes to resurrect his wife by regrowing her; *Short Circuit* (1986) about the lightning-struck robot Number Five, whose name irresistibly prompted the advertising campaign to echo *Frankenstein* by announcing, "It's alive!"; or even *Electric Dreams* (1984), which queries the distinction between human and computer love.

In all four versions of *Frankenstein* under consideration, the same crucial philosophical questions about creation, science, and social responsibility play major, if varying, roles. However, the answers to these questions, as indicated by the fates of key characters, may differ markedly—from Shelley's warning about hubristic self-confidence to Brooks's boisterous reassurance about human possibilities. While students may initially gain a greater appreciation for the complexities of horror films, which in itself is not bad, they must also inevitably see the continued relevance of Shelley's work for contemporary society. That reason alone amply justifies detouring, as some may see it, onto the Hollywood sidetrack.

The Films of *Frankenstein*

Wheeler Winston Dixon

While not every college student has had the opportunity to read Mary Wollstonecraft Shelley's *Frankenstein*, most students have seen one or more of the many filmic versions of her novel. Since some students bring to their first reading of *Frankenstein* considerable experience with these cinematic adaptations, instructors should understand the history of the films, including the technological and the economic factors that strongly influenced the form in which they were produced and released. Although this brief essay does not touch on every film version of *Frankenstein*—to say nothing of the many other genre films that partake of the themes explored in the novel (often without acknowledging it)—it does discuss the four major periods to date in *Frankenstein*'s filmic career.

The first film adaptation of *Frankenstein*, released on St. Valentine's Day, 14 February 1910, by the Thomas A. Edison Company, was directed by J. Searle Dawley, with Charles Ogle as the monster. For more than sixty years, the film was thought to be lost. It was generally assumed that the film's negative had failed to survive the twin dangers of cellulose nitrate decomposition and haphazard archival storage. Then, after more than half a century, the film surfaced in a private cinema archive. After all the years of neglect, it was found to be in surprisingly good condition, with little negative damage.[1] Even before this discovery, some publicity materials were available on the 1910 *Frankenstein*, including a few production stills—one a closeup of the monster (see the cover of the paperback edition of this volume)—and the production "pressbook." From these documents (which are preserved in the Museum of Modern Art Film Archives, New York, and partially reprinted in Huss and Ross's *Focus on the Horror Film*), historians were able to get a fairly good idea of what the production looked like. The pressbook features a scene-by-scene description of the film, with the complete text of all the intertitles used throughout the work. The film runs 975 35mm feet or about eleven minutes at today's standardized projection speed of twenty-four frames a second and tells the story of the novel in twenty-five individual tableaux, each of which advances the plot with dizzying speed.

The rediscovered 1910 Edison film is still not generally available for private or public viewing; indeed, even in 1987, most film histories were still treating the film as lost. However, two sequences from the film, both in their original color tints, were incorporated in the 1976 British television series *The Amazing Years of Cinema* (episode: "The Monsters"): the scene of Frankenstein writing a letter to Elizabeth on the eve of his creation of the monster and the creation sequence itself. My comments here are based on the pressbook materials and a viewing of excerpts from the 1910 film.

In the first shot of the film, an interior scene of a room, Frankenstein leaves his home for study at the university. In the very next shot, we have jumped two years into the future, and Frankenstein, working in the college laboratory, "has discovered the mystery of life" (the quote is from the pressbook). In the film's third shot, Frankenstein is shown writing his betrothed: "In a few hours I shall create into life the most perfect human being that the world has yet known." We see a close-up of the letter in Frankenstein's hand, followed by a wide shot of Frankenstein in his study, rising from his chair, confidently striding off to create his "most perfect human." However, the film tells us, "Instead of a perfect human being, the evil of Frankenstein's mind creates a monster." In shots 5–18, the bulk of the film, we see Frankenstein synthesizing a monster in a gigantic, smoldering vat, as the film alternates shots of Frankenstein's reactions with shots of the "monster forming," in color tints of orange and yellow painted directly on the film (color photographic film had not been invented yet). Frankenstein's laboratory is a Grand Guignol chamber of horrors. A human skeleton is tossed on a chair to the left of the frame; the set is dominated by an enormous cauldron at the back, framed on either side by riveted metal doors. This is no temple of scientific experiment: it is an alchemist's lair, echoing Mary Shelley's mention of Cornelius Agrippa, Albertus Magnus, and Paracelsus in the novel. Frankenstein hurriedly mixes some fluids and powders in an earthen bowl, consults a manual for a moment, and then pours this mixture into the vat. The mixture explodes in a flash of smoke and flame. He spoons more material into the cauldron, exultantly closes the doors, and waits for the Creature to materialize. As he peers through the peephole, we suddenly see from Frankenstein's point-of-view the monster's creation, a syntactical alteration of some sophistication for the period. The use of reverse-motion footage allows the skeletal form of the monster to assemble out of nothingness. As the smoldering, infernal Creature is born, Frankenstein is unable to control his sense of triumph. Watching the monster being created from the slime and mire of a gigantic, steaming tub, we see flesh compose on bone, eyes find sockets, limbs take on human aspect: the sequence proceeds like a magic ritual. The supernatural overtones are more apparent here than in any later version of the novel. Despite the Edison Company's professed intention to bowdlerize *Frankenstein*, this is a graphic, harrowing, and convincing sequence. Many exhibitors found the film too horrid to show their patrons: it is easy to see why.

In shot 19, the monster shambles through a doorway to confront his creator, and we are told by the intertitle that "Frankenstein [was] appalled at the sight of his evil creation." The creation sequence abruptly ends, and in the next shot we see the sleeping Frankenstein tormented by nightmares of the being he has created. In shot 21 Frankenstein returns to his home; the monster has apparently followed him because in shot 22 the intertitles tell us that "haunting his creator and jealous of his sweetheart, for the first time the monster sees himself." The description of the accompanying action tells us that "Frankenstein sees monster. Monster sees himself in glass and struggles with Frankenstein tearing from his waistcoat the flower that his fiancée had given him." This brief evidence of infantile jealousy is the only real conflict we see between Frankenstein and his creation. The next shot, number 23, jumps forward to the night of Frankenstein's wedding, with the intertitles announcing that "on the bridal night Frankenstein's better nature assert[ed] itself." We see "Frankenstein [being] congratulated by his friends," followed by the film's final two shots, as described in the pressbook:

> [T]he monster broken down by his unsuccessful attempts to be with his creator enters the room, stands before a large mirror holding out his arms entreatingly, but gradually the real monster fades away, leaving only the image in the mirror. A moment later Frankenstein enters.
>
> Standing directly before the mirror we see the remarkable sight of the monster's image reflected instead of Frankenstein's own. Gradually, however, under the effect of love and his better nature, the monster's image fades and Frankenstein sees himself in his young manhood in the mirror. His bride joins him, and the film ends with their embrace, Frankenstein's mind now being clear of the awful horror and weight it has been laboring under for so long.

This brief film presents little more than a sketch of the novel. The Edison Company noted in their pressbook that they had "carefully tried to eliminate all the actually repulsive situations, and to concentrate upon the mystic and psychological problems that are to be found in this weird tale." The graphic sensationalism of the film's creation sequence seems to contradict this claim. Yet the Edison Company insisted that the

> story of the film brings out the fact that the creation of the monster was only possible because Frankenstein had allowed his normal mind to be overcome by evil and unnatural thoughts. With the strength of Frankenstein's love for his bride and the effect of this upon his own mind, the monster cannot exist.

This pressbook text is obviously intended to explain the film's last two shots, in which Frankenstein's spiritual dedication to his new bride simultaneously redeems him and allows for the "evaporation" of the monster before the looking glass.

In 1931, James Whale directed the first sound version of *Frankenstein* for Universal Pictures, under the supervision of the producer Carl Laemmle, Jr. The script of the 1931 film had a rather convoluted genesis. The original novel was in the public domain and so could be used by anyone. Universal, however, based its version of *Frankenstein* on an Americanized version of Peggy Webling's 1930 London stage play of the novel and then brought in John L. Balderston (who had worked with Hamilton Deane in adapting his play of *Dracula* for Universal earlier in 1931) to help with the screenplay. The final shooting script was credited to Garrett Fort and Francis Edward Faragoh, both competent studio writers, and was based on Webling's play as edited by Richard L. Schayer, head of Universal's story department. Also involved in the scripting was the director Robert Florey, who worked on an initial draft of the scenario with Fort and even directed a two-reel (20-minute) test sequence to help "sell" the film to Laemmle (Curtis 72–77). In the midst of all this collaborative wrangling, Mary Wollstonecraft Shelley does receive a credit, although it is not one that I suspect she would be overly fond of: "From the novel of Mrs. Percy B. Shelley." The finished film script has little in common with her novel, but it is still an effective, if slightly dated, piece of gothic filmmaking, highlighted by Boris Karloff's adroit performance as the monster and by the atmospheric, forced-perspective sets used throughout the film. With this 1931 film Whale created a series of iconic conventions that rapidly became clichés in the decade and a half that followed and that, until the advent of the 1957 and 1976 productions, severely limited any serious approach to the novel's actual concerns.

That said, one must acknowledge the many successes of the film. Whale executes beautiful dolly or tracking-camera shots, unusual for the early sound period, that allow the camera to float among the actors, participating in the action it records. Karloff effectively evokes sympathy and empathy for the monster, who is not allowed a single line of dialogue and who could easily have been rendered an insensitive brute. The sets, strongly influenced by the 1919 German film *The Cabinet of Dr. Caligari* (Curtis 79), present a nightmarish, expressionist backdrop for both indoor and outdoor sequences. Although there are a few genuine outdoor scenes, most of the film was shot indoors to allow Whale precise control of the lighting and sound recording. Whale also has an excellent sense of dramatic pacing, which, for the first half of the film at least, keeps the plot moving forward with grisly assurance. In the first reel, Henry Frankenstein (Victor in the novel) is a near-demonic presence, maniacally dedicated to proving his theory that he can give life to an artificially constructed human being. The first ten minutes of the film reveal that Henry is willing—even eager—to exhume freshly buried corpses, to cut down executed criminals from the gallows, or to break into a medical school auditorium to steal a human brain, all in order to create his "child." He is assisted by Fritz, a hunchbacked halfwit ably played by Dwight Frye (who specialized in these roles; he also played the part of Renfield, Dracula's pathetic assistant, in the 1931 film version of Bram Stoker's novel). Henry cuts himself off from fiancée, father, former teachers, and friends to pursue his experiments in a lonely, ruined castle, a visually ideal location for experiments that the film represents as beyond the boundaries of acceptable scientific inquiry. Perhaps the most serious thematic deviation from the novel occurs when Fritz, sent by Frankenstein to steal a "normal, healthy brain" from the Goldstadt Medical College, bungles the assignment by dropping the normal brain and makes off with an "abnormal, criminal brain" described as exhibiting a "distinct degeneration of the frontal lobes." Because the brain comes from the skull of a brute who led a life of "violence, brutality, and murder," the unfortunate creature who receives it should be doomed to a similar existence. But Karloff's monster acts quite reasonably throughout the film, killing Fritz only after being continually tormented with a lighted torch and savagely whipped by the hunchback. The famous scene in which Karloff meets Little Maria, who shows him the only kindness in the film, further demonstrates that the plot device involving the substituted brain is both unnecessary and inconsistent with the film's own action. Watching Maria throw flowers in the water, Karloff smiles and laughs for the first time in the film; when there are no more flowers to be thrown in the water, the monster reaches out to Maria in a spirit of childlike play and throws her in the water, thinking that she, too, will float. Maria drowns, of course, but her death cannot be construed as an act of violence on the monster's part. It is simply an accident that sets up the final third of the film, in which the villagers form a lynch mob to avenge Maria's death. With Henry as one of their leaders, the villagers track the monster to a windmill, which they set on fire, ostensibly killing the Creature.

The scene of Maria's accidental drowning was censored by the Motion Picture Distributors Association of America (now the Motion Picture Association of America) on the film's initial release, and this censorship substantially altered both the tone of the film and the director's intent in staging the scene in the first place. In most surviving prints, including the one still circulating on home videocassette, we see Maria and the monster throwing the flowers in the water, then the monster reacting with bewilderment when the flowers run out, and finally Karloff, with a playful, childlike smile, reaching in a close-up for Maria. The film cuts at this point to the villagers dancing in celebration of Henry's impending wedding, and when next we see Maria, she is being carried as a corpse by her father to the town square, where he demands that his fellow citizens help him track down the "fiend" who "murdered" her. The footage of the monster playfully tossing Maria into the water, her drowning, and the monster's worried and bewildered response to her misfortune has all been excised. Contemporary industry censors "reasoned" that the scene of Maria being thrown in was too horrific to be shown; it would have to be implied. The cut has precisely the opposite effect, making the monster seem a genuinely malicious murderer and not a pathetic and well-meaning creature whose miscalculation has resulted in a child's accidental death. This deleted sequence was exhumed by Universal for their videodisc release of the film in 1987. The reinsertion of these shots alters the film utterly, making the Creature's eventual death an agonizing martyrdom. Indeed, this deleted footage leads one's sympathies to rest entirely with the monster and not with Henry, who is seen at the film's end recovering in bed while his wife Elizabeth caresses him, secure in the lap of bourgeois luxury. The restored, complete, and uncensored version is now readily available in videocassette and 16mm formats: one hopes that Universal will now add this newly discovered footage to all the available versions.

The Bride of Frankenstein, produced in 1935, immediately succeeded the 1931 production. James Whale again directed, but the film is discernably a baroque exercise, shamelessly camped up rather than sincerely felt. Even at this relatively early stage in filmmaking, sequels had become calculated, cynical enterprises, dictated predominantly by the first film's resounding success at the box office. By far the most interesting thing about *Bride* is Elsa Lanchester's double role. In the opening sequence she portrays Mary Shelley, pressed by both Lord Byron (Gavin Gordon) and Percy Shelley (Douglas Walton) to relate "what happened next" after the monster's supposed demise in the 1931 film. Lanchester's appearance at the end of the film as the bride of the monster is one of her most indelible pieces of work as an actress: she remained identified with it for the rest of her long career. But Karloff's performance as the monster and the film as a whole are both badly undermined by unnecessary and tedious additions and digressions. The 1931 original was a straight-ahead horror film, grim and relentlessly uncompromising. In *Bride*, Whale indulges excessively in tilted camera angles and allows the plot to be sidetracked into a long and wearisome sequence in which Ernest Thesiger's Dr. Pretorius displays a gallery of miniature humans he has created. Whale also gives the actress Una O'Connor (as Minnie, the Frankensteins' house servant) unlimited range to harangue the audience with her synthetic Irish brogue. Significantly, compared with the original film, this film did very little business at the box office. Moreover, Karloff, after only one more sequel, abandoned the character of the monster permanently. One of the film's few achieve-ments is Franz Waxman's intelligently romantic score, which is generously used throughout the film and which, in variously edited versions, popped up in other Universal films for the next fifteen years, including the *Flash Gordon* serials. *The Bride of Frankenstein* is also available for 16mm and videocassette rental.

Before continuing on to the 1957 British production *The Curse of Fran-kenstein*, I need to say a few words about the balance of the Universal Frankenstein series. In rapid succession, Universal produced *Son of Fran-kenstein* (1939); *The Ghost of Frankenstein* (1942); *Frankenstein Meets the Wolf Man* (1943); *House of Frankenstein* (1944); *House of Dracula* (1945), in which the Frankenstein monster appears in a brief cameo; and finally and ignominiously, *Abbott and Costello Meet Frankenstein* (1948). *Son of Frankenstein*, directed by Rowland V. Lee, featured Karloff for the last time in the role of the monster. Despite its good cast, including Basil Rath-bone, Lionel Atwill, and Bela Lugosi, the film is even more formulaic than *The Bride of Frankenstein*. Apart from a few good scenes—those involving the monster's kidnapping of Frankenstein's child and featuring the de-pendable Lionel Atwill as the local police inspector whose arm has been "torn out by the roots" during the monster's previous rampages—the film is flat and obligatory. By the time of the film's release Mary Shelley's mon-ster was associated more with the Universal mythos than with the Greek legend whose Prometheus features in the novel's subtitle. The studio be-came increasingly dependent on trotting out the Frankenstein monster, as well as Dracula and the Invisible Man, at regular intervals to generate much-needed cash.

By the time *The Ghost of Frankenstein* appeared in 1942, Universal had become a different studio altogether. The Laemmles, Jr. and Sr., sold their interest in the studio on 14 March 1936 (Curtis 138), and although the decline in quality was not immediately apparent, the new regime clearly placed profit before quality. By the 1940s, the Universal Studio had be-come completely identified with the production of B horror films, some good and some bad, and with the long-running Abbott and Costello series. *The Ghost of Frankenstein* was accorded a much lower budget than any of the previous Frankenstein films, although it did have the talents of Cedric Hardwicke, Lon Chaney, Jr., Lionel Atwill, and Bela Lugosi. Erle C. Ken-ton directed, but the film was hopelessly hampered by a short shooting schedule and its low budget. *Frankenstein Meets the Wolf Man* (1943) demonstrated that Universal no longer had confidence in just one monster to bring in people at the box office. The film, directed by Roy William Neill (who also directed most of the Universal *Sherlock Holmes* series with Nigel Bruce and Basil Rathbone), is simply an atmospheric rendering of by now very familiar territory. *House of Frankenstein* and *House of Dracula*, both released in 1945 and directed by Erle C. Kenton, gather the Frankenstein monster, Dracula, the Wolf Man, and other assorted Universal properties into ridiculous assemblages of slightly more than an hour's length apiece. Whatever dignity the series once possessed was completely sacrificed in these last two films and particularly, in 1948, in *Abbott and Costello Meet Frankenstein*. In this last film, Dr. Frankenstein does not even appear: the monster has by now entirely subsumed the identity of its creator. In the film, Dracula supervises the monster's ritual return to consciousness. Clearly, the series had long ago abandoned any hope of coherence or continuity.

One interesting footnote to the Universal series is the 1958 production *Frankenstein 1970*. Although the film was produced by Allied Artists, not Universal, it carries on, for one film, many of the iconic structures and thematic concerns of the Universal cycle. In this film, Boris Karloff appears as a descendant of Victor Frankenstein, who, in 1970, is a recluse in an ill-kept castle, bankrupted by his re-creation of his ancestor's experiments. To raise money, Karloff allows a television crew to film a documentary on the Frankenstein legend in the castle. When body parts prove in short supply, he eliminates members of the film crew. As the creator of the monster, Karloff is at his least sympathetic as a grim, acid-scarred fanatic. Alternately narrating and starring in the sensationalist film-within-a-film that frames and mirrors *Frankenstein 1970*'s action and performing needlessly grisly experiments in his laboratory, Karloff gives us Frankenstein as a fading huckster, forced to make commercial compromises with those who exploit the legend of his family. When the face of the monster is finally revealed to the audience in the climatic moments of the film, it is the face of Karloff—perhaps the only time one actor portrayed both roles in the same film. Poor production values and shoddy execution relegate the film to the category of an interesting oddity. Nevertheless, the film has an interesting premise, and it is certainly worth viewing.

In 1957, Hammer Films, a British production company with studios at Bray, England, produced the stylish *The Curse of Frankenstein*, starring Peter Cushing as Baron Victor Frankenstein and Christopher Lee as the monster. Directed by the gifted British gothicist Terence Fisher, from a script by James Sangster, this was the first color Frankenstein feature and the first that did not use Jack Pierce's patented Universal design for the monster. Much has been written about the Hammer production company; David Pirie's excellent book *A Heritage of Horror: The English Gothic Cinema, 1946–1972* is particularly useful and informative. Simply put, Hammer revived and rejuvenated the classic horror films of the 1930s and 1940s, taking them far more seriously than Universal did its original films except for Whale's first *Frankenstein* (1931). Apparently audiences in 1957 were ready for a new wave of gothic horror films quite unrelated to the Universal cycle. Then, too, since many viewers were unfamiliar with the older Frankenstein films, Hammer found an opportunity to reinvent the iconic structure of the earlier series. Like Universal, Hammer followed *The Curse of Frankenstein* with numerous sequels. For most viewers, however, this first film in Hammer's Frankenstein series is the most successful. Although *The Curse of Frankenstein* does not follow the plot of the novel with great fidelity, it nevertheless seems more in tune with the world of Mary Shelley's work than any of the films (save, perhaps, the 1931 original) in the Universal series do.

The Curse of Frankenstein did incorporate two of the basic tenets of the Universal 1931 screenplay: the defective brain—this time a brain damaged during a laboratory fight but used nevertheless—and the unspoken but still clearly delineated concept of the nobility of the Frankenstein family. Peter Cushing, magnificent as Frankenstein, is even more aristocratic than Colin Clive had been. A former member of the Royal Shakespeare Company, Cushing had apprenticed with Laurence Olivier and had spent many years on the London stage before venturing into television and films full-time in the mid 1950s. Christopher Lee, who was to have a considerable effect as Dracula in Terence Fisher's *Horror of Dracula* in 1958, had been working in films since the late 1940s, doing small roles and acting as a stunt double for Stewart Granger. At six feet, two inches tall, Lee had found it difficult to get leading parts, but for the Creature's role his gaunt, towering figure proved ideal. Lee's makeup, by Philip Leakey, was designed to be as repellent as possible, with acid-scarred skin, stitches running randomly over the Creature's face, and flaps of excess flesh dangling from hands and neck.

Director Fisher and his cast and crew lavished immense care on the production of *The Curse of Frankenstein*, using sets and costumes that were as accurate to the period as possible. The laboratory sequences, although lacking some of the superficial pyrotechnics of the Universal series, have a convincing early nineteenth-century air about them. Leyden jars and chemical storage batteries abound in the laboratory set, and the electricity used to revive the monster combines lightning and artificial electricity generated by a primitive spinning-wheel generator. Although the flavor of the film's physical details is scrupulously maintained, this is primarily an actor's film. Peter Cushing's performance as Baron Victor Frankenstein dominates the proceedings. The film's central interest resides in Frankenstein's continuing attempts to reanimate the dead and in his willingness to sanction moral and ethical liberties in doing so. Unlike Colin Clive, who seemed in the grip of a mad, feverish desire that invariably crumbled during the climax of each of the James Whale films, Cushing is unremittingly arrogant, foppish, superior, and chillingly self-centered in the Hammer series. In his creation of the monster, Cushing's Frankenstein is assisted not by a half-witted hunchback but rather by talented members of the medical profession whom he coerces into submission. The Baron's unwilling assistant, Krempe, in *The Curse of Frankenstein* is simply the first in a long line of medical students, country doctors, and retired professionals whom Cushing manages to bend to his will. Moreover, Cushing's Frankenstein does not hesitate to murder his mistress, the servant girl Justine (Valerie Gaunt), when he tires of her, by the simple expedient of locking her in a room with the monster, who obligingly dispatches her. The next morning, idly buttering some toast at breakfast, Cushing suggests that she has "probably run off with one of the village Lotharios. . . . She always was a romantic young thing." To obtain a brain for his creation, Frankenstein arranges the "accidental" death of one of his more illustrious colleagues, Professor Bernstein. His murder of Bernstein is so coldly calculated that any audience sympathy for Frankenstein's character evaporates from that point forward: with this act, he has sealed his generic fate. In his final moments in the prison cell, Cushing's Frankenstein begs Krempe to corroborate his story of the monster's creation and subsequent rampage, yet Krempe refuses further complicity, knowing that his refusal will ensure Frankenstein's execution, which is richly deserved. In many of Terence Fisher's films, friendship—and the sacrifices and responsibilities it entails—emerges as a dominant theme. Because Frankenstein callously breaches the limits of friendship and loyalty, he earns the deadly retribution that Fisher's film delivers to him.

Christopher Lee's interpretation of the monster (called "The Creature" in the film's opening titles) is entirely different from Karloff's. In the first film, Karloff was allowed a few grunts or growls when he was menaced with Fritz's torch or a childlike whimper of pleasure when he made friends with Little Maria. Lee's monster is a shambling, mute agent of destruction, whose first act on being brought to life is the attempted murder of Frankenstein by strangulation. Frustrated in this attempt, he escapes to the countryside, where he immediately and without provocation murders an old blind man and his young son. Lee's monster is simply that—a monster—and the audience never builds up any sympathy for, or identification with, his characterization. In view of Cushing's pervasive hold on the narrative, Lee's portrayal does not emerge as a serious defect in the film's construction. If the monster had been given the power of speech, however, he could well have emerged as a formidable counterbalance to the machinations of Frankenstein. Fisher does explore this possibility in the later Frankenstein films, but these efforts suffer from the sense of mechanical repetition that pervades most sequels, and the creation-versus-creator conflict is never fully or convincingly developed.

In 1973, as the Hammer cycle was winding down with the production of Terence Fisher's *Frankenstein and the Monster from Hell* (the last film of the Hammer Frankenstein series and Fisher's last film as director), a 200–minute adaptation of *Frankenstein* was made for television, entitled *Frankenstein: The True Story*. Although the telefilm was well acted by James Mason, David McCallum, Michael Sarrazin, John Gielgud, and Leonard Whiting, it was overlong, and Jack Smight's direction did little to help matters. Whiting did his best as Frankenstein, while Sarrazin was intermittently effective as the monster. *Frankenstein: The True Story* suffers from the same defects as most television miniseries: it is poorly paced, slowly plotted, and designed primarily to get the most out of the "name" cast through the use of interminable sequences of static exposition. As this largely unsuccessful production is not generally available in 16mm or videocassette format, it is not listed in the selected filmography.

In 1976, a small Swedish company, Aspekt Film, produced *Victor Frankenstein* (titled *Terror of Frankenstein* in the United States), a theatrical feature film that was considerably better. Although it suffered from poor distribution in its initial United States release, the film has since been shown extensively on television, attracting some well-deserved, serious critical attention. *Victor Frankenstein* is, quite simply, the best screen adaptation to date of Mary Shelley's work. Aspekt Film and director Calvin Floyd managed to make the most of a very small budget by taking Hammer's physical production strategy one step further: the film was shot entirely on location, without any new sets at all. Costumes, dressings, and technical props are reduced to a minimum. Per Oscarsson's makeup as the Creature is understated, and the film eschews shock effects and standard horror-film iconography almost entirely. More important, the production follows Shelley's novel more faithfully than any other film version. At the beginning, Frankenstein is picked up by Robert Walton, the captain of an explorer vessel temporarily icebound on the way to the North Pole. After a brief convalescence on board, Frankenstein relates his story to the captain in flashback. The balance of the film follows Mary Shelley's scenario almost without variation.

Per Oscarsson's monster speaks, from the moment of its creation: the Creature in *Victor Frankenstein* behaves with all the moral complexity with which Mary Shelley originally endowed it. Desperately lonely, jealous of Frankenstein's family and associates, the Creature Oscarsson portrays is a cunning, instinctively evil child—determined to get what it wants, no matter the cost. Karloff and Lee had done yeomanly service with an essentially mute role; in *Victor Frankenstein*, Shelley's monster is allowed to speak, act, and reason as a separate entity, with free will and mobility. For the first time, it emerges as an intellectual adversary, not just a physical brute whose intelligence is ruled by infantile rages and fears. This is a truly horrific creation—not the lumbering giant of the Universal series or even Lee's more athletic interpretation for Hammer. Oscarsson's monster is the feared dopplegänger fully come to life. He needs no mediating agent: he can control Frankenstein with his own will, his own desires. Dressed in rough garb, with stitches running around his wrists and neck, thick black lips, and yellow, watery eyes (just as Mary Shelley specified), this solitary, isolated humanoid is fiercely jealous both of his creator and of Frankenstein's link to the rest of humankind. He is the ultimate outsider, unique and terrifyingly alone.

Connections to the Faust legend are definitely apparent. Victor and his friend Henry Clerval are seen as little more than overgrown adolescents, obsessed with ancient sorcerers, dabbling in black magic. Although Victor is clearly possessed by his desire to create life, the film also gives the strong sense that his experiments are motivated in part by sheer boredom: he is an aristocrat with sufficient means to support himself and much idle time to occupy. As in the 1910 Edison film, Frankenstein is seen as a fallen figure who, his scholarly instinct gone awry, embraces the darker powers of nature to achieve his ambition. He seems to fall to pieces as the film progresses. His health, good looks, and humor are replaced by a hollow pallor as he is increasingly brought under the monster's sway. This struggle of wills reaches its climax when the monster insists that Victor fashion him a mate. In this pivotal scene and in the rest of the film, the conflict between Frankenstein as the mother/father and the monster as willful child is brilliantly explicated.

Numerous thematic and visual contrasts are rigorously worked out during the course of the film. The characters are all dressed like dandies, but they live in houses of drab, cold stone. The Creature is an unnatural construct of Frankenstein's making, but he is happiest in his walks through the Irish countryside, imagining himself to be a part of the nature that surrounds him. The narrative of the film is inherently unrealistic, yet director Calvin Floyd stages his scenes with a quiet, assured naturalism. Color is effectively muted, as are the camera movements. No baroque dollies are used, just slow, calm motions toward, or away from, the actors. Often, Floyd seems to "throw away" detail shots that significantly add to the depth of the film. In one memorable instance, Frankenstein's increasing lack of humanity is pointed up by a simple, two-shot sequence. In the first shot, Frankenstein sits at his work desk, absorbed in his labors. For a moment, he looks up and then to the right of the frame. Immediately after this, Floyd shows a mercifully brief close-up of a monkey writhing against the leather straps that confine it to a hard wooden chair. The piteous expression on the monkey's face is all we need to see: Frankenstein obviously has no compassion for this "inferior creature." In another sequence, Clerval scales the walls of a sheer cliff to spy on Frankenstein, who is attempting to create a mate for the monster on an isolated island. As Clerval reaches the top of the cliff, he is intercepted by the monster, who first offers him a hand up and then, after a moment's reflection, tosses him into the sea. The matter-of-fact way in which this scene is photographed, in a modified first-person documentary style, underscores its violence.

With Floyd's film, the Frankenstein series moves away from the excessively stylized approach of the earlier versions, toward a naturalism that lets the story tell itself without melodramatic embellishment. One of the most striking things about *Victor Frankenstein* is its technical and physical simplicity. Stripped of all the traditional filmic trappings that have become associated with the series, the story of Frankenstein is more terrifying: it becomes plausible. In *Victor Frankenstein*, the series finally reaches a level of maturity not approached by any of the other films discussed here. Floyd is content to let the ideas of the novel come through in his work, without resorting to conventional horror-film imagery. He takes his imagistic strategies directly from the novel, not from Hollywood. Paradoxically, for this reason a number of critics have dismissed the film as a faithful, yet uninspired, version of the book. To me the film is inspired, but not by any of its many predecessors. *Victor Frankenstein* places faith in and draws inspiration from the novel itself, succeeding in a way that none of the other versions can: it is Mary Shelley's own vision, faithfully translated to the screen.

Mary Shelley's tale has only been brought to the screen once with even a modicum of fidelity (not counting the 1973 television version). Yet in the 1910, 1931, 1957, and particularly the 1976 productions, the essence of her novel survives the many emendations made to her plot. Even the assembly line of screenwriters who worked on the 1931 production could not entirely abrogate her central themes: the creation of a being from the remnants of human beings; the questions of birth, life, and death and of the immortality of the soul; and the ways in which one's life can be changed irrevocably by research when that research outstrips its human needs. The Edison film, now restored, shows how early narrative filmmakers were fascinated by the novel's central themes: the creation of life and the questions of physical and spiritual life and death. The Universal and Hammer films, imperfect though they are, do address many of the central issues of Mary Shelley's work, and thus they can serve as an incomplete, yet tantalizing, introduction to the novel. *Victor Frankenstein* demonstrates how a faithful production of the novel can in many ways outstrip the previous film adaptations. There will no doubt be many more versions of *Frankenstein*. The summer of 1986 saw a remake of *The Bride of Frankenstein* (entitled simply *The Bride*), with the rock singer Sting as Frankenstein and *Flashdance*'s Jennifer Beals as the bride of the monster. Although the definitive production of *Frankenstein* may be in the future, all the films discussed here may serve as keys to the novel, as seen through the mirror of Hollywood invention or through a faithful adaptation of the original text. The best of these films demonstrates that when the task is approached with taste and skill, it is possible to transfer the gothic sensibility from the novel to the film essentially without compromise—an endeavor I feel certain Mary Wollstonecraft Shelley, visionary that she was, would enthusiastically have approved.

NOTE

[1]Ron Magliozzi of the Museum of Modern Art Film Studies Archive (New York) asserts that all surviving prints of the 1910 *Frankenstein* were acquired by a single private collector who for years refused to loan or even to screen the film for researchers. While Magliozzi reports that the film is not collected in any archive associated with the International Federation of Film Archives (IFFA), a copy of the film exists in the private archive of Al Dettlaff of Milwaukee, Wisconsin.

CONTRIBUTORS AND SURVEY PARTICIPANTS

The following scholars and teachers generously agreed to participate in the survey of approaches to teaching *Frankenstein* that preceded preparation of this volume. Without their assistance, their support, and their many suggestions, this volume would not have been possible.

Marcia Aldrich, Michigan State University; Brenda Ameter, Indiana State University; John Anzalone, Skidmore College; Stephen C. Behrendt, University of Nebraska, Lincoln; Betty T. Bennett, American University; Sylvia Bowerbank, McMaster University; Jerome Bump, University of Texas; Paul A. Cantor, University of Virginia; Syndy M. Conger, Western Illinois University; William Crisman, Pennsylvania State University, Altoona; Beth Darlington, Vassar College; Wheeler Winston Dixon, University of Nebraska, Lincoln; Richard J. Dunn, University of Washington; Deborah S. Ellis, Case Western Reserve University; Paula R. Feldman, University of South Carolina; Michael Fischer, University of New Mexico; Barbara Gelpi, Stanford University; Linda Georgianna, University of California, Irvine; Joan F. Gilliland, Marshall University; Douglas K. Gray, Pontifical College Josephinum; Burton Hatlen, University of Maine; Devon Hodges, George Mason University; Terrence Holt, Rutgers University, New Brunswick; Richard Isomaki, West Virginia University; Mary Jacobus, Cornell University; Donovan Johnson, University of California, Irvine; David Ketterer, Concordia University, Sir George Williams Campus; Mark Kipperman, Northern Illinois University; U. C. Knoepflmacher, Princeton University; Paul A. Lacey, Earlham College; Alice Levine, Hofstra University; Herbert J. Levine, Franklin and Marshall College; William J. Lohman, Jr., University of Tampa; Harriet E. Margolis, Florida Atlantic University; Irving Massey, State University of New York, Buffalo; William McDonald, University of Redlands; Karen McGuire, Pasadena City College; Anne K. Mellor, University of California, Los Angeles; Elsie B. Michie, Louisiana State University; Michael Valdez Moses, Duke University; Kevin O'Neill, University of Redlands; E. Susan Owens, Ursuline College; Mary Poovey, Johns Hopkins University; Susan Rosowski, University of Nebraska, Lincoln; Paul Sherwin, City College of New York; Patricia L. Skarda, Smith College; R. D. Stock, University of Nebraska, Lincoln; Patrick Story, George Mason University; Mary K. Thornburg, Ball State University; Martin Tropp, Babson College; James Twitchell, University of Florida; William Veeder, University of Chicago; William Walling, Rutgers University, New Brunswick; Susan J. Wolfson, Rutgers University, New Brunswick; Art Young, Clemson University; Theodore Ziolkowski, Princeton University.

WORKS CITED

Aldiss, Brian Wilson. *Frankenstein Unbound*. London: Cape, 1973.

Atwood, Margaret. "Speeches for Dr. Frankenstein." *The Animals in That Country*. Toronto: Oxford UP, 1968. 42–47.

Bacon, Francis. *A Selection of His Works*. Ed. Sidney Warhaft. Toronto: Macmillan, 1965.

Baldick, Chris. *In Frankenstein's Shadow: Myth, Monstrosity, and Nineteenth-Century Writing*. Oxford: Clarendon, 1987.

Blake, William. *Blake: Complete Writings*. Ed. Geoffrey Keynes. Oxford: Oxford UP, 1969.

––––––. *The Poetry and Prose of William Blake*. Ed. David V. Erdman. New York: Doubleday, 1970.

Bloom, Harold. "*Frankenstein*: Or, The New Prometheus." *Partisan Review* 32 (1965): 611–18. Rpt. as afterword in *Frankenstein*, ed. Bloom, 212–23.

––––––, ed. *Mary Shelley's* Frankenstein. New York: Chelsea, 1987.

Brooks, Peter. " 'Godlike Science/Unhallowed Arts': Language, Nature, and Monstrosity." Levine and Knoepflmacher 205–20.

Burke, Edmund. *A Philosophical Enquiry into the Origin of Our Ideas of the Sublime and Beautiful*. 1757. Ed. J. T. Boulton. Notre Dame: Notre Dame UP, 1968.

Byron, George Gordon, Lord. *The Complete Poetical Works*. 5 vols. Ed. Jerome J. McGann. Oxford: Clarendon, 1980–86.

Cameron, Kenneth Neill, ed. *Romantic Rebels: Essays on Shelley and His Circle*. Cambridge: Harvard UP, 1973.

Cameron, Kenneth Neill, and Donald H. Reiman, eds. *Shelley and His Circle*. 8 vols. Cambridge: Harvard UP, 1968–86.

Cantor, Paul A. "The Nightmare of Romantic Idealism." *Creature and Creator: Myth-Making and English Romanticism*. Cambridge: Cambridge UP, 1984. 103–32.

Clairmont, Claire. *The Journals of Claire Clairmont*. Ed. Marion Kingston Stocking. Cambridge: Harvard UP, 1968.

Clifford, Gay. "*Caleb Williams* and *Frankenstein*: First-Person Narratives and 'Things as They Are.' " *Genre* 10 (1977): 601–17.

Coleridge, Samuel Taylor. *Poetical Works*. Ed. Ernest Hartley Coleridge. London: Oxford UP, 1912.

Curtis, James. *James Whale*. Metuchen: Scarecrow, 1982.

Dante Alighieri. *The Inferno*. Trans. John Ciardi. New York: NAL, 1982.

Dinnerstein, Dorothy. *The Mermaid and the Minotaur*. New York: Harper, 1976.

Dowden, Edward. *The Life of Percy Bysshe Shelley.* 2 vols. London: Kegan Paul, 1886.

Dunn, Jane. *Moon in Eclipse: A Life of Mary Shelley.* London: Weidenfeld, 1978.

Dunn, Richard J. "Narrative Distance in *Frankenstein.*" *Studies in the Novel* 6 (1974): 408–17.

Dussinger, John A. "Kinship and Guilt in Mary Shelley's *Frankenstein.*" *Studies in the Novel* 8 (1976): 38–55.

Edison Company Pressbook. *Frankenstein.* New York: Museum of Modern Art Film Studies Archives, 14 Feb. 1910.

Ellis, Kate. "Monsters in the Garden: Mary Shelley and the Bourgeois Family." Levine and Knoepflmacher 123–42.

Favret, Mary. "The Letters of *Frankenstein.*" *Genre* 20 (1987): 3–24.

Florescu, Radu. *In Search of* Frankenstein. Boston: New York Graphic Society, 1975.

Foucault, Michel. *Discipline and Punish—The Birth of the Prison.* Trans. Alan Sheridan. New York: Random, 1979.

———. *Madness and Civilization: A History of Insanity in the Age of Reason.* Trans. Richard Howard. New York: Random, 1973.

Freud, Sigmund. *The Interpretation of Dreams.* Trans. and ed. James Strachey. London: Hogarth, 1953.

Frye, Northrop. Introduction. *Fables of Identity: Studies in Poetic Mythology.* New York: Harcourt, 1963. 1–3.

Gilbert, Sandra M., and Susan Gubar. *The Madwoman in the Attic: The Woman Writer and the Nineteenth-Century Imagination.* New Haven: Yale UP, 1979.

Glut, Donald F. *The* Frankenstein *Catalogue: Being a Comprehensive Listing. . . .* Jefferson: McFarland, 1984.

———. *The Frankenstein Legend: A Tribute to Mary Shelley and Boris Karloff.* Metuchen: Scarecrow, 1973.

Godwin, William. "Of Health, and the Prolongation of Human Life." *An Enquiry concerning Political Justice, and Its Influence on Morals and Happiness.* Ed. F. E. L. Priestley. 3 vols. Toronto: U of Toronto P, 1946.

Grylls, Rosalie G. *Mary Shelley: A Biography.* London: Oxford UP, 1938.

Heath-Stubbs, John, and Phillips Salman, eds. *Poems of Science.* Harmondsworth: Penguin, 1984.

Hill, J. M. "*Frankenstein* and the Physiognomy of Desire." *American Imago* 32 (1975): 332–58.

Holmes, Richard. *Shelley: The Pursuit.* New York: Dutton, 1975.

Homans, Margaret. *Bearing the Word: Language and Female Experience in Nineteenth-Century Women's Writing.* Chicago: U of Chicago P, 1986.

Huss, Roy, and T. J. Ross, eds. *Focus on the Horror Film.* Englewood Cliffs: Prentice, 1972.

Iser, Wolfgang. *The Act of Reading: A Theory of Aesthetic Response.* Baltimore: Johns Hopkins UP, 1978.

Jameson, Fredric. *The Political Unconscious: Narrative as a Socially Symbolic Act.* Ithaca: Cornell UP, 1981.

Jennings, Richard. "La Fenêtre Gothique: The Influence of Tragic Form on the Structure of the Gothic Novel." Diss. Ball State U, 1983.

Johnson, Barbara. "My Monster/My Self." *Diacritics* 12 (1982): 2–10.

Kaplan, Morton, and Robert Kloss. *The Unspoken Motive: A Guide to Psychoanalytic Literary Criticism.* New York: Free, 1973.

Keats, John. *Complete Poems.* Ed. Jack Stillinger. Cambridge: Harvard UP, 1982.

——— . *The Letters of John Keats.* 2 vols. Ed. Hyder Edward Rollins. Cambridge: Harvard UP, 1958.

Ketterer, David. *Frankenstein's Creation: The Book, the Monster, and Human Reality.* Victoria: U of Victoria P, 1979.

Kiely, Robert. *The Romantic Novel in England.* Cambridge: Harvard UP, 1972.

Knoepflmacher, U. C. "Thoughts on the Aggression of Daughters." Levine and Knoepflmacher 88–119.

Lamprecht, Sterling Power. *The Moral and Political Philosophy of John Locke.* New York: Russell, 1962.

La Valley, Albert J. "The Stage and Film Children of *Frankenstein*: A Survey." Levine and Knoepflmacher 243–89.

Le Guin, Ursula. *The Left Hand of Darkness.* New York: Walker, 1969.

Levine, George. "The Ambiguous Heritage of *Frankenstein*." Levine and Knoepflmacher 3–30.

——— . "*Frankenstein* and the Tradition of Realism." *Novel* 7 (1973): 14–30.

——— . *The Realistic Imagination: English Fiction from Frankenstein to Lady Chatterly's Lover.* Chicago: U of Chicago P, 1981.

Levine, George, and U. C. Knoepflmacher, eds. *The Endurance of Frankenstein: Essays on Mary Shelley's Novel.* Berkeley: U of California P, 1979.

Lyles, W. H. *Mary Shelley: An Annotated Bibliography.* New York: Garland, 1975.

Macherey, Pierre. *A Theory of Literary Production.* London: Routledge, 1978.

Marshall, Mrs. Julian. *The Life and Letters of Mary Wollstonecraft Shelley.* 2 vols. London: Bentley, 1889.

Marx, Karl. *Selected Writings.* Trans. and ed. David McLellan. Oxford: Oxford UP, 1977.

Mellor, Anne K. "*Frankenstein*: A Feminist Critique of Science." *One Culture: Essays in Science and Literature.* Ed. George Levine. Madison: U of Wisconsin P, 1987. 287–312.

——— . *Mary Shelley: Her Life, Her Fiction, Her Monsters.* New York: Methuen, 1988.

——— . "On Romanticism and Feminism." Mellor, *Romanticism* 3–9.

————. "Possessing Nature: The Female in *Frankenstein*." Mellor, *Romanticism* 220–32.

————, ed. *Romanticism and Feminism*. Bloomington: Indiana UP, 1988.

Merchant, Carolyn. *The Death of Nature: Women, Ecology, and the Scientific Revolution*. San Francisco: Harper, 1980.

Miyoshi, Masao. *The Divided Self: A Perspective on the Literature of the Victorians*. New York: New York UP, 1969.

Moers, Ellen. "Female Gothic." Levine and Knoepflmacher 77–87.

————. *Literary Women: The Great Writers*. Garden City: Doubleday, 1976.

Moi, Toril. *Sexual/Textual Politics: Feminist Literary Theory*. London: Methuen, 1985.

Moretti, Franco. *Signs Taken for Wonders: Essays in the Sociology of Literary Forms*. London: Verso, 1983.

Nelson, Lowry, Jr. "Night Thoughts on the Gothic Novel." *Yale Review* 52 (1963): 236–57.

Nemerov, Howard. "Cosmic Comics." Heath-Stubbs and Salman 293–94.

Newman, Beth. "Narratives of Seduction and the Seductions of Narrative: The Frame Structure of *Frankenstein*." *ELH* 53 (1986): 141–63.

Nitchie, Elizabeth. *Mary Shelley: Author of* Frankenstein. New Brunswick: Rutgers UP, 1953.

Oates, Joyce Carol. "Frankenstein's Fallen Angel." *Critical Inquiry* 10 (1984): 543–54.

O'Flinn, Paul. "Production and Reproduction: The Case of *Frankenstein*." *Popular Fictions: Essays in Literature and History*. Ed. Peter Humm, Paul Stigant, and Peter Widdowson. London: Methuen, 1986. 196–221.

Pirie, David. *A Heritage of Horror: The English Gothic Cinema, 1946–1972*. London: Gordon Fraser, 1973.

Pirsig, Robert. *Zen and the Art of Motorcycle Maintenance*. New York: Morrow, 1984.

Poovey, Mary. *The Proper Lady and the Woman Writer: Ideology as Style in the Works of Mary Wollstonecraft, Mary Shelley, and Jane Austen*. Chicago: U of Chicago P, 1984.

Rabkin, Eric S. *The Fantastic in Literature*. Princeton: Princeton UP, 1976.

Rimmon-Kenan, Shlomith. *Narrative Fiction: Contemporary Poetics*. New York: Methuen, 1983.

Rosenblatt, Louise M. *The Reader, the Text, the Poem: The Transactional Theory of the Literary Work*. Carbondale: Southern Illinois UP, 1978.

Rubenstein, Marc A. " 'My Accursed Origin': The Search for the Mother in *Frankenstein*." *Studies in Romanticism* 15 (1976): 165–94.

Saberhagen, Fred. *The Frankenstein Papers*. New York: Baen, 1986.

Schiller, Friedrich. "Der Verbrecher aus verlorener Ehre" [The Criminal from Lost Honor]. *Erzaehlungen*. Vol. 16 of *Schiller's Werke: Nationalausgabe*. Ed. Hans Heinrich Borcherdt. Weimar: Böhlaus, 1954. 7–29.

Schug, Charles. "The Romantic Form of Mary Shelley's *Frankenstein.*" *Studies in English Literature* 17 (1977): 607–19.

Schopf, Sue Weaver. " 'Of What Strange Nature Is Knowledge!': Hartleian Psychology and the Creature's Arrested Moral Sense in Mary Shelley's *Frankenstein.*" *Romanticism Past and Present* 5 (1981): 33–52.

Scott, Peter Dale. "Vital Artifice: Mary, Percy, and the Psychopolitical Integrity of *Frankenstein.*" Levine and Knoepflmacher 172–202.

Shelley, Mary Wollstonecraft. *The Annotated* Frankenstein. Ed. Leonard Wolf. 1831 text. New York: Potter, 1977.

———. *Falkner.* London, 1837. Folcroft: Folcroft, 1975.

———. *Frankenstein: Or, The Modern Prometheus.* 1831 text. Berkeley: U of California P, 1984.

———. *Frankenstein.* Ed. Harold Bloom. 1831 text. New York: Signet-NAL, 1965.

———. *Frankenstein.* Ed. Maurice Hindle. 1831 text. New York: Penguin, 1986.

———. *Frankenstein.* Ed. Diane Johnson. 1831 text. New York: Bantam, 1981.

———. *Frankenstein.* Ed. M. K. Joseph. 1831 text. Oxford: Oxford UP, 1969.

———. *Frankenstein.* Ed. James Kinsley and M. K. Joseph. 1831 text. Oxford: Oxford UP, 1980.

———. *Frankenstein.* 1831 text. Philadelphia: Running, 1987.

———. *Frankenstein.* Ed. James Rieger. 1818 text. Chicago: U of Chicago P, 1984.

———. *History of a Six Weeks' Tour through a Part of France, Switzerland, Germany, and Holland.* With Percy Bysshe Shelley. London: Hookham, 1817. Rpt. in *The Complete Works of Percy Bysshe Shelley.* Ed. Roger Ingpen and Walter E. Peck. 10 vols. London: Benn, 1926–30. Vol. 6. 85–152.

———. *The Journals of Mary Shelley, 1814–1844.* Ed. Paula Feldman and Diana Scott-Kilvert. 2 vols. Oxford: Clarendon, 1987.

———. *The Letters of Mary Wollstonecraft Shelley.* Ed. Betty T. Bennett. 3 vols. Baltimore: Johns Hopkins UP, 1980–88.

Shelley, Percy Bysshe. *The Complete Poetical Works of Percy Bysshe Shelley.* Ed. Thomas Hutchinson. Oxford: Oxford UP, 1960.

———. *The Letters of Percy Bysshe Shelley.* Ed. Frederick L. Jones. 2 vols. Oxford: Clarendon, 1964.

———. *Zastrozzi and St. Irvyne.* Ed. Stephen C. Behrendt. Oxford: UP, 1986.

Sherwin, Paul. "*Frankenstein*: Creation as Catastrophe." *PMLA* 96 (1981): 883–903.

Sidgwick, Henry. *Outlines of the History of Ethics for English Readers.* London: Macmillan, 1954.

Small, Christopher. *Ariel like a Harpy: Shelley, Mary, and* Frankenstein. London: Gollancz, 1972. Rpt. as *Mary Shelley's* Frankenstein: *Tracing the Myth.* Pittsburgh: U of Pittsburgh P, 1973.

Snow, C. P. *The Two Cultures: And a Second Look.* Cambridge: Cambridge UP, 1964.

Spark, Muriel. *Child of Light: A Reassessment of Mary Wollstonecraft Shelley.* Hadleigh, Eng.: Tower, 1951. Rev. and rpt. as *Mary Shelley: A Biography.* New York: Dutton, 1987.

Spivak, Gayatri. "Three Women's Texts and a Critique of Imperialism." *"Race," Writing and Difference.* Ed. Henry Louis Gates, Jr. Chicago: U of Chicago P, 1986. 262–80.

Sterrenburg, Lee. "Mary Shelley's Monster: Politics and Psyche in *Frankenstein.*" Levine and Knoepflmacher 143–71.

Stevick, Philip. "*Frankenstein* and Comedy." Levine and Knoepflmacher 221–39.

Sunstein, Emily. *Mary Wollstonecraft Shelley: Romance and Reality.* Boston: Little, 1989.

Swingle, L. J. "*Frankenstein's* Monster and Its Romantic Relatives: Problems of Knowledge in English Romanticism." *TSLL* 15 (1973): 51–65.

Taylor, Henry. *Autobiography of Henry Taylor, 1800–1875.* 2 vols. London: Longman, 1885.

Thompson, G. R., ed. *The Gothic Imagination: Essays in Dark Romanticism.* Pullman: Washington State UP, 1974.

Thornburg, Mary K. Patterson. *The Monster in the Mirror: Gender and the Sentimental/Gothic Myth in* Frankenstein. Ann Arbor: UMI Research, 1987.

Thornburg, Thomas R. "The Quester and the Castle: The Gothic Novel as Myth, with Special Reference to Bram Stoker's *Dracula.*" Diss. Ball State U, 1970.

Tracy, Ann B. *The Gothic Novel: 1790–1830.* Lexington: U of Kentucky P, 1981.

Tropp, Martin. *Mary Shelley's Monster: The Story of Frankenstein.* Boston: Houghton, 1976.

Varma, Devendra P. *The Gothic Flame: Being a History of the Gothic Novel in England: Its Origins, Efflorescence, Disintegration, and Residuary Influences.* London: Barker, 1957.

Veeder, William. *Mary Shelley and* Frankenstein: *The Fate of Androgyny.* Chicago: U of Chicago P, 1986.

Vlasopolos, Anca. "Mary Wollstonecraft's Mask of Reason in *A Vindication of the Rights of Woman.*" *Dalhousie Review* 60 (1980): 462–71.

Walling, William. *Mary Shelley.* New York: Twayne, 1972.

Weiskel, Thomas. *The Romantic Sublime.* Baltimore: Johns Hopkins UP, 1976.

White, Newman Ivey. *Shelley.* 2 vols. New York: Knopf, 1940.

Wilkie, Brian, and James Hurt, eds. *Literature of the Western World.* Vol 2. New York: Macmillan, 1984.

Wordsworth, William. *The Poetical Works.* 5 vols. Ed. Ernest de Selincourt and Helen Darbishire. Oxford: Clarendon, 1940–54.

INDEX

Modern Language Association of America
Approaches to Teaching World Literature
Joseph Gibaldi, series editor

Achebe's Things Fall Apart. Ed. Bernth Lindfors. 1991.
Arthurian Tradition. Ed. Maureen Fries and Jeanie Watson. 1992.
Atwood's The Handmaid's Tale *and Other Works*. Ed. Sharon R. Wilson, Thomas B. Friedman, and Shannon Hengen. 1996.
Austen's Pride and Prejudice. Ed. Marcia McClintock Folsom. 1993.
Beckett's Waiting for Godot. Ed. June Schlueter and Enoch Brater. 1991.
Beowulf. Ed. Jess B. Bessinger, Jr., and Robert F. Yeager. 1984.
Blake's Songs of Innocence and of Experience. Ed. Robert F. Gleckner and Mark L. Greenberg. 1989.
Brontë's Jane Eyre. Ed. Diane Long Hoeveler and Beth Lau. 1993.
Byron's Poetry. Ed. Frederick W. Shilstone. 1991.
Camus's The Plague. Ed. Steven G. Kellman. 1985.
Cather's My Ántonia. Ed. Susan J. Rosowski. 1989.
Cervantes' Don Quixote. Ed. Richard Bjornson. 1984.
Chaucer's Canterbury Tales. Ed. Joseph Gibaldi. 1980.
Chopin's The Awakening. Ed. Bernard Koloski. 1988.
Coleridge's Poetry and Prose. Ed. Richard E. Matlak. 1991.
Dante's Divine Comedy. Ed. Carole Slade. 1982.
Dickens' David Copperfield. Ed. Richard J. Dunn. 1984.
Dickinson's Poetry. Ed. Robin Riley Fast and Christine Mack Gordon. 1989.
Eliot's Middlemarch. Ed. Kathleen Blake. 1990.
Eliot's Poetry and Plays. Ed. Jewel Spears Brooker. 1988.
Ellison's Invisible Man. Ed. Susan Resneck Parr and Pancho Savery. 1989.
Faulkner's The Sound and the Fury. Ed. Stephen Hahn and Arthur F. Kinney. 1996.
Flaubert's Madame Bovary. Ed. Laurence M. Porter and Eugene F. Gray. 1995.
García Márquez's One Hundred Years of Solitude. Ed. María Elena de Valdés and Mario J. Valdés. 1990.
Goethe's Faust. Ed. Douglas J. McMillan. 1987.
Hebrew Bible as Literature in Translation. Ed. Barry N. Olshen and Yael S. Feldman. 1989.
Homer's Iliad *and* Odyssey. Ed. Kostas Myrsiades. 1987.
Ibsen's A Doll House. Ed. Yvonne Shafer. 1985.
Works of Samuel Johnson. Ed. David R. Anderson and Gwin J. Kolb. 1993.
Joyce's Ulysses. Ed. Kathleen McCormick and Erwin R. Steinberg. 1993.
Kafka's Short Fiction. Ed. Richard T. Gray. 1995.
Keats's Poetry. Ed. Walter H. Evert and Jack W. Rhodes. 1991.
Kingston's The Woman Warrior. Ed. Shirley Geok-lin Lim. 1991.
Lessing's The Golden Notebook. Ed. Carey Kaplan and Ellen Cronan Rose. 1989.
Mann's Death in Venice *and Other Short Fiction*. Ed. Jeffrey B. Berlin. 1992.
Medieval English Drama. Ed. Richard K. Emmerson. 1990.
Melville's Moby-Dick. Ed. Martin Bickman. 1985.

Metaphysical Poets. Ed. Sidney Gottlieb. 1990.

Miller's Death of a Salesman. Ed. Matthew C. Roudané. 1995.

Milton's Paradise Lost. Ed. Galbraith M. Crump. 1986.

Molière's Tartuffe *and Other Plays*. Ed. James F. Gaines and Michael S. Koppisch. 1995.

Momaday's The Way to Rainy Mountain. Ed. Kenneth M. Roemer. 1988.

Montaigne's Essays. Ed. Patrick Henry. 1994.

Murasaki Shikibu's The Tale of Genji. Ed. Edward Kamens. 1993.

Pope's Poetry. Ed. Wallace Jackson and R. Paul Yoder. 1993.

Shakespeare's King Lear. Ed. Robert H. Ray. 1986.

Shakespeare's The Tempest *and Other Late Romances*. Ed. Maurice Hunt. 1992.

Shelley's Frankenstein. Ed. Stephen C. Behrendt. 1990.

Shelley's Poetry. Ed. Spencer Hall. 1990.

Sir Gawain and the Green Knight. Ed. Miriam Youngerman Miller and Jane Chance. 1986.

Spenser's Faerie Queene. Ed. David Lee Miller and Alexander Dunlop. 1994.

Sterne's Tristram Shandy. Ed. Melvyn New. 1989.

Swift's Gulliver's Travels. Ed. Edward J. Rielly. 1988.

Thoreau's Walden *and Other Works*. Ed. Richard J. Schneider. 1996.

Voltaire's Candide. Ed. Renée Waldinger. 1987.

Whitman's Leaves of Grass. Ed. Donald D. Kummings. 1990.

Wordsworth's Poetry. Ed. Spencer Hall, with Jonathan Ramsey. 1986.

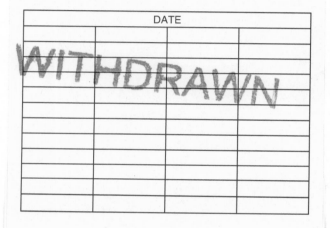